History and Imagery
in British Churches

HISTORY AND IMAGERY IN BRITISH CHURCHES

M. D. Anderson

JOHN MURRAY

Printed in Great Britain by
R. & R. Clark, Ltd.,
Edinburgh

0 7195 2232 3

CONTENTS

Contents ix

LIST OF ILLUSTRATIONS

PLATES

FIGURES

* *From a drawing by W. H. Price*
† *From W. G. Collingwood's 'Northumbrian Crosses', by kind permission of
   Messrs. Faber & Faber Ltd.*
‡ *From a drawing by W. M. Keesey*

ACKNOWLEDGMENTS

I acknowledge with gratitude the help of all those who have
allowed me to reproduce the photographs and drawings used
for the illustrations of this book. In addition to those mentioned
in the list of illustrations, I am grateful to the daughters of the
late Professor E. W. Tristram for giving me permission to
reproduce his copies of the wall-paintings at Claverley and
South Newington. The staff of the National Buildings Record
have given me much help in collecting the illustrations and my
thanks are also due to Miss Dorothy Liptrap for drawing the
map.

PREFACE

THIS BOOK represents a fusion of two earlier volumes: *Looking for History in British Churches*, which dealt chiefly with the evidence of secular history to be found in churches, and *The Imagery of British Churches*, which discussed the religious and allegorical meanings of such imagery. A much simplified version of this second work constitutes the middle section of this book, with the addition of some new material on the influence of vernacular sermons and religious drama.

The material taken from *Looking for History* has been divided between the first and third parts of this book and rearranged. Part I deals with the survivals of pre-Christian beliefs and customs that are illustrated in medieval churches and with some of the political and social forces that affected church building up to the 12th century. Part III is concerned with the traces left upon later churches by various groups of people, such as great nobles, merchants, or pilgrims and, finally with the daily life of the common people as it was portrayed by ecclesiastical craftsmen at various periods.

B

INTRODUCTION

SINCE few methods of education offer such an ideal combination of pleasure and profit as foreign travel, we accept the axiom that travel broadens the mind without troubling overmuch to question its truth. We do not really believe that a few days spent in a land whose language we may not know deepens our insight into its political and economic situation, yet memories of sunlight upon shuttered houses, of the lilt of babbling voices in a market-place, or even of fiercely mingled smells from a back street, do give a vivid actuality to everything we hear or read about that country when information about lands as yet unseen is quickly forgotten. Our minds react in somewhat the same fashion to the study of events far removed from us, not in space but in time. We visualise the 18th century fairly easily, not only because we have portraits to show us what the people looked like, and letters and diaries to disclose their thoughts and expressions, but because we still occasionally live in their houses, sit in their chairs and use their tea-things. Our very finger-tips are in contact with the period. This personal awareness is much more difficult to achieve in the case of the Middle Ages. Letters, and diaries, the raw material from which social historians reconstruct a living impression of the opinions and manners of a former age, are rare treasures for the student of medieval life, and their strange script and archaic phraseology baffle the ordinary reader. The only first-hand source of information which is easily accessible to everyone is the structure and decoration of a medieval church, but how few of the thousands who yearly visit the parish churches of England even attempt to decipher the record of human life which these embody!

This book is therefore not concerned with the architectural history of the churches, or with the changes in ritual that have modified their plans and fittings, but solely with the record of men's lives and thoughts which is incorporated in their structure and imagery. The actions of our ancestors in peace and war, at work or play, the learning of scholars translated into vividly dramatic language by poets, playwrights and preachers and its distortions by the popular imagination of ignorant craftsmen, all these have left their marks somewhere—if we are prepared to look for them. This is an inheritance which belongs alike to all English people, even though some of them no longer count themselves as Christians, and the beauty and interest of our churches are something very precious which all should unite to preserve.

If constrained by an enquiring foreigner to draw a 'typical English village' most of us would start with the church. Whether we showed a battlemented tower at the end of a street in which medieval cottages alternate with petrol pumps, or a slim spire rising from a huddle of roofs to dominate a wide expanse of fields, would depend partly upon our powers of draughtsmanship and partly upon the type of country which, to us, means home. In any case, the scene could not be typical without the church which was, for centuries, the focal point, not only of the religious life of the parish, but also of its civil administration.

The medieval parishioners were encouraged to take pride in the beauty which they, and their forefathers, had conferred upon their parish church, by the frequent reading of the Bede Roll which commemorated past benefactors. Even the poorest and most remote village church contained some precious object before the Reformation. When repairs to the structure were required, enlargements planned, or the need for new bells, windows or vestments considered, the parish, as a corporate body, discussed ways and means of providing them. A lucky chance has preserved the financial records of the rebuilding of Bodmin church in 1469–72[1] and, glancing through the receipts, one gets a moving impression of a little community pooling all its resources to glorify God through the beauty of their new nave. Most of the money was raised through forty local guilds, five of them craft guilds and the rest social or religious communities. Every inhabitant seems to have been expected to give something, either money, goods or free labour, and some men were fined, or had household goods seized, because they had not fulfilled their obligations. Many gave produce to be sold, a goose, or a lamb;

Cicely Searle gave her 'crokke' (a cauldron) and the Vicar contributed his whole year's salary. References to some of the chief contributors can be seen in the church; the arms of Thomas Luccombe are carved on the roof bosses and the merchant's mark of Bartholomew Trote on the bench-ends. At St Neot's in Cornwall, some of the 16th-century stained glass windows were given by 'The Wives', 'The Sisters' and 'The Young Men' of the parish respectively.

Ecclesiology is a subject as flexible in the nature of its rewards as it is varied in its interest. From the heights of learning a scholar sees every scrap of surviving evidence in its true relation to the whole landscape of history, and traces to the horizon of knowledge the roads by which strange designs came to an English church. The enquiring amateur wanders in happy confusion, feeling his mind enriched by the mere process (if I may coin a word) of 'peradventuring' in churches; while the hurried tourist looks at all places of reputed interest but sees very little.

We live in an age when pictures, either moving across a screen or reproduced in newspapers, probably exercise a stronger influence upon the popular imagination than at any time since the Middle Ages, and visual aids are an accepted form of education. We are therefore, perhaps, almost too ready to accept the statement that the stained glass, wall-paintings and sculpture of a medieval church were designed to serve as 'the picture book of the unlearned'. It is only when we look more closely at some of the strange subjects represented in what is left of our medieval imagery that we begin to question whether this statement can be true and, if so, how this remarkable picture book was meant to be interpreted. Undamaged illustrations of Scriptural subjects are easily recognised and the attributes which identify the saints most commonly found can be memorised with little effort, but much remains which might either express recondite symbolism or merely reflect the artists' unbridled fantasy. Thus, all too often, the visitors to our old churches pass on with a merely aesthetic appraisal and so miss the deeper significance which these battered, faded images reveal to those who love and understand them.

How deeply we can penetrate the meaning of medieval

symbolism depends largely upon our own religious convictions. The image which evokes in one mind the intense response of personal mysticism, will only stir another to a scholarly interest in solving antiquarian puzzles. The mystics need no guidebook, for their world is timeless, but the general public would visit old churches with a more reverent interest, and a deeper understanding of the medieval mind, if they understood the general principles of medieval iconography, which was, literally, a system of 'picture-writing' designed to impress certain lessons upon the minds of the worshippers, while also beautifying the churches, to the greater glory of God. This book will therefore deal with the popular, rather than the scholarly, interpretation of medieval imagery, so that its readers may look at what remains of this great medieval Picture Book through the eyes of ordinary people, like themselves, but who were alive when these churches were being built.

No other country has so many parish churches, of such a wide variety, within so small a space, as England, and these churches have also a richness of individuality, a faulty, human loveworthiness, which give them an incomparable charm. A fine English church is as strongly characterised by its locality as the speech of its parishioners used to be. Its shape and substance tell us of the geology of the district, and of the lines of transport by which its stones were brought to the site. The extent to which the building has been altered records the fluctuating prosperity of its parishioners at various periods. Its decoration may show us legends and designs from many different civilisations, or satirical commentaries on contemporary life which offer interesting parallels to their literary equivalents. We may mark with reverence the highest flights of medieval mysticism, recognise memorials of the outstanding personalities and events of British history, or chuckle at the ribald humour of the British working man.

The clocks measure out the centuries from hundreds of church towers; the bells under hundreds of steeples ring out in alarm or victory, happiness or tragedy. As their sound vibrates above the roses and ragged grass of the churchyard, the imagination can take the whole church, or only a single stone, for the starting-point of a journey back through time to when bells first rang from that tower. The life of the Middle Ages is then no longer an incomplete historical record, but a living world in which both bells and dreamer have their being, and perhaps the dreamer will reach even further back in time than the sound of the bells.

PART ONE

The Growth of the Churches

Chapter 1

THE DARK ROOTS

EVEN before we cross the churchyard the remote past lies within the reach of our imagination, for new faiths, like invading armies, must garrison the strongholds of the realms they conquer, and many churchyards have an infinitely longer history as places of worship than even the oldest church built upon them. At Rudston (Yorks), in a round churchyard (a feature which immediately suggests a link with the circular enclosures of the pre-Christian faiths), stand one of the largest monoliths in the country and also a roughly triangular standing stone (Plate 2). The place-name is derived from *rōd-stan*, a rood stone, and, if the original surface of the monolith had not been worn away, we might have seen a cross roughly incised upon it, as a token to all passers-by that this ancient pagan monument had been converted to a landmark beneath which Christian people should gather for worship. An interesting anecdote in the 7th-century Life of St. Samson of Dol describes how the saint, during his sojourn in Cornwall, came upon a group of people who were worshipping 'an abominable image'. St. Samson converted them by means of a miracle and straightway commemorated the event by cutting a cross upon a menhir which had been connected with their pagan worship. At least five megaliths in western Wales are called 'Carreg Samson',[1] and, while this is no proof that this saint here repeated his recorded action, it may indicate that other early Christian teachers followed his example. It has been suggested[2] that the peculiarly British tradition of the great standing crosses of the Anglo-Saxon period derived from the menhir-cult of the Celtic world, adapted to Christian use. Some standing stones in Brittany have had crosses incised upon them and, in the romanesque period, menhirs were sometimes carved into actual crosses, though the very thick bases of these reveal their original form.[3] So we may wonder whether some lofty Saxon cross shaft, standing in a churchyard, was originally placed there as a pagan monolith, but it is a very risky guess!

So many churches stand in, or near, prehistoric earthworks, or stone circles, that it seems clear that such sites were deliberately chosen for Christian worship. At Knowlton Rings (Dorset) a ruined church stands in the centre of a circular earthwork which has two entrances and is thought to have been constructed as a place of worship nearly four thousand years ago. At Yspitty Cynfyn (Cards) four stones, the highest about 11 feet above ground, stand in the churchyard, forming an arc, and two other survivors from a stone circle are used as gateposts.[4] Close to St. David's we can see the ruins of St. Non's Chapel surrounded by standing stones, and, near by, a well which long enjoyed a reputation for healing powers. The legend that, when St. Non reached this divinely appointed spot, where her son, St. David, was to be born, she found an oasis of summer sunshine though all the country round was lashed with storms, suggests that she took over something more than a mere site of worship from the earlier Nature cult.[5] Such examples as these, and they could be multiplied many times, should encourage the visitor to ancient churches to be on the alert to notice masses of rock, either built into the structure or standing near it, and to recognise in the swell of a mound, or the strange line of a fosse the traces of prehistoric occupation. Such awareness should, however, be safeguarded by a readiness to admit, on closer study, that the supposed megalith is merely an outcrop of natural stone, and the 'ancient earthworks' are only traces of a medieval moat, or even an unromantic modern ditch!

The policy of the early Church towards such continued occupation of a sacred site is expressed in the instructions which Pope Gregory sent to St. Augustine by Mellitus: 'Do not pull down the fanes. Destroy the idols; purify the temples with holy water; set relics there; and let them become temples of the true God. So the people will have no need to change their places of concourse, and where of old they were wont to sacrifice cattle to demons, thither let them continue to resort on the day of the saint to whom the church is dedicated, and slay their beasts, no longer as a sacrifice, but for a social meal in honour of Him whom they now worship.' Gregory the Great was wise in his forecast of what happened; the annual fairs in the churchyards, the Church 'ales' and other convivial festivals continued, but all memory of their pagan origin was lost.

Parish churches often stand on rising ground and, when the hill is a natural eminence, many reasons, such as desire to avoid risk of floods or to make the new church a conspicuous landmark, might have led to this choice of site. But sometimes the hill is not natural. Excavations have proved that Fimber church (Yorks) stands upon a Bronze Age barrow which was later used as an Anglian burial-place,[6] and the place-name of Edlesborough (Bucks) suggests that the mound on which the fine parish church stands, in a round churchyard, was raised as the barrow of Eadwulf (Plate 1). Barrows are quite commonly to be seen in, or near, churchyards, as, for instance, at Brinklow (Warcs) or Berwick (Sussex). The famous tumulus at Taplow (Bucks) stands in the original churchyard.

The dedications of hill-top churches, whether they stand on artificial mounds like the Hampshire churches of Cheriton, Corhampton and Sopley,[7] or on natural peaks like St. Michael's Mount, are interesting. The most frequent hill-top dedication is to St. Michael, and the *South English Legendary*,[8] compiled in the 13th century, contains several legends illustrating the archangel's predilection for hill-top shrines. This passage is followed by a section describing how, after Lucifer had been overthrown by the loyal angels led by St. Michael, the less sinful among the fallen angels were allowed to haunt the earth, dwelling in woods and on high hills and known to men as 'elves'. The evil practices of these elves, as described in the *Legendary*, form an interesting chapter in medieval demonology but do not concern us here unless the story, told of many churches, of how supernatural powers destroyed by night what had been built each day, represents a folk-memory of nocturnal raids by pagans, whether Saxon or British, who resented this invasion of their holy places.[9] At Winwick (Lancs) a pig carved on the west front of the church is said to have carried stones from the unfinished church to a new site, in its mouth. In this case the pig seems to have been an agent of God for the new site was one hallowed by the blood of St. Oswald, so this legend links on to the belief, perhaps based on the tradition of the founding of Rome, that a white sow and her farrow would mark a divinely chosen spot. This episode figures in the legends of SS. Brynach and Brannock (who may be the same person) and the sow and farrow are often seen on bosses and bench-ends in the West-country churches such as Broad Clyst, Spreyton, Ugborough and Sampford Courtney, all in Devon.

The early Christians, while denying the divinity of the pagan gods, did not question their potency as devils. The struggle between Christians and heathens on earth was matched by perpetual warfare in the spirit world, and the Norman tympana which show St. Michael fighting the dragon of Evil, like those at Moreton Valence (Glos) (Plate 18), or Hoveringham (Notts), express something more than abstract symbolism. The Celts of the British Isles had sacred mounds which were considered as the dwelling-places of gods,[10] and it would have been in accordance with the general practice of early Christianity to build churches upon these mounds in order to prevent the recrudescence of pagan worship. To guard such a position of danger, which patron saint could be more suitable than St. Michael? In Wales his dedications are thrice as numerous as in England, and Llanvihangel (the church of the angel) is a common element in place-names. Over the whole country St. Michael ranks fourth in order of popularity for dedications, but in Northumberland and Shropshire he ranks second, many of the churches standing on hills,[11] while in Lincolnshire he falls back to seventh place and in Kent to eighth. The obvious inference would seem to be that the Roman and Anglo-Saxon invasions had cleared the south-eastern hills of their superstitious associations before the advent of Christianity, but archaeological problems are rarely as simple as that! The evidence of place-names (without which we should know very little of the local centres of the heathen English worship and nothing definite about the places at which individual gods were honoured) makes it clear that the Anglo-Saxons did worship at hill-top shrines.[12] The element *Hearh*, which we know from literary sources to mean temple, or idol, seems to imply, in such place-names as Harrow-on-the-Hill, a hill sanctuary.

Another dedication frequently to be found in hill-top churches is that to St. Catherine, whose cult was introduced into England at the time of the Crusades. Her legend is a mysterious and composite one. Episodes of the life of a princess in Alexandria were connected with a body found buried on the top of Mount Sinai by the story of angels carrying the body of the virgin martyr to this lofty burial-place, the suggested prototype of all her hill-top shrines. It may have been merely the association with Alexandria, the site of the most famous lighthouse of antiquity, which led to St. Catherine being specially associated with beacons on sea or land routes, a connection particularly marked in England, but it is also possible that her cult absorbed some of the rites of an early fire-goddess. In the time of Edward II, provision was made for a priest who would keep a light burning, during stormy weather, on the octagonal tower of the ruined chapel on St. Catherine's Point, in the Isle of Wight, to warn mariners off that dangerous shore before a lighthouse was built. There are no early records to tell whether the ruined chapel of St. Catherine on the rock which guards the entrance to Tenby harbour was ever a lighthouse, but its position strongly suggests it. The little hill-top church of St. Catherine at Abbotsbury (Dorset) certainly had a beacon in its tower intended particularly to guide mariners.

St. Catherine figures, more often than any other female saint, in the decoration of English churches, always identified by the wheel of her martyrdom. The similarity between this wheel, with its slanting spikes, and the flames of a conventionalised solar disc can hardly fail to strike anyone who bears in mind the other fiery associations of this saint. Wheels wrapped in straw or wooden discs which were trundled flaming over the fields to ensure their fertility continued to figure in the fire festivals of Europe until recent times.[13] The legends of several saints originated in popular misunderstanding of older symbols and, in the case of St. Catherine, this process has completed a full circle and the saint is once more connected with a revolving firework.

Another saint who may have had pagan antecedents is St. Apollonia, who was invoked by sufferers from toothache because her figure was identified by a tooth held in a pair of long forceps. She appears on the painted rood-screens of Ashton (Devon), Ludham (Norfolk) and Westhall (Suffolk), also in windows at Ludlow, Norwich St. Stephen's, Norton (Suffolk) and Mells (Somerset). Teeth, being less subject to decay than any other part of the body, were considered as emblems of immortality in many primitive religions, a symbolism still perpetuated in the savage medicine-man's necklace of teeth. A pair of leaden forceps found in the Temple of Apollo at Delphi was presumably connected with worship, since they were too soft for use in extractions, and as this saint's feast day, on February 9th, falls within two days of the Roman feast of Apollo, known as the Apollonia, it seems likely that her legend developed from the attempts of the early Church to obliterate the pagan associations of a festival whose observance it would have been dangerously unpopular to oppose.[14] In the same way the August feast days of various saints called Hippolytus, who all suffered martyrdom by being dragged by wild horses, replaced the association of the heroic son of Theseus and Hippolyta with a pagan festival held that month. One of these saints is represented in the glass at Wiggenhall St. Mary Magdalene (Norfolk).

Our sense of continuity with the beliefs of the ancient Britons is never stronger than when we stand by one of the holy wells which are to be found near many churches. The saint whose name the well now bears was almost certainly first associated with it in the role of a sentinel, to defend Christianity against the stealthy persistence of the old Nature worship. The penitentials of the 7th century imposed a three years' fast upon those who offered sacrifices to fountains, a denunciation repeated in the laws of Canute and by Archbishop Anselm in the 11th century.[15] While the custom of decking the wells on certain feasts persists in several places, notably at Tissington (Derbs), who shall say that the last survival of water worship has ceased to be practised in Britain?

The in-dwelling divinities of springs and streams, whom the early Britons worshipped, retained their dignity under Roman rule. When the well dedicated to the British water-nymph Coventina, near the Roman Wall at Carrawburgh, was cleared out, some 15,000 coins and other offerings, dating from pre-Roman days up to the 4th century A.D., were discovered. An altar to the Goddess Verbeia, presumed to have been the divinity of the River Wharfe, which is now in the church at Ilkley (Yorks), was dedicated to her honour by Roman legionaries from eastern Gaul.[16] The Anglo-Saxon invasion caused extensive depopulation of the south-eastern district, and few of the wells and streams retained their Celtic names or their supernatural associations. The contrast between the large numbers of holy wells in Celtic districts and their rarity in areas of Anglo-Saxon settlement is striking: Cornwall has 40 holy wells, Shropshire 36 and Northumberland 35, compared with meagre totals of 6 in Surrey, 3 in Wiltshire and only 1 in Essex.

In most cases the association of the spring with its titular saint is merely an extension of the dedication of the church, but in a few instances the origin of the spring is said to mark the spot where he, or she, was martyred or buried. The most famous example of such a well is at Holywell (Flints), where one of the most copious springs in Britain fills a star-shaped basin in the crypt of a chapel built by the mother of Henry VII, marking the spot of St. Winifred's death.[17]

Pure water for baptisms was a primary need for every Christian community, and the existence of a good spring may sometimes have determined the site of the first church. In both Wales and Cornwall we find small chapels, often in ruins, beside the holy wells, which were used as baptisteries, and also, sometimes, in connection with the healing properties of the well. Not far from the church of St. Cleer, near Liskeard (Cornwall), a much restored chapel guards a holy spring in whose waters lunatics used to be ducked until they became quiet—either through the merits of the water or from being half-drowned![18]

Occasionally the procedure by which the saint named the well was apparently reversed. Two Yorkshire churches, Giggleswick and Middleham, are dedicated to St. Alkelda, a shadowy saint who was said to have been strangled by the Danes. Her legend is illustrated on a fragment of old glass at Middleham and, more fully, in a modern window at Giggleswick. One interpretation of this dedication is that the saint's name is a corruption of Halig-Keld (a holy well), for in each of these two places there is a holy well.[19]

Perhaps the superstition that the north side of the church was the devil's side originated, as a typically British compromise, in the days when Christianity battled with the heathen gods for possession of sites of worship. Its effects are often clearly visible. Most churches stand on the northern part of their churchyards and the principal entrance is almost always by the south door, unless some very cogent reason of convenience favours a north entry. At the beginning of the present century there were many churchyards in which the south side was so crowded with graves that enlargement had been necessary, although hardly a mound marked the sward to the north.[20] When Parliament made it obligatory for ground to be reserved in the churchyards, though unhallowed, for the burial of criminals, suicides and unbaptised infants, these plots were always situated to the north of the church.[21] Such was its ill-repute that an unexplained burial there might have been considered an implication of guilt, and a gravestone at Epworth (Lincs) bears the inscription:

> That I might longer undisturbed abide
> I choos'd to be laid on this Northern side.

Christianity took over more than the sites of pagan worship. Primitive man's desire to propitiate the supernatural powers, in order to induce Nature to provide more plentifully for his physical needs, had to be satisfied, and so certain forms of Christian ritual were devised to replace pagan observances. As a result of this tolerant diplomacy, medieval churches occasionally show us memorials of pre-Christian rites.[22]

From the earliest dawn of civilisation men seem to have disguised themselves as animals for ritual practices, probably intended to secure good luck in hunting. On the walls of the Caverne des Trois Frères at Ariège there is a prehistoric drawing of a man wearing antlers on his head and dressed in skins. In England during the 7th century Archbishop Theodore ordered those who transformed themselves into the semblance of wild animals to do penance for three years 'because this is devilish',[23] but, in spite of the denunciations of the Church, the antics of men disguised with masks representing the heads of animals formed part of many medieval revels. Under the licence of the Feast of Fools, when rulers made abdication of their powers to the most grotesque regents, clergy and laity alike disguised themselves and held mock services. A misericord in St. David's Cathedral which shows an animal mask with a veil pinned to the centre of its forehead and falling back behind its ears (Plate 8), may represent one of the masks used in the Feast of Fools, the veil being meant to conceal the wearer's head and neck. A more direct survival of the prehistoric hunter's magic can be seen at Abbots Bromley (Staffs) where the six sets of reindeer's horns and the hobby-horse, used in the annual Horn Dance, are kept in the church. Three of the horns are light and three are dark. Originally the dance took place in the church, later the music was played from the church porch while the dancers footed it in the churchyard, and now the 'deer' are hunted through the streets. Officially the dance commemorates the restoration of certain forest rights in the reign of Henry III, but neither in the Middle Ages nor today do official explanations always tell the whole truth!

Strange as it seems, the medieval clergy did not oppose the inclusion of some crude symbols derived from the old fertility rites among the designs used to decorate churches. In an article in the *Anthropological Institute Journal* for 1934 Dr. M. A. Murray illustrated several examples carved upon English churches of the grotesque female figure known as the Sheila-na-Gig and noted its affinity with the Egyptian goddess Baubo. At Whittlesford (Cambs) the Sheila-na-Gig is carved over a window of the church tower, accompanied by a sinister, human-headed, quadruped.[24]

Man the hunter, who lived entirely upon the flesh of the animals he killed and the wild fruits of the earth, was succeeded by Man the tiller of the soil who, in his turn, devised magic rites to induce the spirits of vegetation to favour the work of his hands. The forms taken by some of these rites persisted in the many examples of tree worship which are recorded in *The Golden Bough* as surviving among the primitive peasantry of Europe. The Church's long struggle against survivals of tree worship is dramatically illustrated on an alabaster panel, now in the Victoria and Albert Museum, which shows St. Boniface overthrowing the tree sacred to Thor, at Geismar. The bishop and his clergy are shown on horseback and St Boniface raises his hand in a gesture of command as demons flee from the tangled wreckage of the fallen oak.[25]

Broadly speaking, the rites of the tree worshippers fell into two groups. In the first, the tree itself was reverenced as the shrine of the in-dwelling divinity; in the second, a youth, or a maiden, clothed and masked with foliage, was led through the fields to ensure their fertility. Both varieties survived in medieval England, the first as the dance round the maypole, the second as the Jack-in-the-Green, or Green Man.

I have never seen a representation of a maypole in any church, although the medieval carvers included most common sports among their subjects. Perhaps the pagan origin of the dance was too clearly remembered. An alternative form of this pagan rite, in which the worshippers moved in a circle round the tree, or some other object, considered sacred, was sometimes transferred to the church, and known as the 'clipping' (or embracing) of the building. This custom has been revived in some places and at Painswick (Glos), by a confusion in etymology, it has regained its association with trees, for it takes place in that most beautiful of all English churchyards, when the ninety-nine yew trees (the hundredth tree is said always to die) have been freshly clipped.

The personification of the spirit of the tree may have lost its pagan associations in the minds of the people at an early stage, or else the origin of the decorative motive to which it probably gave rise was forgotten. So far from banning it, the Church allowed the foliate mask to become one of the few recurrent themes in the inexhaustible variety of designs which the carvers lavished upon capitals and corbels, spandrels, bosses and misericords (Plate 12). C. J. P. Cave photographed over 300 bosses bearing this human face peering through a screen of leaves which generally, but not always, spring from two stems issuing from its mouth.[26] Even before medieval foliage sculpture had quickened to its spring, we can see conventionalised leaves coming from the mouth of a mask on the Norman capitals of the doors at Oxhill (Warcs) and Longdon (Staffs). Various types of foliage, natural or conventionalised, are found surrounding these masks, such as wild apple and bryony at Southwell,[27] but in the majority of cases it is the oak, the holy tree of the Druids and of many pagan faiths. Various explanations of the device have been given; on the shrine of St. Frideswide at Oxford it is said to commemorate the occasion when the saint was forced to hide in a wood, but the most convincing explanation of its widespread popularity is that which connects the foliate mask with the many-aliased personage also commemorated by the numerous inn signs of 'The Green Man'.[28] Until the beginning of the 20th century many places kept up the traditional ceremony of the Green Man who rode, or walked, through the streets with his head and shoulders hidden by a wicker cage thickly covered with leaves, only allowing him to peer through a narrow aperture. At Castleton (Derbs) the Garland King and his Queen still ride through the village on horses bedecked with flowers. The King is covered by the traditional cage surmounted by a posy of flowers and, at the end of the day, this cage is hoisted up to the top of the church tower. The modern association with the Restoration of Charles II fails to convince when we compare this ceremony with its counterpart in German folklore, where the cage is broken up and planted in the fields to make them fertile.[29] On a roof boss at Pershore (Worcs) the foliate head wears a crown.

The Castleton Garland King may be the civilised descendant of the wicker giants which used to figure in midsummer processions in many parts of Europe and which were sometimes crammed with live cats, snakes and other animals before being burned at the end of the festival.[30] The sinister beauty of some foliate masks, such as that on a misericord in Holy Trinity church, Coventry (Plate 12), may therefore carry our imaginations backwards through time to the grim statement of Julius Caesar regarding the human sacrifices of the Druids in Gaul: 'some tribes make great images whose limbs, woven of wickerwork, they cram with live victims and then place fire below and slay them by the flames.'[31]

A new faith must perforce accept the challenge of its older rivals and equal, if not surpass, all that these have claimed to achieve. While the purely festive rites of the Green Man might be left to the laity, the Church had to satisfy the desire of its converts for some means by which the protection of the deity might be invoked for their crops. In the Rogationtide processions the priest led his flock through the fields, all bearing flowers or branches of foliage, and the springing crops were solemnly blessed. In the Labours of the Months, often illustrated in all forms of medieval art, one of the spring months is usually represented by a figure holding up bunches of flowers or leaves, as on the misericord in Worcester cathedral (Plate 11). One of the bench-ends at Blythburgh (Suffolk) represents a priest, in cassock and biretta, holding up a bouquet. The Christian feast of Easter took its English name from the Anglo-Saxon goddess of spring, Eostre, and some of the rites of her festival, following the pattern of still older forms of worship, were probably incorporated in these flower-bearing processions of medieval Rogationtide.

Perhaps the most impressive example of this historic continuity is the May Cross which stands upon the roodscreen of Charlton-on-Otmoor church (Oxon). This is made of foliage and is renewed each May day, when the new Cross is carried to the church by girls dressed in white. Early 20th-century records state that it was formerly carried through the parish with songs and dances and that its form was then recognisably human, with a face and hands made of flowers and smaller bunches of flowers down the vertical shaft, referred to by older villagers as 'my Lady's buttons'.³² Contemporary engravings show two crosses of unequal size which broaden at the base like a bell skirt, so 'my Lady' probably had once a Lord.

Although Corn Dollies are now chiefly made as a decorative handicraft, there are a few places where they retain their association with the 'Last Sheaf' of the harvest which was richly decked to be the dwelling of the Corn Spirit during the winter. As such, it was given a place of honour at the Harvest Feast and taken to church. Corn Dollies hang in the porches of Overbury and Beoley in Worcestershire and figure in Harvest Festival decorations elsewhere. At Garway in Herefordshire a wreath of holly used to be hung in the church tower and it was considered an ill omen if it fell down during the year.

Our chief source of information about the Celtic gods of Britain are the references to them in Roman dedications and, because the churches were often used to shelter any interesting antiquities discovered in the parish, some of these altars and inscribed stones may be seen there. Where no question of political opposition was involved, the Romans preferred to absorb, rather than suppress, the religious cults of the races they had conquered, and so these references to Celtic gods usually occur in composite Romano-British forms, like the famous Sul-Minerva of Bath.

At Caerwent (Mon) there is an altar in the church porch, dedicated to Mars-Ocellus, a composite deity in whom the worshippers honoured both the Roman, and one of the many Celtic, gods of war. Another altar, in the crypt at Hexham, was dedicated by an officer of the Sixth Legion to the British god Maponus, here equated with Apollo.³³ A stone in the porch of Lanchester (Durham) is dedicated to an otherwise unknown goddess 'Garmangabis' and to the divinity of the Emperor Gordian III, by the detachment of Suebi which bore his name.³⁴ The Dea Brigantea, titular deity of the Brigantes, is only known to us through dedications of the Roman period.³⁵ A settlement of Brigantes near Waterford may have introduced into Irish mythology the goddess Brigit, controller of poetry and wisdom, and some of the customs by which the Irish peasantry celebrated the Feast of St. Bridget suggest that she may have taken over the functions of the Celtic goddess as patron of crops and fire.[36] Missionaries from Ireland in the 10th century dedicated churches in north-west England to Irish saints, and so, in these churches dedicated to St. Bridget, or St. Bride, we may allow our imaginations to catch a faint echo of the Dea Brigantea's name in the lands where she was once honoured.

This tolerance of unimportant Celtic cults is in striking contrast to the hostile attitude of the Roman Empire towards early Christianity, the immense political implications of which were immediately recognised. This is illustrated by the dedication of St. Alban's cathedral to the young Roman official who was executed during the Diocletian persecution because, although still a pagan, he had sheltered a Christian priest. The scene of his martyrdom is carved upon the base of his early 14th-century shrine in the cathedral, whose Saxon builders drew largely upon the ruins of Verulamium for their building stone.

Reminders of purely Roman gods are often found in churches. In the porch at Middlebie (Dumfries) is a stone dedicated to Jupiter by German legionaries. A stoup at Michaelchurch (Herefs) has been cut from an altar inscribed DEO TRI(VII) BECCICIS DONAVIT ARA(M) which probably stood at a road junction. A bull, appropriate sacrifice to a male god, which is carved on an altar in the church of Stone-in-Oxney (Kent), suggests that this may have been dedicated to Mithras, the favourite god of the Roman soldiers, and an altar to the Mother Goddesses, another cult much favoured by the Legionaries, serves as a font in the church of Lund (Lancs).[37] On neither of these two last is there any inscription, but, although the three figures on the face of the stone at Lund are too battered for us to see whether they are the seated women holding baskets of fruit which generally represent the Mothers, the dancing figures carved in lower relief on the sides of the stone seem to be akin to the 'dancers' which appear at Pallanza and Avigliano, in Italy, on stones dedicated to the Mothers. In the church at Aldborough (Yorks) there is a damaged statue of Mercury, and a figure of Aesculapius is set in a niche on the south wall at Tockenham (Wilts).[38]

A Roman altar in St. Swithun's church in Lincoln is dedicated jointly to the *Parcae* and to the *numina Augustorum*.[39] The dedicator,

C. Antistius Frontinus, is described as *Curator ter* and was perhaps an official of a guild in which the Curator acted as Treasurer. A dedication to the Fates (who decided man's span of life) made by such an official suggests that the altar may have belonged to a burial club, which maintained a communal tomb, or a cemetery, where the memory of its members was kept green by ritual ceremonies. This altar may therefore be considered as foreshadowing the functions of some of the religious guilds of the Middle Ages which played such an important part in shaping the development of our churches.

One is inclined to take for granted that these pagan customs were allowed to continue as part of Christian usage because their origin had been forgotten, but this was not always the case. In *Mirk's Festial*, a 14th-century sermon manual,[40] the preacher explains, in his sermon on the Feast of the Purification of the Virgin, that this was called Candlemas because Pope Sergius, seeing Christian men and women drawn to the 'mawmetry' of the old Roman custom of carrying lighted candles through the streets in honour of the goddess Februa and her son Mars, commanded that they should carry them to church instead, in honour of the Blessed Virgin and her Son. The figures holding candles which appear in scenes of the Presentation in the Temple in the windows of Canterbury cathedral, Malvern Priory and Thursley (Surrey) are thus a reminder of this long process of tolerant absorption.

As we climb steep slopes to hill-top churches, gaze at battered altars converted into fonts, or meet the enigmatic eyes of foliate masks which recall both prehistoric sacrifices and medieval jollifications, we can hardly fail to be impressed by a sense of historical continuity. Absorbing rather than destroying, enriched from the strangest variety of sources, the stream of English history flows on steadily, all the stronger because its course has not been marked by the smoking cataracts of sudden, violent change.

Chapter 2

MILESTONES IN THE DARK

THE YEARS between the departure of the Roman Legions and the arrival of St. Augustine's mission have been called 'the two lost centuries of English history' for written evidence is scarce and unreliable and their authentic story can only be deciphered with the spade. This darkness throws its shadow back in time and we know little of the social conditions and the spread of Christianity during the last phase of Roman Britain. So the few scraps of evidence which we find in some churches have a rarity value. For example, in the porch at Caerwent (Mon) a large stone, perhaps once the base of a statue, bears an inscription recording its erection by the *respublica civitatis Silurum*, in honour of Tiberius Claudius Paulinus, Commander of the Second Legion in the early 3rd century, who had been Governor of Narbonne and Lyons before he came to defend the wild Welsh borders of the Roman Empire.[1] The Silures had been among the most stalwart opponents of Roman domination and this reference to their 'commonwealth' shows that they had been allowed to maintain something of their tribal organisation, by the same imperial diplomacy which we have already noted as applied to the Celtic gods.

The greater importance, and final victory, of the Anglo-Saxon invaders tend to obscure our memory of the Irish Picts who were the first to assail the crumbling defences of Roman Britain, but the churchyard wall of St. Cybi's at Holyhead almost certainly formed part of one of the forts built to defend the 'Irish Shore' against them.[2] These defences were over-run and, by the late 4th century, the Irishmen were masters of the greater part of Wales, as well as of Devon, Cornwall and part of Somerset. In the south transept of Nevern church (Pembs) we can see a memorial of these early invaders: a stone inscribed with the name of Maglocunus, son of Clutorius. Along the edge of this stone are cut thin grooves, looking like a first exercise in the straight strokes of shorthand; an inscription in the Ogham script which they brought from Ireland to the areas they conquered.[3] Some Irish manuscripts have given the key to this script, in which the distinction between the letters consists in the number of notches, from one to five, on the angle at which they are cut and their position above, below, or through a line which is often represented by the edge of a block. Welsh bilingual inscriptions have confirmed this trans-literation and, in the church at Towyn (Merioneths), there is a four-sided pillar, ascribed to *c.* 650, on which is the earliest known inscription in the Welsh language.[4]

The Christian communities in Roman Britain have left little visible evidence of their existence. If we judge by the small scale of the foundations of the only unquestionably Roman church, at Silchester (Hants), they were neither numerous nor wealthy. The fact that several Roman villas have been excavated near churches, or on sites known by such names as Church Field, or Chapel Close, has however given rise to a theory that Roman land-owners who became Christians may have built private chapels or adapted a room in their villas to serve as a place of worship.[5] The Roman villas at Chedworth (Glos) and Frampton (Dorset) were certainly occupied by Christians, for the Chi-Rho monogram, Fig. 1 (see p. 26) figured on a tile at one and a mosaic floor at the other. By A.D. 350 the owners of the Roman villa at Lullingstone (Kent) had been converted and had constructed a series of rooms devoted to Christian worship. In one of these, presumably the house-chapel, the walls were painted in fresco with a row of human figures in an attitude of prayer, together with large repre-sentations of the Chi-Rho. This symbol also appeared in an ante-chapel beyond which there was a vestibule with an outer door, perhaps intended for the admission of neighbours who were also Christians.[6] There is some evidence that these rooms went on being used after the rest of the building was abandoned and, much later, a small chapel was built near its site. At Woodchester (Glos) a magnificent Roman mosaic floor lies under part of the church-yard and similar floors have been uncovered under churches at Caerwent, Widford (Oxon) and Wimborne Minster (Dorset). These *may* indicate continuity of worship on the site since the 3rd century, but this would be a rash assumption to make without further evidence.

In the cities, where we might expect to find more important evidence, the constant process of destruction and rebuilding has obliterated the record of archaeology, and it is in the relatively unchanged Celtic country that we must seek for evidence of the continuous survival of Christianity in Britain during the Dark Ages. Bede gives us a starting-point, both in time and place. He tells us that, at the end of the 4th century, St. Ninian, a British Christian of gentle birth, returned to his native country after studying at Rome and under St. Martin of Tours.[7] On the wild shores of Galloway he built a stone church (perhaps with the help of craftsmen brought from Gaul), the pallor of whose new masonry won it the name of the *Candida Casa*. The ruins of the medieval Priory of Whithorn (Wigtownshire) may mark the site of this chapel, but the corrupt Anglicised version of its name is their only other connection with it. The authentic relics of St. Ninian's mission are the early gravestones at Whithorn and Kirkmadrine on the next peninsula, which, by the peculiarities of their inscriptions, can confidently be ascribed to the period following the Roman withdrawal.[8] Several of these stones stand in the Cave of St. Ninian, whither the saint is said to have withdrawn for solitary contemplation, and the early crosses cut upon its rock walls seem to support this tradition.

The fact that this early Christian settlement was in direct contact with Rome, and the work which won for St. Ninian the title of 'The Apostle of the Picts', caused his name to be revered in the medieval Church. Four English churches are known to have had ancient dedications to him, as well as those in Scotland. The mitred figures holding fetters which are carved on Prince Arthur's chantry in Worcester Cathedral and on the tomb-chest of Sir Ralph Grey at Chillingham (Northumb) can only be tentatively identified as St. Ninian since they might equally well represent St. Leonard. A more certain representation occurs on one of the panels from a rood screen, preserved in the church of Fowlis Easter (Angus). St. Ninian is here shown as a bishop, with one hand raised in blessing, and manacles on his wrist. The lion of Scotland appears on the foot of his rochet.[9]

With the fine points of scholarship relating to the inscriptions on the Galloway stones I cannot deal, but something must be said of the Chi-Rho monogram which appears on several of them. A monogram of the first two letters of the Greek word Χριστός was used as an abbreviation for the name of Christ in inscriptions in

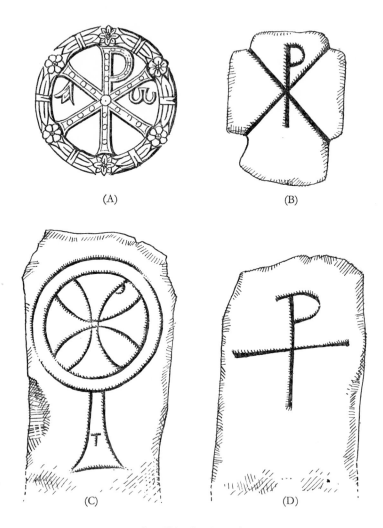

(A)

(B)

(C)

(D)

Fig. 1. The Chi-Rho Sacred Monogram

(A)—Example of the wreathed monogram from the Catacombs.
(B)—Cross of St. Just-in-Penwith.
(C)—Gravestone at Whithorn.
(D)—Gravestone at Penmachno.

the catacombs as early as the 3rd century (Fig. 1) and became widely popular as a sacred emblem after the Emperor Constantine had placed it upon the shields of his soldiers and made it the crowning feature of his official standards. According to Eusebius, the monogram on the banner of Constantine was surrounded by a gem-studded golden crown, and Professor Baldwin Brown suggested that this circular frame was the origin of the Celtic wheel-head cross.[10] No form of Chi-Rho is to be found upon the ancient Christian monuments of Ireland, so that its rare appearance in parts of Celtic Britain may fairly be taken as evidence of the survival of Christian belief among the Romano-Britons, as opposed to the later revival inspired by missionaries in close contact with Ireland. Originally the sacred monogram followed the correct form of the Greek letters, the P rising from the X, but another form, based on a cross with a horizontal transom, was common in Gaul from the late 4th to the mid 6th century. An open loop to the Rho is a sign of later date. It is this form which we find on the stones at Kirkmadrine, evidence which fits in well with the tradition about St. Ninian's mission, while the number of early gravestones, and certain variations in their inscriptions, testify that the community was not swept away in the collapse of the Roman defences.

There are only about thirteen examples of stones inscribed with the Chi-Rho in Britain, of which two are in Wales, at Penmachno and Treflys in Caernarvonshire, and six in Cornwall.[11] References to 'a heap of stones' on the memorial to Carausius at Penmachno, and to a 'tumulus', in an inscription at Hayle (Corn) support the statements in the Lives of the saints that these inscribed stones were set up on burial-mounds. Very rarely do they give any specific indication of date, an exception being the memorial of Avitorius at Penmachno, which was definitely set up in the time of Justinus the Consul.

We do not know how many Romano-British settlements in south Wales had been converted to Christianity by the time the last Legions sailed for Gaul, but the Faith survived, though the empire crumbled. Among the inscribed stones at Margam (Glam) is a pillar, usually ascribed to *c.* 550, commemorating Bodvoc, son of Catogirnus, great-grandson of Eternalis Vedomavus. Such inscribed pillars are generally Christian monuments, so we have here perhaps a record of several generations of a noble Celtic family with Roman traditions, and probably Christians.[12]

During these unchronicled centuries Christian teachers, either British-born or coming from Ireland, moved about the country-side of Wales and, from there, passed into the south-western countries of England. Because the Celtic church did not associate new churches with the names of particular saints, these became known by the name of the missionary who had founded them. Thus, when St. Teilo established Christian communities in a particular district, their churches were called 'Teilo's churches' and this title, later treated as a dedication, is preserved in such place-names as Llandilo, Llandeloy, or Llantilio, even though the dedication of the church may have been changed. This custom has thus preserved for us a record of some outstanding person-alities of the 5th and 6th centuries and those who have the know-ledge and industry to analyse the names of villages, valleys, rocks and holy wells, as well as the dedications of churches, can recon-struct the spheres of influence of many early Celtic saints.[13]

One of the outstanding figures of the 5th century was St. Dubritius, whose sphere of activity seems to have been in south-west Herefordshire, Brecon and Glamorgan. The Warwick chronicler, Usher de Primordiis, tells us that Dubritius was the son of Pepiau, of the family of King Brychan, who ruled over Erchenfield.[14] A district of Herefordshire is still called Erchen-field, and it includes the churches of Whitchurch, Ballingham and Hentland, all dedicated to St. Dubritius, as is also the Hereford-shire church of St. Devereux.

The district to which St. Dubritius brought Christianity was extended westward by St. Illtyd who, according to his medieval biographers, was an Armorican soldier in the train of King Arthur who was converted by St. Cadoc.[15] The churches dedicated to him are confined to south Wales, with the exception of Llanelltyd (Merioneths). He was appointed by St. Dubritius to be the head of the monastery at Llantwit Major (Glam) a centre of learning which numbered among its pupils such outstanding personalities as SS. David, Samson of Dol and Paul Aurelian as well as the gloomy historian Gildas. It was famous for its classical studies, which may indicate a survival of Roman culture, since Roman remains have been found there. Among the remarkable collection

of pre-Conquest carved stones preserved in the fine church of
the medieval monastery, is a carved cross-shaft known as the
Cross of St. Illtyd,[16] and the bell of the 15th-century Town Hall
is inscribed: SANCTE ILTUDE ORA PRO NOBIS.

Among the next generation of saints, who worked in the 6th
century, St. Teilo seems to have covered the whole area opened
up to Christianity by his predecessors. There are twenty-nine
dedications or place-names referring to him in south Wales and
others in Cornwall and Brittany.[17] The tradition that his head-
quarters were at Llandeilo, in the Towey valley, is supported by
the fact that churches dedicated to him are found more frequently
towards the west. A modern church now serves Llandeilo (Pembs),
but the remains of its predecessor can still be seen. The interior
of the ruined nave, which has a stone bench against the wall, is
only 18 feet by 8½ feet, but, small and ancient as it is, this church
is later than St. Teilo's day, and the only relics of his period
remaining there are two stones beside the wicket-gate. These
record in Ogham and Latin script ANDAGELL FILI CAVETTI, and
COIMAGNI FILI CAVETTI, whom, in the absence of any definite
knowledge, we are free to imagine as having been the saint's
disciples. Near by is St. Teilo's Well from which pilgrims used to
drink, using as a goblet a human skull, reputedly that of the saint.
St. Teilo is generally considered as having been the first Bishop
of Llandaff, although the title is sometimes given in error to St.
Dubritius. Medieval tombs commemorating the two saints stood
one on each side of the presbytery and that of St. Teilo retains
its place today. An effigy of a bishop which now lies in a recess on
the north wall may have come from the tomb of St. Dubritius.

The fame of St. David makes his activities hard to trace through
the medium of dedications, for he, alone among the purely Welsh
saints, was officially canonised in the 12th century. This honour
almost certainly led to more churches being dedicated to him,
including probably those in Yorkshire and Nottingham. His Life
tells us that, after being educated at Llantwit, he founded a small
monastery near his birthplace from which he evangelised the
surrounding district. The great purple and silver cathedral of St.
David's, lying in its grassy hollow like a barbaric jewel in a velvet
case, still marks the site of that small monastery, and the name and
legends of St. David are an integral part of the history of Wales.

Here I will only recall one episode: the church of Llandewi Brefi (Cards) stands upon a mound which is said to have risen miraculously beneath the feet of St. David as he addressed a synod summoned there to enact canons of discipline, so that his voice should be more clearly heard. The present church only dates from the 13th century, but built into the west wall are fragments of a memorial stone to Idnert, last Bishop of the see of Llanbadarn Fawr, founded by the Breton saint, St. Padarn, in the 6th century and merged with the see of St. David's during the Middle Ages.

St. Illtyd and St. Padarn came from Brittany to Wales, but the tide of influence was soon to turn, and one of the chief results obtained by recent researches into church dedications has been the proof that south-west England and also parts of Brittany were evangelised from Wales. Cornwall and the coastal districts of Somerset are rich in dedications to saints who have the focal point of their cult in Wales, and if we pass through Breton villages whose churches are dedicated to saints with strange, Welsh-sounding names we should remember that the founders of the bishoprics in Brittany were often monks of British origin.[18]

One such band of pious travellers was led by St. Samson of Dol whose followers included several saints commemorated in Cornish dedications: SS. Austell, Gwythian, Mewan and Winnow. Their churches lie mostly between Padstow, where they landed, and Golant.[19] Dedications to St. Samson at St. Kew and Golant mark both ends of their journey across the Cornish peninsula. While their leader founded these settlements, St. Mewan founded churches at St. Mewan and Mevagissey, and a holy well and chapel at Menacuddle also bear his name. St. Austell's foundation is marked by a fine medieval church, on the tower of which appear statues of the founder, dressed as a pilgrim, and St. Samson in bishop's robes. St. Sampson's, on Guernsey, may mark either a stage in the journey by sea, or a temporary retreat to a lonely island. In Brittany St. Samson seems to have landed in the estuary of the Rance, for he and his followers are commemorated by many dedications in the surrounding country. Yet, in spite of this widespread fame, only six English churches are dedicated to St. Samson, and the only further representations of him known to me are in windows at St. Samson's Golant and Wiggenhall St. Mary Magdalene (Norfolk).

Before he started on his journeys, St. Samson was for three years Abbot of Caldey, an island inseparably associated with the memory of the early Celtic saints. The little priory church, whose short spire leans westward, as if warped by the winds, probably dates from the 12th century, but its small dimensions and cobbled floors convey a sense of much greater antiquity. To the south of the chancel arch stands a stone inscribed in faint Ogham characters and damaged Latin script, which has been the subject of much controversy. That the inscription invites 'all those who walk in this place to pray for the soul of Cadwgan' is generally agreed, but whether or not the remaining words state that Illtyd fashioned the cross is undecided, and estimates of date vary from the 6th to the 9th century. Wronoc, the 9th-century monk who wrote the Life of St. Paul Aurelian, tells us that St. Illtyd spent much time on Caldey, together with SS. David, Paul and Samson, and the Life of St. Samson says that Dubritius was wont to spend the season of Lent on Caldey Island. There was certainly a close connection between Caldey and Llantwit Major, and the saints who taught on the mainland may well have come here to restore their strength in healing loneliness. From Caldey we can see the long rise and fall of the mainland cliffs and at the limit of westward vision, St. Govan's Head juts into the sea like the bows of a battleship. There, in a narrow crevasse among its rocks, stands a tiny chapel guarding a holy well. Tradition says that no one can count correctly the number of steps which lead down to the hermitage where St. Govan retired to end his days, and that the hollow in the living rock which we enter from the chapel was miraculously opened to hide him from pirates. The present chapel is medieval and has no pretensions to beauty, but its very insignificance, compared to the surrounding grandeur of Nature, makes it the more fitting memorial to the men who brought Christian culture to this wild countryside and later faced the even more arduous task of carrying their message to unknown lands in Cornwall and to the communities of Britons beyond the seas.

D

Chapter 3

THE FIRST CHURCH BUILDERS

WITH the coming of the Celtic missionaries from Ireland and Iona to north-western England, and the arrival of St. Augustine's mission to Canterbury, the lights begin to go up once more on the stage of English history, and some of the churches which they built are still standing. But before turning to look at these early buildings, let us consider some evidence of a phase in Christian worship which preceded the building of even the earliest Anglo-Saxon churches.

The concept of a parish church, with its particular priest serving the spiritual needs of each small community, was foreign to the Celtic monks who converted a great part of England. A Celtic bishop was often the head of a monastery to which the missionaries, who worked wherever opportunities offered for converting the heathen, could return to recreate their spiritual forces by loneliness and prayer. The first rallying-point of the newly converted was thus the spot at which the travelling teacher stopped to preach and baptise, and a rude cross made from two pieces of wood may first have marked the site where the congregation should await his coming. Reverence expressed in craftsmanship soon embellished this symbol of the Faith, and some of the surviving stone crosses show features which suggest a richly carved wooden original. Thus, the curious form of the cross shafts at Gosforth (Fig. 3) and Beckermet in Cumberland, with a circular base shaved down to form four flat sides higher up the shaft, reflects the laborious attempt of the stone carver to follow what had been the line of least resistance to his predecessor, ornamenting only the upper part of a wooden stem. The interlacing band below a change of plane, on the stone crosses at Ilam and Leek in Staffordshire, or Brailsford (Derbs), is reminiscent of a metal collar strengthening a wooden post. The circular boss which occurs in the centre of many cross heads can hardly have originated with the stone carvers, who had to sink a large field to allow for its projection, but a wood carver would naturally tend to stress the decorative effect of the nail securing the transom to the shaft.¹

In the Life of St. Willibald (born *c*. 700) we read that great and good men were wont to erect a cross, rather than a church, on their estates and Joceline of Furness, the 12th century biographer of St. Kentigern, tells us that, when the saint preached in a mountainous district near Carlisle, he set up a cross 'where now has been reared in the name of the saint, a stately church'.² This site is thought to be that of St. Kentigern's church at Crosthwaite (Cumb). In many churches the remains of Saxon crosses can be seen, many of them reduced to fragments of the shaft, sometimes recovered from medieval walls whose builders had regarded them merely as convenient blocks of stone. Four early crosses were built into the tower of Middleton (Yorks).

The finest of these Saxon crosses are the masterpieces of early British sculptors and their stylistic differences indicate the cultural associations of the various Saxon kingdoms. Thus the graceful figure sculpture on the fragments of a 7th-century cross from Reculver, now in the crypt of Canterbury cathedral, suggests that the artistic traditions of Roman Britain had survived more strongly in Kent than in other parts of the country and prepared the ground for the reintroduction of classical models by the followers of St. Augustine. The figure of a dancing man, holding aloft a branch of foliage, on the 9th-century cross shaft in the church of Codford St. Peter (Wilts), has Frankish affinities recalling, perhaps, the years of exile which King Egbert of Wessex spent at the court of Charlemagne, although the general character of the carving is essentially English.³ The great crosses of Bewcastle (Cumb) and Ruthwell (Dumfries) show that the art of Northumbria's Golden Age was partly inspired by Mediterranean examples. A characteristic form of decoration on Saxon crosses is the foliate scroll, generally of vine leaves, and sometimes with birds pecking at the grapes, as at Bewcastle and on a fragment from the Easby cross, now in the Victoria and Albert Museum. This design, derived from late Roman architecture was reproduced by early Christian artists in Byzantium, Egypt, Syria and Italy. It is possible that the Northumbrian carvers took as their models small works of art, perhaps carved in ivory or bone, imported from these countries.⁴

When the people gathered for worship, a small portable altar, like that of St. Cuthbert preserved in Durham cathedral, was

probably set up at the foot of the cross. This was inconveniently
exposed to the vagaries of the British climate so the next development was the building of a small chapel to protect it. The base of
the Reculver cross has been excavated and shown to be contemporary with, or even earlier than, the church which Bassa, the mass
priest of King Egbert of Kent, built within the Roman fort in
669, for a pink *opus signinum* pavement is stopped against it on
two sides, though this is now concealed by the turf. E. L. Cutts[5]
quotes an ancient foreign canon requiring rectors to build such
chapels, and suggests that the generally accepted medieval custom
by which the rector was responsible for the structure of the
chancel and the parishioners for that of the nave, derives from
the phase when the congregation had to build their own shelter
if they wanted it. Whatever its origin may have been, the custom
had a marked effect upon the growth of the parish churches as
can be seen by comparing the modest Early English chancel of
such a church as Blakeney (Norfolk) with the splendid nave built
by its wealthy 15th-century parishioners. A magnificent exception
to this rule is the fine chancel of Norbury church (Staffs.) (Plate 80)
built by a 14th-century rector, Henry Kniveton.

Most of the earliest churches were probably built of wood and
our only example of what they may have looked like is the early
11th-century wooden church at Greensted (Essex) where the nave
walls are made of halved tree trunks, set vertically with the flat
surface facing inwards. Although this primitive method of construction was probably used for many country churches in the 7th
century, others may have been built with timber framing filled in
with wattle and daub, for the walls of the late 10th-century tower
at Earl's Barton (Northants) are decorated, not only with the
vertical stone pilaster strips characteristic of the grander Anglo-
Saxon buildings, but also with angled strips which resemble the
struts of medieval half-timbered construction.[6] It looks as if the
Saxon masons, still uncertain of how to design in stone, had
copied the familiar conventions of wooden architecture. They
were not always highly qualified, and when we see some of their
first experiments in building arches we can imagine the feelings of
relief with which some early Saxon church builders appropriated
complete Roman archways from ruined buildings, as well supplies
of cut stones. At Britford (Wilts) the arch of the original south

door is turned in re-used Roman bricks. Some of these are wedge-shaped for use as voussoirs, but the Saxon mason had so little understanding of the principles of arch construction that he set many of them with the thick end to the centre, relying on the varying thickness of his beds of mortar to turn the arch. At Wootton Wawen (Warcs) the springings of the Saxon arches have been laboriously cut out of solid stone.

Corstopitum was one of the most important stations on the Wall and we enter the parish church of Corbridge (Northumb) through a west porch, large in proportion to the rest of the building, under a magnificent archway, 16 feet in height, and with Roman mouldings. The whole arch is, presumably, a Roman gateway from Corstopitum, and the marks on the stones of the surrounding wall suggest that these came from the same source. The church contains many detached Roman stones, including the top of an altar. At Escomb (Durham) an almost unaltered Saxon church has thick walls built largely of squared stones, showing Roman tooling, which probably came from Binovium (Binchester). The most striking feature of this interior is the chancel arch, perhaps a gateway of the ruined fort. Both here and at Corbridge the massive jambs and voussoirs are so deep that they form a lining to the arch.

In the belfry opening of the Saxon tower at Wickham (Berks), a Roman dwarf pillar, little more than 3 feet high, is used to divide a two-light window in the manner characteristic of Saxon architecture. Dwarf pillars such as this have been found on several sites of Roman buildings, and the success with which they could be re-used may have led to their reproduction when the supply was exhausted. From a very early period Saxon builders used small lathe-turned balusters as a decorative feature, as for instance in the porch of Monkwearmouth (Durham), but here the classical divisions of base, shaft and capital have been ignored, although the mouldings show skilled craftsmanship. The use of a lathe would have been familiar to many builders in wood.

In the Celtic monasteries oratories for individual monks were often scattered over a large area with a church, and sometimes a refectory, serving as meeting places. The whole was usually surrounded by some kind of defensive wall. The monks were glad to inherit from the Romans, not only the worked stone with which to build their churches, but also the shelter of their abandoned forts. The most interesting example of this is at Bradwell-on-Sea (Essex) where the church of St. Peter-on-the-Walls is almost certainly that built by St. Cedd *c.* 653, in the Roman fort of Othona, when he established a monastery at 'Ythancester'. Blocked arches on the outer walls of this little church show that it once shared with the Roman-built church at Silchester and many churches in North Africa, the peculiarity of two irregularly placed transeptal projections.[7] Of these the *prothesis*, entered from the nave, served for the reception of offerings while in the *diaconicon*, opening into the chancel, the holy vessels were kept. The foundations of the 7th-century church at Reculver (Kent) lie within the Roman fort of Regulbium and at Burgh Castle (Suffolk), where St. Fursa is said to have founded a monastery, the isolated parish church stands near the Roman walls. Churches also stand within the Roman forts of Dover, Portchester and Lympne, but they appear to be of later foundation.

What were presumably the grandest Anglo-Saxon churches have all been pulled down and rebuilt at later periods; the Normans had all a victor's contempt for the achievements of those whom they had conquered. We can only form an idea of their probable magnificence by taking characteristic features from this or that more modest building and combining them in our imaginations with the references of the early chroniclers. We know from Jarrow and Bradford-on-Avon that Saxon churches were often high in proportion to their width, and sometimes very long as well. Brixworth (Northants), which must have been one of the finest churches built north of the Alps at that period, gives us a sense of scale, and the delicacy of their sculptural ornaments may be gauged by the fragments at Breedon-on-the-Hill (Leics) or Sompting (Sussex). The vigorous rhythms of their figure sculpture can be typified by the flying angels of Bradford-on-Avon. We know from records that the walls of churches were sometimes adorned with paintings and if these reflected the influence of the monastic artists who produced some of the superb pre-Conquest manuscripts, they must have been splendid indeed.

From such nostalgic imaginings of what was built, we must now turn to the scanty memorials of those responsible for the building of some very early churches. Visible record of the identity of the church builder is very rare but an inscribed stone in the church of St. Mary-le-Wigford, Lincoln (which still retains its Saxon tower) states that: EIRTHIG HAD ME BUILT AND ENDOWED IN PRAISE OF CHRIST AND MARY. Who Eirthig was, whether missionary or convert, we do not know. A more interesting memorial is the inscription over the south door of Warnford (Hants): WILFRID FUNDAVIT BONUS ADAM RENOVAVIT, which records both the foundation of the church by St. Wilfrid, during his exile in Wessex in 675, and the 12th-century rebuilding by Adam de Port.

A connection with St. Paulinus, who worked in Northumbria under King Edwin, but returned to Kent with the widowed queen Ethelburgha after the King's death in 633, may perhaps be traced on the Saxon sundial above the south door of Kirkdale church (Yorks). The inscription tells us that 'Orm the son of Gamal bought St. Gregory's Minster when it was broken and fallen down, and made it anew from the ground, to Christ and St. Gregory, in the days of Edward the King and Tosti the Earl'. It ends, 'Hawarth me wrought and Brand, priests'. The dedication to the great Pope suggests an early foundation[8] and as Paulinus is known to have preached on the Yorkshire moors it is likely that the first church marked one of his missionary stations. The nave of Kirkdale is still much as Orm built it, between 1055, when Tosti became Earl of Northumberland, and 1065, when he was banished for crimes which included the murder of Gamal, Lord of Kirby Moorside.

Above the south door of Edstone church (Yorks N.R.) there is a sundial of Anglo-Danish character inscribed 'Othan has wrought me' (*Othan me prohtea*) but this may not have referred to the whole church.

In most places it is the position of the church rather than its structure which recalls the first builders. The support of the Anglo-Saxon leaders, whether king or thegn, was essential for the conversion of their followers and close contact had to be maintained with them. Just as the *cathedra* of a bishop was sited where the King usually held his court, so the church built with the aid of a local thegn was usually near his hall. The priest who officiated in it was also his chaplain, a tradition which persists in the peculiarly English custom by which the Lord of the Manor can nominate a priest to his local benefice, subject only to the approval of the bishop. In cases where the Domesday Survey records that one man held lands in various parts of the country, there is frequently only mention of a church in one place, presumably his favourite residence, and sometimes it is definitely stated that this church stands on his demesne.[9] The Domesday Survey tells us that the wealthy Saxon, Cheping, had a church near his home at Headbourne Worthy (Hants) but none is mentioned on his other estates in Hampshire. We often see a village church standing either within the park of the great house, or else close to its gates, as though the relative positions of the thegn's hall and the church which served as his private chapel had remained unchanged, but it would be rash to assume in all such cases that the first church was built there by a Saxon thegn, for at no time have the Lords of the Manor welcomed an unnecessarily long journey to church.

Above the original west door of Cheping's church at Headbourne Worthy, which is now enclosed within a later tower, we can see the battered outline of a magnificent Saxon rood group carved on the surface of the wall and a similarly defaced Saxon rood at Breamore may have been built in emulation. If our imaginations restore to these pathetic outlines carvings of the quality of the Romsey Rood, or the flying angels beside the chancel arch at Bradford-upon-Avon (Wilts), we shall do fuller justice to the memory of some of these Saxon church builders. The coffin lid of a member of the Cheping family, if not of the Lord of the Manor himself, can be seen in the church of Stratfield Mortimer (Berks). It is inscribed: ✠ VIII KL'. OCTB FUIT POSITUS AEGELWARDUS FILIUS KYPPINGUS IN ISTO LOCO. BEATUS SIT OMO QUI ORAT PRO ANIMA EIUS. ✠ TOKI ME SCRIPSIT.

In East Anglia, particularly in Suffolk, the Domesday Survey records cases of churches owned, and therefore presumably built, by groups of freemen of very modest means. At Culpho the church, endowed with ten acres of land, stood on the holdings of five freemen who owned only twenty-one acres between them. The ownership of the church (and the Survey brings out the essentially proprietary character of the early organisation) might be divided; at Wantisden (Suffolk), half of the church was attached to the holdings of twenty-two freemen, while the remaining quarters were held by two freemen and one freeman respectively.

Other examples of such part-ownership of a church are referred to at Braiseworth, Helmingham and Creeting St. Peter. The fact that the Derbyshire church of Brailsford, which has a fine Saxon cross and some traces of pre-Conquest masonry, stands outside the village, is probably explained by the entries in the Domesday Survey recording that Brailsford and the neighbouring manor of Ednaston each owned 'half a church'.[10] Communal ownership of town churches is recorded in Norwich and Hedon (Yorks) at a much later date.

The Saxon towers of such churches as Bosham and Singleton in Sussex and Deerhurst (Glos) have upper chambers with doors, or long windows, opening into the nave. It has been suggested that these chambers served as the private oratory of the thegn, but, alternatively, they may have been used for the sacrist and have given access to a western gallery from which the watcher could say the night offices without descending into the nave.[11] If the Saxon thegns of Deerhurst did use the tower of the monastery church as a private oratory, they must have found the arrangement unsatisfactory, for, in 1056, Duke Odda built a small chapel near by where Masses could be said for the soul of his brother, Elfric.[12] It is less than 40 feet long and has both nave and chancel, with a narrow arch separating them. For many years it served as a farm building but has now been restored and is as fairly representative of the private chapel of a pre-Conquest Lord of the Manor as any building we shall find in England.

Chapter 4

THE MARTYRDOM OF KINGS

THE CONVERSION of the Anglo-Saxon kings was of paramount importance to the early Christian missionaries. Backed by the king's favour, they could extend their teaching throughout his realm and converts would flock to hear them, but the death of a Christian king and the succession of a pagan one could quickly undo all that they had achieved.

It was, therefore, natural that Anglo-Saxon royalties, whether mighty kings or obscure princesses, should become such an integral part of the history of the early Church in Britain that their names are still remembered in the lands they ruled. Churches are dedicated to them, and their figures are represented in sculpture, stained glass and wall-painting. In the 14th and 15th centuries there was a marked recrudescence of interest in the saints of Anglo-Saxon England, occasioned perhaps by a rising sense of English nationalism, as opposed to either Norman or Saxon, or merely by the desire of those concerned with the administration of churches where such saints were buried to attract more pilgrims. Elaborate tombs were built at the places where tradition told that even uncanonised kings were buried; a fine altar-tomb which is said to mark the burial-place of King Athelstan stands in the north aisle at Malmesbury.*

The lives of these royal saints as recorded by monastic chroniclers and illustrated by ecclesiastical artists, represented the average medieval Englishman's knowledge of Anglo-Saxon his-

---

* Allusions to this great King are also to be found in other churches. A window in York Minster which illustrates the life of St. John of Beverley includes one panel showing a king kneeling before an altar on which lies a sword. This refers to the incident when Athelstan laid his sword upon the saint's shrine, before the Battle of Brunanburgh, promising to redeem it should he defeat the Danes. He did redeem his sword but later bequeathed it to the Minster where it was laid in the tomb of St. John. The arms which medieval heralds ascribed to King Athelstan (*Per saltire gules and azure, a cross botonny argent*) appear in the windows of Milton (Dorset) and Muchelney (Somerset), for in both places he was reputed to have founded the Abbey. In Milton Abbey he is shown in a medieval painting presenting a model of a church to a kneeling Abbot.

tory. Thus, although their representation in medieval churches may not teach us any new facts, and the events depicted may never have happened, we have the interest of looking at this early period through medieval eyes.

There were no martyrdoms due to religious intolerance in Anglo-Saxon England, although the early Church bestowed the title of martyr upon several Christian princes who were killed by their political opponents, for canonisation then took place by popular acclamation, without the elaborate procedure which was instituted later.[1] Although strong support given to the Church, and a contemporary reputation for personal piety, distinguished some of the Saxon kings who were later revered as saints, a violent death seems to have been an essential qualification until the case of Edward the Confessor. Had Penda, King of the Mercians, not slain so many Christian kings in battle, our churches would be less informative about the history of the 7th century, but his campaigns were probably launched from desire for plunder rather than in support of paganism. A pagan Penda remained to the end of his days (although the 19th-century carvers of the west front of Lichfield cathedral have represented him in a central position, clasping the Cross), but Bede tells us that he did not oppose the teaching of Christianity in Mercia, only despising 'those instructed in the faith of Christ whom he discovered to have not works of faith'.[2] This insistence upon martyrdom as a prelude to canonisation has made the record of the churches historically unbalanced. Princes who did great service to the spread of Christian teaching in England have no memorial while others, memorable only for their tragic end, are commemorated by dedications and find their place in the iconography of medieval art. Without the support of King Ethelbert of Kent, St. Augustine would have found it hard to establish his mission in pagan England, yet no church is dedicated to this monarch, while sixteen, including the cathedral of Hereford, are dedicated to Ethelbert of East Anglia, of whom we only know that he was murdered by Offa of Mercia under suspicion of being a spy. Yet the loyal supporter of St. Augustine is not without his memorial. Canterbury was a town of secondary importance in Roman Britain and St. Augustine had intended to establish archbishoprics in London and York, but, when he came to England, he found that Ethelbert had made Kent the dominant kingdom of the Heptarchy so the capital of Kent became, and still remains, the Metropolitan See of England.[3]

King Edwin of Northumbria was the first of the Anglo-Saxon kings to be canonised, but although his conversion seemed to assure the acceptance of Christianity in the whole area from the Humber to the Forth, the church of Coniscliffe-on-Tees (Durham) is the only one still dedicated to him. A statue on the west front of Wells cathedral (that fine medieval sculpture gallery of national and scriptural history) has been identified as St. Edwin on the grounds that the figure stabbing itself, carved on the base, may refer to the attempted assassination of this king by an emissary from the King of Wessex.

After a short interval, Edwin was succeeded upon the throne of Northumbria by Oswald, distinguished alike as saint and ruler, who made his kingdom predominant in the Heptarchy during the eight years of his reign, and to whom sixty-two British churches are still dedicated.[4] One of these, the little chapel of St. Oswald, near Chollerford (Northumb), is sometimes claimed as marking the site of the Battle of Heavenfield, by which he won back his kingdom. Oswald had spent his youth as an exile in Scotland, and it was to Iona that he appealed for a teacher to reconvert Northumbria. The church of Bamburgh, once capital of Northumbria, is dedicated to St. Aidan, that teacher whose gentleness won all hearts and for whom the king was proud to serve as interpreter. When King Oswald ordered the silver dish, from which he was about to eat, to be broken up and given to the poor who had gathered about his gates to beg for alms, St. Aidan exclaimed: 'May this hand never wax old!' and after the King's death his hand was found to be incorruptible and was preserved as one of the chief treasures of Peterborough cathedral, having been stolen from Bamburgh by a monk, Vynegot.[5] The statue of St. Oswald on the west front of Wells is identified by the dish which he holds (Plate 5).

St. Oswald fell in the battle of the 'Maserfield', the location of which is disputed between Oswestry (Salop) and Winwick (Lancs). A stone of uncertain date set in the wall at Winwick bears an inscription stating that King Oswald was here slain, and we may imagine the man holding two handbells, carved on a pre-Conquest cross shaft in this church, ringing the knell of the great Northumbrian king. When his dismembered body was recovered by the army of his brother Oswy, it was first buried at Bardney (Lincs), where the parish church contains a stone said to have covered his grave. It was subsequently translated, by Ælfled, daughter of Alfred the Great, to the Abbey of St. Oswald at Gloucester, of which only scanty ruins now remain. At this period the translation of the body of a dead person implied recognition that the deceased had been a saint.[6] His head was originally buried at Lindisfarne, but, when the Viking raids made the monks flee to the mainland carrying with them the body of St. Cuthbert, they put the head of St. Oswald in the same coffin, and its frontal bone was found when the coffin was opened in 1899. It is for this reason that we commonly see St. Cuthbert represented as a bishop carrying a king's head in his hand, as in the statues of Henry VII's chapel, Westminster, and the Chapel of the Nine Altars, Durham, a window at Methley (Yorks) or the painted screen of Nayland-on-Stour (Suffolk). Single figures of King Oswald appear in windows at Cockayne Hatley (Beds), brought there from a church in Yorkshire, York Minster and All Souls Chapel, Oxford. His cult was evidently much more widely spread than that of St. Edwin, despite the similarity of their stories, and it was not even limited to England, for the cathedral of Zug in Switzerland is dedicated to him.[7]

In 1841 a Saxon-inscribed stone was discovered at Collingham (Yorks) and is now in that church. Its wording was then thought to read: 'Œdibloed this set after her nephew, after the King Auswini, pray for the soul', and to imply that it was here that St. Oswin, King of Deira, was murdered at the order of his brother, King Oswy of Bernicia. Later critics have doubted both this reading of the inscription and the possibility of its being of 7th-century workmanship. Although a wide area round the shrine at Tynemouth to which St. Oswin's relics were translated after the Norman Conquest was known as St. Oswin's Peace and regarded as a sanctuary, no church retains a dedication to him. On the other hand, five ancient dedications are known to St. Edward, King and Martyr,[8] although it is improbable that his stepmother had him murdered at Corfe Castle for reasons connected with his faith. A low-vaulted chapel of curious construction in the church at Wareham (Dorset), St. Edward's Chapel, is said to reproduce the structure of the little wooden chapel in which his body was buried, until popular indignation brought about its translation to Shaftesbury, where the great Abbey was dedicated in his name. His statue at Wells stands upon the crouching figure of the cruel Queen Ælfryth and holds in one hand the broken stem of the goblet from which he was drinking when his murderers struck him down.

Lest I should be accused of suggesting that the study of medieval iconography is a safe way of learning history I must mention one case in which the unbiased record of early charters has been contrasted with the legend of the pious chroniclers of the Middle Ages. Legend tells us that St. Kenelm succeeded his father, King Kenulph of Mercia, in 819, while still a child, and that he was murdered by Ascobert, the lover of his elder sister Quendreda, who coveted the throne. The guilty queen gave out that the child had disappeared mysteriously and threatened with death anyone who should even mention his name, but a white dove let fall a scroll before the Pope, as he celebrated Mass in St. Peter's, on which was written:

> In Clent, at Cowbach, lieth under a thorn
> His head off-shorn, Kenelm, king-born.

The Pope instructed the Archbishop of Canterbury to investigate this accusation and the searchers were guided to the grave by the lowing of a white cow. Beside the body they found a blood-stained knife and, from the empty grave, a fountain gushed forth which later attracted pilgrims from all over the country. The blocked arches by which these pilgrims once approached the holy spring can still be seen under the east end of St. Kenelm's church on the Clent Hills and a modern window in the nave illustrates his legend. Kenelm's body was borne with pomp to his father's capital of Winchcombe. As the procession entered the town, Quendreda was reading the psalter backwards, for some dark charm, and when she came to the words 'this is the work of them who defame me to the Lord and speak evil against my soul' her eyes were torn from their sockets by divine vengeance and the page was splashed with blood.[9] The story, which appears first in a comparatively simple form in the 11th-century chronicle of Florence of Worcester, gathered miraculous elements with each retelling, but the documentary evidence suggests that Kenelm either died as a child during his father's lifetime (he is mentioned in charters as early as 803 but not after 811) or was grown up when, according to the Anglo-Saxon Chronicle, Kenulph was succeeded by his brother, Ceolwulf. Kenulph was alive in 821 and Quendreda was certainly Abbess of Southminster (probably Minster in Thanet) by 824 if not earlier, an appointment which would hardly have been made had she been generally thought to have been miraculously blinded as a punishment for fratricide.[10]

When the foundations of Winchcombe Abbey were excavated in 1815, two stone coffins were found, a large one containing the bones of a grown man and a smaller one in which were the bones of a child and also a long-bladed knife.[11] The bones immediately crumbled to dust but the coffins remain in Winchcombe parish church. Since Leland's Itinerary of 1549 states that Kenulph and Kenelm were buried in Winchcombe Abbey, it seems probable that these coffins were theirs, and that the monks of Winchcombe, eager to enhance the sanctity of the young Mercian prince, slandered Quendreda in order to match the female-murderess element in the legends of both St. Ethelbert and St. Edward. The statue of St. Kenelm at Wells stands upon the figure of a crouching woman, falling forwards on to an open book (Plate 6).

An incident of the Viking wars frequently represented in churches is the martyrdom of St. Edmund who succeeded to the throne of East Anglia about 855. In 870 he was defeated by a Danish army and was put to death because he refused to abjure Christianity. The bosses of the cloister at Norwich show us his birth (with a crowned queen in bed and the Hand of God issuing from a cloud to point out the child held by a nurse in the background) and a battered representation of his martyrdom. A more spirited carving of this is shown on a misericord at Norton (Suffolk) and it also appears on the bosses of St. Edmund's chapel Tewkesbury, in wall-paintings at Troston (Suffolk), Hemblington (Norfolk) and Stoke Dry (Rutland) and the glass of the Lady Chapel of Bristol cathedral.[12] A picturesque element in the legend is that of the faithful wolf which guarded the King's head through the night, allowing no Dane to come near, and yielded it up to the King's attendants in the morning. To eyes accustomed to the pictorial shorthand of medieval iconography, any vaguely dog-like animal with a crowned head between its paws would suggest the whole legend of St. Edmund, and it is thus that we see it on bench-ends at Hoxne, Hadleigh and Stonham Aspall in Suffolk, at Walpole St. Peter (Norfolk) (Plate 7), on the stone parapet of Pulham St. Mary (Norfolk) and on a stone seat in Ely cathedral. The martyr's body was taken first to Bury St. Edmunds; thence, under threat of fresh Danish attacks, to London, and then back to Bury in 1013. During this last journey the body rested at Greensted (Essex) where the one surviving wooden church was probably built to give it temporary shelter. The cult of the saint was widespread. Sixty-one English churches are dedicated to him, the finest being that at Southwold (Suffolk) where an inscription in crowned letters, inlaid in stone on flint, above the west door, reads: SCT EDMUND ORA PRO NOBIS. His figure is generally identified by his crown and the arrows which he holds, as on the painted screens of Barton Turf, Barnham Broom, and Trimingham in Norfolk; Guilden Morden (Cambs) and in the east window of Long Melford (Suffolk). Sometimes the attributes appear alone, as on the porch of Fressingfield (Suffolk), and they were often represented on the shield-shaped marks of the medieval bellfounders of East Anglia.

As Christianity became the unchallenged religion of Western Europe the Church became more critical of the claims of murdered monarchs to be considered as saints. The transformation of the choir and transepts of Gloucester cathedral marks this changed attitude. When Edward II was murdered at Berkeley Castle in 1327* the Abbeys of Bristol and Malmesbury pusillanimously refused to give his body burial, but the Abbot of Gloucester went in solemn procession to fetch it. Popular imagination was inflamed by the crime to such an extent that the weak and favourite-ridden monarch was hailed as a martyred saint, and the miracles wrought by his relics brought throngs of pilgrims to the beautiful shrine erected by Edward III on the north side of the choir (Plate 81). Their offerings almost rebuilt the Abbey as a testimony to their belief in the sanctity of the dead king, but Edward II was not canonised.[13]

---

* The death-agony of Edward II is represented on two bosses in the transept of Bristol cathedral. One of these is reproduced by C. J. P. Cave in *Roof Bosses in Medieval Churches*, and shows the King, naked save for his crown, pointing to the spot where the red-hot iron entered his body.

The commercialism which was one of the chief abuses of the medieval Church makes itself apparent in the case of Henry VI. His noted piety and the sinister indications of violence which attended his death made him a martyr by popular acclamation, but the Archbishop of York forbade the veneration of his statue on the rood-screen of the Minster.[14] In a letter, written in 1504, Pope Julius II stated that miracles had been wrought by the intercession of the dead king, but at this period the power of deciding whether a suggested saint should be canonised was the prerogative of the Pope, and heavy dues were levied by the Papal Court. Henry VII parsimoniously refused to pay these, and the sanctity of Henry VI remained a matter of public opinion which, to judge by the frequency with which we find him represented in churches, was fully in his favour. He appears on nine painted rood-screens in East Anglia alone, amongst them Binham, North Elmham and Barton Turf in Norfolk, and Eye and Nayland-on-Stour in Suffolk. He also appears on a panel, now attached to the pulpit at Sturminster Marshall (Dorset). It is, however, as sovereign rather than saint that he set his mark upon the ecclesiastical architecture of his country, and we owe to him two of the finest monuments of late Gothic building, the chapels of his foundations of Eton College and King's College, Cambridge.

The cult of martyred kings was not confined to the Middle Ages. On the very day when King Charles I was buried, a book entitled *Eikon Basilike* appeared in London and was immediately accepted by all Royalists as an authentic portrayal of the King in the role of a martyred saint. It recorded his meditations on the troubles of his reign, his prayers and the Christian fortitude with which he foresaw his probable execution. In spite of all attempts to suppress the book it sold so widely that it was reprinted thirty times within a year.[15] So fervid a cult of the new saint naturally left its mark upon some churches. Five churches are dedicated to Charles I: Newtown (Salop), Falmouth, Peak Forest, Plymouth, Tunbridge Wells and Shelland (Suffolk). At Lambourn (Berks) there is a 17th-century alabaster relief showing the King's head in profile being crowned by angels. On the back of a set of royal arms, now hanging in the tower of Burstwick church (Yorks E.R.) there is a rough painting of the King's execution, obviously copied from the woodcut at the top of some contemporary

E

broadsheet. At Little Compton (War), the village to which Archbishop Juxon retired after the execution of his royal master, a modern window first shows him with Charles and his family in prison and then assisting both at the execution and funeral of the King.

Perhaps the most interesting memorial of King Charles' death is the chronogram* cut on a beam in the porch of Brookthorpe church (Glos) which reads:

ter DenO IanI Labens reX soLe CaDente	(= 1212)
CaroLVs eXVtVs soLIo sCeptroqVe seCVre	(= 436)

(= 1648)

'In the afternoon of 30 January the falling king was stripped of throne and sceptre by the axe'.

and gives the date of the King's execution according to the Old Style calendar.

The vindictive oppression of the Royalists under the Commonwealth is frequently recorded in epitaphs, as, for instance, that of Colonel John Salkeld at Rock (Northumberland) which tells us that he served King Charles 'with a constant, dangerous and expensive loyalty'. After so many reminders of the terrible cost in human suffering of religious fanaticism, it is comforting to find, at Staunton Harold (Leics) an inscription which expresses the spirit of healing tolerance. Above the florid west door, whose classical details and heavy swags of fruit are the only obvious indications of the late date of the church, is a tablet with this

---

* A chronogram is a sentence of which certain letters express a date while the sentence itself alludes to the event which then took place. Every letter which represents a Roman numeral must be counted, and as it is thus difficult to avoid too large a total in any but the shortest sentences, the date is often doubled or tripled. As X is a rare letter W has the value of 10 and U is reckoned, and often written V; J is the equivalent of I. Although a possible chronogram is known dating from the 13th century, the device did not become current until the 15th century. The majority of chronograms are in Latin and come from Catholic countries, the Jesuits being particularly adept at their composition. Sculptured chronograms are rare in England. There is one on the tomb, in Westminster Abbey, of Ludovic Stuart, Duke of Richmond and Lennox, the cousin of James I. It reads: 'an IgnorantIs bUIa prInCeps et VIr MagnUs ob IIt hoDIe' = 1623. (W. L. White, 'Chronograms', *The Library*, iv. 59 ff.)

inscription: 'In the year 1653, when all things sacred were throughout the nation either demollisht or profaned, Sir Robert Shirley, baronet, founded this church, whose singular grace it is to have done the best things in the worst times and hoped them in the most calamitous'[16].

Chapter 5

SCANDINAVIAN BRITAIN

ROM THE END of the 8th century onwards, raiding Vikings
ravaged the coasts of Britain and the monasteries, often built
on islands or exposed promontories, were among their chief
objectives. Later rebuilding has obliterated most traces of these
raids, but the marks of fire are said to be visible on some stones
at the east end of the church of Barton-upon-Humber (Lincs)
burned by the Danes in 867. Two great Saxon churches in East
Anglia, North and South Elmham, were also burned and the
foundations of the former were covered by an early Norman
earthwork which suggests that this church was still ruinous in the
11th century. The Normans would hardly have destroyed an
existing cathedral to build a castle.[1]

There has always been a tradition that Danes caught pillaging
on the East Coast were flayed alive and their skins nailed to the
church doors. Fragments of the skins of fair-haired persons have
indeed been found under the ironwork of church doors at Hadstock (Essex) (this is now in the Saffron Walden Museum) and
Copford (Essex), but human skin was also found upon doors in
Westminster Abbey, so this hideous penalty may have been applied
to any captured church robber.[2]

Another problem connected with the Viking raids is that of the
origin of the East Anglian round towers. Many of the round
towers in Ireland are known to have been built as places of
defence in which the villagers could withstand the assault of the
Vikings for the short time which their forays usually lasted, and
it has been suggested that the East Anglian round towers had a
similar purpose. In Norfolk there are 129 such towers[3] and 41
more in Suffolk, situated mostly close to the favourite landing-
places of the Vikings in the estuaries of the Yare and the Waveney.
Some of these round towers, if we discount later alterations, show
features suggestive of defence; no windows near the ground, and
those of the first floor very narrow; no west entrance and, on the
east side, a narrow arched doorway, the sill of which is at least

10 feet above the ground. The most formidable of them, from the raiders' point of view, would have been Wortham (Suffolk) which has an interior diameter of 29 feet with walls 4 feet thick.[4] This, like the round towers at Barsham, Bungay, Hengrave and Wissett in Suffolk, was probably built early in the 11th century. Any of these towers might have played a useful part in coastal defence, both as observation posts from which early warning of approaching forays could have been given by means of their bells, and as places of defence when no better strongholds were available, but that they were actually built for defence remains unproven. The absence of good building stone to make angle quoins would have been a sufficient reason for the persistence of this form, which also occurs in the lower stage of the flint tower at Little Shefford (Berks).

During most of the 10th century Viking raids ceased and the children of earlier invaders settled down to cultivate the lands they had won, but, in the reign of Ethelred the Unready (978–1016), the raids began again. By 1010 the whole of southern England was being ravaged and one of the reasons why only one pre-Conquest chalice survives (the Trewhiddle Chalice in the British Museum) may be that so much church plate was melted down during Ethelred's unsuccessful attempts to buy off the Danes. In 1011 they attacked Canterbury and the 12th-century roundel of stained glass in the Cathedral represents this siege (Plate 20). For three weeks St. Alphege, then Archbishop, defended the city which was eventually taken by treachery. Another medallion in this window shows the Archbishop being forced aboard a Danish ship where his captors pelted him to death with bones, during a drunken orgy, after he had refused to ask for ransom. Five English churches are dedicated to him at Canterbury, Greenwich, Seasalter (Kent), London Wall and Solihull (War) and he is represented in windows at Great Malvern (Worcs), New College Oxford and Alfriston (Sussex).

It was not only upon the East Coast that the fury of the Norsemen descended. St. David's cathedral was thrice burned by the Danes and an 11th-century cross in the south transept is a memorial to the sons of Bishop Abraham who fell during the last attack, in 1078. The concealed position of the great Norman cathedral, which is revealed with startling suddenness to the stranger who wanders, unprepared, through the medieval gateway from the town, is another reminder of the danger of sea-borne raids. It was better to remain invisible, and not until comparative safety had been achieved in the Middle Ages did the builders of St. David's and Llandaff allow their bell-towers to top the cover of the hills which hid both cathedrals from the sea.

The long ships from the Norwegian fjords generally followed the Outer Line which carried some of them on adventurous journeys to Greenland and North America, whilst others, steered more cautiously round the north coast of Britain, overran the Orkneys and parts of south-west Scotland, established the Kingdom of Dublin, and later, turning eastward once more, settled colonies in the English counties of Cumberland, Westmorland, Lancashire and Cheshire. Churches dedicated to Irish saints in these counties recall these Norse settlements to which, in the 10th century, missionaries from Ireland brought the message of Christianity. The evidence of the dedication is sometimes supported by the presence of monuments dating from this period, as, for instance, the wheel-head crosses at Topcliffe (Yorks N.R.) where the church is dedicated to St. Columba, or at the two churches dedicated to St. Bridget at West Kirby (Ches) and Brigham (Cumb).

The wheel-head cross is one of the most characteristic forms of Norse sculpture, as opposed to the Anglian type in which the arms of the cross are left free. We have already noticed that a cross enclosed in a circle was incised upon the stone slabs of some early Celtic monuments, but its use as the head of a free-standing cross, with the interstices of the arms pierced through the thickness of the stone, seems to have originated in the Isle of Man, where early examples are plentiful, and to have been imported into England by the Norsemen. A map of England showing the distribution of the remaining wheel-head crosses (Fig. 2) immediately reveals their interest as evidence of the cultural relations between different parts of Scandinavian Britain.[5] They are most frequent on the coast of Cumberland, opposite the Isle of Man, and in Yorkshire, with a fair number in the area lying between these two districts, a reminder that, in the first part of the 10th century (and none of the Yorkshire crosses is earlier) there was much travel between Ireland and York, since the kings of Northumbria reigned

SKETCH MAP
THE DISPERSION OF
WHEEL-CROSSES

St Vigeans +

dalton +
Barochan +

Lesmahagow +

GALLOWAY

Rockcliff
+
+Bromfield
Gilcrux ++Aspatria +
+Dearham Penrith Stanwick Kirklevington
Brigham K.Stephen + + +
Gosforth + Gilling Brompton-side
Lezayre +Muncaster Finghall + N'. + K.Moorside +Sinnington
Ballaugh ++ + + +allerton + + Middleton
Michael + Lonan Urswick + +Malton +Ellerburn
Braddan + Corchan +Burton Topcliffe+Stonegrave + + +Driffield
Gargrave Bilton + York N.Frodingham
Otley + + +
Leeds + K.Wharfe

penmon W. Kirby Winwick Conisbro'
Hilbre I. + + +
Diserth + + Bromborough Disley
Maen-y- + Neston +
chwyfan Chester
Rolleston
+
Whissonsett
+
Barnack + +Helpston

Mears Ashby Willingham
Cambridge +
Stapleford+ Fulbourn

+Nevern
St Davids
Carew
+ Gnoll
Margam
+ +Coychurch
Penally +
Merthyr mawr +
Llantwit

Lanherne St Teath
+Cardynham
+St Neot
Lanivet
llack
Sancreed

FIG. 2.

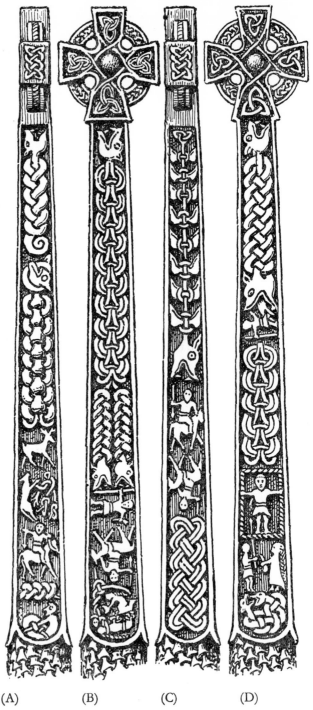

(A)   (B)   (C)   (D)

alternately in both places. A group on the shores of the Mersey estuary and the coast of north Wales is linked with another group in Cambridgeshire and Norfolk by a few isolated examples which seem to mark a route through Disley (Ches), Rolleston (Staffs) and Barnack (Lincs). Other groups of late 10th- or early 11th-century crosses occur on the coast of south Wales and in Cornwall, within an easy sea journey of the Isle of Man. Sometimes the design of the English crosses shows a close affinity with the Manx monuments; at Kirkby Wharfe, Collingham and Saxton, all in the West Riding, are crosses which have a centre pattern also used by the great Manx carver of the mid-10th century, Gaut Bjarnarson.[6]

The pagan Vikings held that the grave was the habitation of the departed spirit, and the curious tombstones which are known by the misleading name of 'Hog-backs' are the solid stone roofs with which, even after their conversion to Christianity, they covered the burial-places of their distinguished dead. Like the roofs of their wooden houses, the ridges of the long stones curve slightly downwards to the gables, while the sides are sometimes ornamented with patterns imitating tiles. Figures of crouching animals decorate the gable-ends, presumably in the belief, common to many countries, that these would frighten away evil spirits from

---

Fig. 3. The Gosforth Cross

Apparently carved as the block lay on the ground, the design runs alternately up and down the shaft, beginning on the south side and working round in the direction of the sun.

(A)—South side: The Hart and Wolf, a symbol of opposed good and evil common to both Christian and pagan. Sometimes the Hart symbolised Vidar, so the tangle at the feet of the Wolf may represent the broken bonds from which the Fenris Wolf rushes to attack its eventual conqueror.

(B)—West side: Two plaited dragons attacking Heimdal, Warder of Heaven, who holds up his great Horn. Below, Loki lies bound, beneath the snake, while Sygin kneels above him pouring poison from her cup.

(C)—North side: The two horsemen are probably meant to be confronted, one of them being perhaps Surt, the fire-god from the south. The many-winged dragon may be meant for the Ship of Hel, and the whole scene for the gathering of the destroyers before the last fight of the Gods.

(D)—East side: Vidar, the only surviving God, rends open the dragon's jaws, thus ending the old world. The promise of a new world to come with the rebirth of Baldur 'the mighty ruler who orders all' is here related to the death and Resurrection of Christ. The snakes below the figures of Mary Magdalene and Longinus in the Crucifixion panel recall the line of the Völuspà: 'Fares from beneath a dim dragon flying . . . Nidhögg'.

sitting on the roof-tree. On early Irish reliquaries, and in the Bayeux Tapestry, as well as on the surviving Stave churches of Norway, we see roof finials decorated with grotesque animal heads, and the thatchers of East Anglia who gave an upward tilt to their gable-ends (in spite of the practical drawbacks of this custom) unconsciously reproduced the last vestige of a guardian dragon.[7] At Brompton (Yorks, N.R.) about ten hog-backs have been found, of which five are now in the Durham Cathedral Library, and most of these have muzzled bears grasping their gables. The choice may have been dictated by some totem-like association with the families buried here. The appearance of coped gravestones, akin to hog-back tombs, at Lanivet, St. Tudy and St. Buryan, in Cornwall, indicate some peaceful settlement of Vikings, who otherwise only figure in Cornish history as bringers of fire and sword. This settlement may also be responsible for the dedication of Poughill church to St. Olave, the King of Norway whose forceful attempts to convert his subjects to Christianity drove them to revolt and murder him. In Scotland, hog-backs can be seen in the church at Abercorn (West Lothian) and near Inchcolm Abbey (Fife).

Scandinavian settlers in Britain seem to have been converted to Christianity with a curious transitional phase when their old mythology seemed to them equally suitable for the decoration of crosses as the imagery of their new Faith. It has been suggested[8] that the strange iconography of the Gosforth Cross (Cumb) (Fig. 3) may illustrate the chief incidents in the *Völuspà*, a poem of the Edda which gives the Norse forecast of the end of the world which heathen and Christian alike expected to happen in the year 1000. Both its form and the undoubted representation of the Crucifixion make it clear that this was a Christian monument and the carvings show us subjects from Norse mythology later absorbed into Christian iconography. The opposition of the Fenris Wolf, enemy of the powers of Light, and the Hart, Eikthyrnir, from whose horns drip the healing waters of rain, was adapted to symbolise the Passion of Christ and appears on Christian gravestones of the Viking period. The gesture with which Vidar forces open the jaws of Fenris Wolf (here represented as a dragon) is the antetype of that with which Christ forces open the jaws of Hell in such later carvings as the Norman tympanum at Quenington

FIG. 4. A hog-back tomb, Heysham
The four Gods who uphold the arch of Heaven being attacked by their destroyers

(Glos). On a hog-back at Heysham (Lancs) (Fig. 4) there are carvings which also illustrate this theme, showing the four gods who uphold the sky being attacked by their predestined conquerors: Thor by the sea-monster Migard, Odin by the Fenris Wolf, Tyr by Garm and Frey by Surt who flies above, while Loki (the treacherous giant who betrays the Gods) is represented as a wolf. On the other side of the stone is shown the sacred Ash, Yggdrasil.[9] On a slab of stone in the churchyard at Jurby (Isle of Man) and perhaps also on a cross at Staveley (Yorks) we see Heimdal, watchman of the Gods, who sounds the great Gjaller Horn to call them to their last fight. The false Loki, bound and awaiting his punishment, may have inspired the 'bound devil' of the cross shaft at Kirkby Stephen (Westmd). At Quenington Christ is shown trampling upon a demon whose shackled limbs are similarly plaited through rings, in a manner characteristic of 10th-century interlacings, and the same feature occurs in an 11th-century psalter in the British Museum.[10] A craftsman's liking for a design will often outlive his memory of its original significance, and although the literary origin of the Harrowing of Hell is in the apocryphal Gospel of Nicodemus, some of its visual prototypes may have been taken from the Norse legends. Before the 12th century it was much more common in England than elsewhere. Another example of this adapted imagery is the tympanum at Dinton (Bucks) (Plate 14), which shows the fruit of the Tree of Life being devoured by two monsters who make strange symbols for the souls of the righteous but would not be inappropriate as defenders of Yggdrasil, while a fearsome serpent which attacks

FIG. 5. Cross shaft at Halton (Lancs)

the puny St. Michael, on the lintel, recalls the fight of Odin with the Hell-Worm.

Christian subjects appear on the west side of an 11th-century cross at Halton (Lancs) (Fig. 5), but on the east and north sides are carved subjects which any lover of Wagner's *Ring* will recognise as illustrating its prototype, the legend of Sigurd.[11] On the lowest panel of the east side we see Regin the smith, Sigurd's false foster-father, forging the magic sword with a double bellows below his anvil; in the head of the panel are more tools, and a plaited coil illustrating the writhing death-agony of the serpent Fafni, above the headless body of Regin. Above this panel is one showing the scene, also carved on stones at Andreas, Mallew and Jurby in the Isle of Man, of Sigurd roasting the serpent's heart and sucking his burnt fingers.[12] The Sigurd subjects on the Halton Cross may allude to the claim of Earl Tosti, to whom the manor then belonged, to be the descendant of Sigurd. These carvings are very important in the history of literature, for they prove that certain elements, such as the smithy setting and the pit in which the hero hid to attack the dragon, were already in the story by the 10th century. The first of the Old Norse and German written versions only date from the 13th century. Some of the English carvings, whose crude execution makes them obscure, can be identified by comparison with clearer wood carvings, such as those on Veigusdal church in Norway. Sigurd subjects may occur on a cross in Leeds parish church but it is more certain that the carvings show Wayland the Smith holding aloft, by legs and hair, Bödvild, the daughter of the king who had imprisoned and crippled him. His artificial wings and smithy tools can be distinguished in the carving, some details of which are corroborated by fragments of a similar cross, now in the Leeds museum. Many place-names in England testify to the honour in which Wayland the Smith was held, and I have wondered whether the legend of St. Eloy cutting off a horse's leg, shoeing it and then replacing it without scar which is represented on carvings at Freckenham (Suffolk) and Durweston (Dorset), was derived from a wish that Christianity should also have its miracle-working smith.[13] It does not accord with the historical record of the French goldsmith who became Master of the Mint to Clothair II, and was later made a bishop.

The dominant feature of the life of the early Vikings—fighting —is illustrated on some hog-backs; at Gosforth we see two armies meeting. At Lowther (Westmd) a man stands between a line of men bearing shields and a Viking ship; on the reverse a row of female figures, together with snakes, may depict the descent of the soul into Hades, where the hideous hag, Hel, awaits those who die, not as warriors, but of old age or sickness.[14] Single figures of warriors appear on monuments at Nunburnholme (Yorks) and Brailsford (Derbs).

I cannot end this chapter without some mention of Canute, under whose rule the Scandinavian empire reached its apogee, for he was a great church builder, paying special honour to the English saints his pagan compatriots had martyred. He is said to have built a church on the site of each of his battles against Edmund Ironside, by which he won the throne of England, and at Sherston (Wilts) the church stands on the lines of old entrenchments. Ecclesiology may perhaps make a contribution to history in determining the site of the Battle of Ashandun, in East Anglia, where Edmund Ironside was decisively defeated. The church of Ashingdon (Essex) shows no signs of an early foundation, while the traces of an 11th-century church at Hadstock, the next parish to Ashdon (Essex), are now accepted as belonging to the minster built by Canute to commemorate his victory, and the consecration of which he attended in 1020.[15] The citizens of London had been among the most staunch opponents of Canute but, after his final victory, their city prospered greatly, owing to the increased trade between Britain and Denmark, and many Danish merchants became leading citizens of London. The original foundation of St. Clement Danes was a suburban church to serve the needs of the Scandinavian population of the City, and the churches which stand at each side of London Bridge mark by their dedications to the Scandinavian martyrs, St. Olave and St. Magnus, the influence of the new settlers. About thirteen ancient dedications to St. Olave are known in English churches, generally in towns where there was a considerable Danish settlement.

Some churches show traces of the survival of Scandinavian speech under the Normans. An inscription on a stone at Thornaby-on-Tees (Yorks, N.R.) and a 12th-century inscription on the wall of Carlisle cathedral are evidence of this, and the inscription on the detached Norman tympanum at Pennington-in-Furness (Lancs), is couched in a clipped form of Norse which has not yet become English.[16] Indeed, so long as the 'thorn' rune (Y = th) still appears on every 'Ye olde' notice-board, the last trace of runic script can hardly be said to have been obliterated. The late runic inscription on the font at Bridekirk (Cumb) has the additional interest of being a signature. It reads: RIKARTH HE ME IWROKTE AND TO THIS MERTHE GERNR ME BROKTE (Richard he me wrought and to this beauty carefully me brought), and the little figure of a man working with hammer and chisel, which is carved in one loop of the scrolling vine, may have been meant for a self-portrait. The curiously mingled characteristics of this font, which have caused it to be ascribed to dates ranging from the 8th to the 13th centuries, make it a good illustration of the gradual fusion of different racial elements into the full splendour of Norman decorative sculpture.

Chapter 6

THE AGE OF ABBEYS

F OR MANY of us the date of the Norman Conquest marks the
frontier between our shadowy impressions of earlier British
cultures and relatively clear knowledge. Of the great church
of Battle Abbey, founded by William the Conqueror, only the
foundations of the crypt and a few fragments are now left, so
the most interesting ecclesiological memento of the battle of
Hastings is perhaps the 12th-century wall-painting above the
nave arcade at Claverley (Salop) which shows a long line of horsemen engaged in battle (Plate 4). In colouring and design the
painting is reminiscent of the Bayeux Tapestry and a passage in
the 12th-century *Roman de Rou* by Magister Wace records an
exploit by Roger de Montgomery (to whom estates including the
manor of Claverley were subsequently granted) which turned the
tide of battle at a critical moment.[1] Other early authorities deny
that Montgomery was even present at Hastings and the painting
is sometimes described as a Psychomachia,[2] or battle between the
Vices and Virtues. I find this interpretation unconvincing because
there is no differentiation between the champions of good and
evil, as there always is in a genuine Psychomachia, like that on the
font at Stanton Fitzwarren (Wilts) (Plate 16), but this is a good
example of the diverse theories between which students of
medieval imagery must sometimes make their choice.

England was conquered piecemeal, with frequent risings which
were so savagely repressed that, in 1069, William is said to have
left no house standing between York and Durham, and no human
being alive whom his soldiers could find to kill. The first churches
shared the fate of the villages and it was nearly a century before
the gradual repopulation of the Yorkshire Wolds led the Norman
landowners to build the simple aisleless churches which stand
there still.

Above the south door of the church at Weaverthorpe (Yorks)
an incomplete inscription ends with these words: ... ✠ IN
HONORE SCI ANDREÆ APOSTOLI HEREBERTUS WINTONIE HOC

Edlesborough Church
Rudston Church and monolith

3 Execution of Thomas, Earl of Lancaster, South Newington
4 Fighting knights, Claverley

St Oswald, Wells Cathedral   6 St Kenelm, Wells Cathedral

7 St Edmund's wolf, Walpole
St Peter

8 Mask, St David's Cathedral

9 Isaac bearing the faggots, Worcester Cathedral
10 Samson with the gates of Gaza, Ripon Cathedral

11 Rogationtide figure and ostriches, Worcester Cathedral
12 Foliate mask, Holy Trinity, Coventry

13 Christ in Majesty, Prior's door, Ely Cathedral

14 The Tree of Life, Dinton

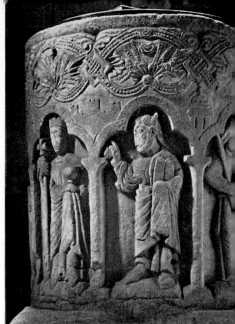

15 Moses between church and synagogue, Southrop font

16 Psychomachia, Stanton Fitzwarren font

17 St George at Antioch, Fordington
18 St Michael and the dragon, Moreton Valence

19 The apse of Copford Church

CANTERBURY CATHEDRAL GLASS
The siege of Canterbury
Pilgrims at the shrine of St Thomas

23 Coronation of the Virgin, Lincoln Cathedral

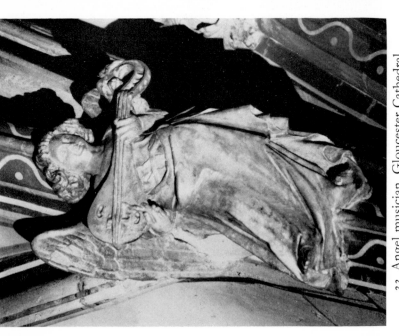

22 Angel musician, Gloucester Cathedral

24 Saxon grave cover, Wirksworth

25 Holy Trinity,
Willoughby-on-
the-Wolds

26 Incarnation of Christ, Ross-on-Wye

SALISBURY CATHEDRAL CHAPTER HOUSE

27 Adam toiling, Cain and Abel sacrificing
28 Noah
29 Abraham serving the angels, and the destruction of Sodom

30 The Sacred Wounds, North Cadbury 31 The Ascension, Launcells 32 The incredulity of

MONASTERIUM FECIT IN TEMPORE RE ... The identity of this Herbert of Winchester has been established by a feoffment made by Thomas, Archbishop of York, 1108–14, to Herbert the Chamberlain which includes Weaverthorpe among the lands named.[3]

The Norman Conquest took place at a time when, in the words of the 11th-century chronicler Raoul Glaber, 'it was as though the very world had shaken herself and cast off her old age, and was clothing herself everywhere in a white robe of new churches'. Monasticism had long been known in Britain, but the Normans brought a fresh stimulus, and the next two centuries may fairly be called the Age of Abbeys, so predominant was the influence of the great monastic houses upon both social life and architectural design.

The Normans disapproved of the ecclesiastical organisation of England and set themselves to improve it. They altered the location of many sees and only ten Saxon cathedrals retained that rank. William of Malmesbury attributed the English custom of siting their cathedrals in the country to the influence of Irish missionaries who 'preferred to bury themselves ingloriously in marshes than to dwell in lofty cities'[4] and he may have been right. The centres of the new Norman dioceses had to be in cities and eight of them were established in wealthy Saxon monasteries founded during the 10th-century monastic revival under St. Dunstan. This led to the exclusively British arrangement whereby the Bishop became the titular Abbot while the executive leader of the monastery was the Prior. It was not an easy relationship and the rebuilding of Winchester cathedral under William of Wykeham was long delayed by friction between the Bishop and the Prior.

As few monastic churches in England still display any pictorial record of their past history, the Founders' Window in the north clerestory of the choir at Great Malvern (Worcs) is of rare interest. Three panels in the upper lights show us the visions of St. Werstan, the Saxon hermit, in which he saw the angels marking the site of his chapel and consecrating the finished building, and his martyrdom which, the window seems to imply, was followed by the dispersal of his followers. The large figures of Edward the Confessor, William the Conqueror and St. Wulstan recall the grants of land made to the first community by King Edward, their

F

confirmation by William I, and the part played by the last Saxon Bishop of Worcester in promoting monasticism in his diocese. Both William and St. Wulstan are shown presenting sealed charters to a small kneeling figure entitled 'Magister Aldewynus' who may have been the first Prior of the new foundation in 1085, but whose identity is not established by contemporary records. Norman nobles enriched the new Priory, and two panels in the lower lights record the donations of Osbert Fitz Pons and of the Earls of Gloucester and Hereford, their charters being represented as books with red seals. A charter of Henry I's reign, still in existence, confirms the Priory in the possession of fisheries given by Osbert Fitz Pons.[5]

The first phase of the monastic revival was dominated by the Benedictine Order, which supported the tenet that the proper use of art was for the highest service, thus justifying those who wished to express their piety in splendour. What this belief meant to English architecture needs no further emphasis than a reminder that every cathedral in which we still admire Norman architecture at its zenith originally belonged to a Benedictine monastery. Canterbury, Durham, Ely, Rochester, Peterborough, St. Albans and Norwich, preserve the stark majesty of their Norman arcades, and Gloucester and Winchester have only been superficially altered. Westminster and Chester alone were entirely rebuilt. When to the consideration of these cathedrals we add the memory of other Benedictine abbey churches, such as Malmesbury, Pershore, Shrewsbury, Sherborne and Tewkesbury, our mental picture of the great Benedictine church of the 12th century begins to take shape, though only as a sketch in monochrome. To appreciate the full effect of the aesthetic revelation which the Benedictines brought to England we must travel hither and thither in memory, gathering stray relics which our imaginations shall refresh and multiply. The 12th-century wall-paintings and windows of Canterbury cathedral survive in part, and to these we must add the masterpieces of the school of metal workers who wrought the Gloucester Candlestick (in the Victoria and Albert Museum) and whose golden and bejewelled shrines are known to us only through the formalised symbols with which contemporary carvers, or illuminators, gave local colour to their backgrounds. Rare textiles were brought from the East to make vestments, cover relics, or to hang round the sanctuary and the fame of the exquisite embroidery done in English nunneries created a demand for *opus anglicanum* in some of the greatest churches of Europe.

The architectural sculpture of the Yorkshire School of the 12th century shows some features in common with Benedictine sculpture in the south and may have been influenced by the wealthy Benedictine Abbey of St. Mary at York, from which came the grandest free-standing statue of this period, the great horned Moses. One characteristic of this Yorkshire school was its use of designs copied from books and at Alne (Yorks, N.R.) the voussoirs of the door are clearly copied from a Bestiary. Not only do they include such rare creatures as the caladrius (a white bird which could foretell the death, or recovery, of a sick person) and the terrobuli (male and female stones which burst into flames when brought together) but the carver has also copied the Latin titles without which these could not have been identified. Alne belonged to the Treasurer of York Minster, who could easily have procured both carvers and their model.

The influence of the Cluniac Order also encouraged artistic splendour, to which the direct dependence of all their houses upon the Mother Church at Cluny tended to give an international character. The chief Cluniac house in England was the great Priory of St. Pancras at Lewes, of which only a few ruins of the domestic buildings remain, and its influence was so dominant that Professor Tristram called the peculiar style of 12th-century wall-painting found in some Sussex churches, notably at Hardham and Clayton, the School of Lewes.[6] Canon Westlake noted a significant resemblance between the painting of the Christ in Majesty above the chancel arch at Clayton and a carving of the same subject in the Cluniac Abbey of La Charité-sur-Loire, and considered that both were probably based upon a design drawn in the *scriptorium* at Cluny.[7] The beautifully carved stone cistern at Much Wenlock (Salop) also suggests comparisons with French sculpture, particularly the capitals at Vézelay.

The sumptuosity of the Benedictine and Cluniac abbeys provoked the Cistercian reaction in favour of simplicity, and although the Cistercians eventually became one of the most powerful organisations in Christendom they did not entirely abandon the austere architectural tradition which they had originated. Their churches were to be colourless, without stained glass or painted walls, and no figures were to be represented there in carving, other than the Crucifix. Since figure sculpture was forbidden, the carvers relied for their effects on the subtle mouldings and foliate capitals. Light and shade took the place of fantastic ornament and, since their abbeys lay in the depth of the country, it was natural that leaves and flowers should replace the weird fauna which had horrified St. Bernard on Cluniac capitals. As we stand in the choir of Abbey Dore (Herefs), which, with Holme Cultram in Cumberland and Margam (Glam), are the only Cistercian abbey churches still in use, we cannot fail to appreciate how much the beauty of our 13th-century architecture owed to the restraining influence of the Cistercians. They chose to build in remote districts, although it is hard to realise that the serene fertility which now surrounds Fountains Abbey was once considered a wild place, more fit for the habitation of devils than of men. At the suppression of the monasteries this isolation led to the ruin of the Cistercian Abbeys, for there was no town to buy the church for £20, as was done at Malvern,[8] but neither were they convenient quarries for later builders. So Fountains, Rievaulx and Tintern, to name but three, remain as ruins of exquisite, lonely beauty.

Cistercian custom, based perhaps on the design of the Mother Church at Cîteaux, did much to establish the English practice of building important churches with a square east end.[9] At Abbey Dore (Herefs) we can still see traces of the screen walls, projecting from the east wall, which enabled this plan to be combined with the need for separate chapels at which the monks who were priests could say their Masses. At Fountains Abbey an eastern transept with nine such chapels provided a model for the famous Benedictine Chapel of the Nine Altars at Durham. Cistercian simplicity also encouraged the building of aisleless cruciform churches, and the influence of their great abbeys in South Wales can be seen in the aisleless churches of many villages in Pembrokeshire, such as Gumfreston and Penally. The Augustinian Canons followed this plan at first but later found the lack of space inconvenient. Several former churches of this Order, such as those at Lanercost (Cumb), Brinkburn (Northumb) and Bolton (Yorks) have later aisles added on the north side only, the south side having been occupied by the cloister.[10]

The structural arrangements of a monastic church have been described in many books, but those who visit, not only cathedrals, but country churches should be on the look-out for unusual features which tell of a monastic origin. The stone pulpit at Beaulieu is the reading-desk of the monastic refectory which has been transformed into the parish church.[11] The fine quality and unusual subjects of the capitals in the chancel at Leonard Stanley (Glos) will not seem surprising when we notice the strange window half-way down the nave, which once lighted the stairway in the wall leading to the rood-screen that divided the part open to the laity from the rest of the monastic church. At Bolton the rood-screen was carried up to the roof and formed so complete a division that, after the Suppression, it became the east wall of the parish church, the monastic choir beyond being allowed to fall into ruins. Sometimes an oddity of design, such as the two towers of Wymondham (Norfolk), records past conflict between the monks and the parishioners who shared the church, over such matters as the ringing of bells, and the close proximity of the parish church to the Abbey of Evesham is due to the peaceful solution of a similar feud.

The unusual plan of the church at Ramsey (Hunts) which conforms closely to that of a medieval hospital, with the nave as its main hall and the chancel for a chapel, has given rise to the theory that it was built in the 12th century as the hospital, or guest house, of the great Abbey and was converted into a parish church in the 14th century, before which date no mention of such a church has survived.

Sometimes the modest *capellae extra portas* which the religious houses erected at their gates, to serve the laity, have survived when their great churches have fallen to decay. Examples of gate chapels still in use can be seen at Kirkstead (Lincs), Merevale (Warcs), Little Coggeshall and Tilty (Essex).[12] These chapels were most frequently built by the Cistercians owing to the greater strictness of this Order about allowing admission to the monastery church.

The effects of the relationship between monasteries and the churches which belonged to them is difficult to estimate. So many estates, including churches, were given to religious communities, usually as part of the perpetual endowment of masses for the soul of the benefactor, that it became a threat to the nation's economy and, in 1279, Edward I passed the Statute of Mortmain which forbade the alienation of lands into 'the dead hand' of permanent communities without special license. At the time of the Dissolution about 63 per cent of the churches in Yorkshire and 50 per cent of those in Lincolnshire were owned by monasteries, although this was somewhat higher than the national average.[13] The effect which monastic ownership had upon the architecture and decoration of the churches was thus obviously widespread and, in the 12th century particularly, may have been aesthetically very important, for the development of local styles of architecture and sculpture at that time centred chiefly on the great religious houses.

When the parishioners had raised the money for a new font or a new series of windows or wall-paintings were to be designed, it seems natural that they should have sought the help of the fine craftsmen who were regularly employed in the workshops of a monastery, or had been drawn thither temporarily by some extensive building operation. The point which can rarely be decided is whether ownership, or contiguity, was the deciding factor in such cases. The remarkable 12th-century wall-paintings at Clayton and Hardham in Sussex almost certainly reflect the influence of the Cluniac Priory at Lewes, to which both churches belonged, but similar paintings (now lost) were found at Westmeston, which had no connection with Lewes beyond geographical proximity. The wooden roof-bosses at Queen Camel (Som) include several rare subjects apparently copied from a much earlier Bestiary which, like the church, may have belonged to Cleeve Abbey,[14] but two other Somerset churches, Sampford Brett and Wootton Courtney, have bosses apparently made by the same carvers,[15] and these churches did not belong to the Cistercians at Cleeve.

The fine Norman fonts at Southrop (Glos) and Stanton Fitzwarren (Wilts) (Plates 15 & 16) look like the products of some great monastery's workshops, but Southrop was owned by the Knights Hospitallers of Quenington, who were not prominent patrons of the arts. Certain iconographical peculiarities of these fonts, including the use, at Stanton Fitzwarren, of a six-winged seraph with a sword as a symbol of the Fall of Man, link these fonts with designs known to have been used in the Priory of Worcester, for works in various media, including probably fine enamels. The carver of the fonts might even have copied his design from an enamelled reliquary decorated with a Psychomachia, like the 12th-century English casket now in the Treasury of the cathedral of Troyes.[16] These few examples must suffice to indicate a complex problem which should be considered by those interested in the history of old churches whenever they find in them ornament of unusually high quality and erudite design, as for instance, the pulpit at Trull (Som) (Plate 47) which belonged to the Priory of Taunton.

From an economic point of view, monastic ownership of a benefice was usually a handicap, for religious communities tended to regard their appropriated livings merely as sources of revenue and neither favoured, nor supported, their schemes for architectural embellishment. For each recorded case in which a chancel was rebuilt by a corporate proprietor, as at Adderbury (Oxon) or Thirsk (Yorks), there are dozens of complaints, from bishops or parishioners, that churches had fallen into ruin because the monastery had drawn all the available money away from the parish. It is noteworthy that in Cheshire, where two-thirds of the livings were owned by religious houses, some of the finest churches are to be found in the remaining parishes. Nantwich was itself collegiate, but the parishes of Bunbury, Malpas, Barthomley and Gawsworth made good use of their independence.[17]

The wealth of the monasteries became their undoing; their temporal interests weakened the spiritual integrity which should have been their defence. An inscription on the choir stalls from St. Agatha's Abbey, Easby, which are now in the church at Richmond (Yorks), states that the abuses of those who live in cloisters are 'costly living, choice food, noise in cloister, strife in chapter, disorder in choir, a neglectful . . . a disobedient disciple, a lazy youth, a headstrong old man, a worldly monk'.[18] The evidence of documents confirms that the Rules had been slackened, although not probably to the extent asserted, for predatory reasons, by the Commissioners of Henry VIII, and many houses would have fallen into decay in any case, from lack of inmates. Even within the monasteries there were those who were ready to help in bringing about the Dissolution, and a characteristically double-faced monument to one of these remains at Burwell (Cambs).[19] When John Lawrence de Wardeboys, the last Abbot of

Ramsey (Hunts), ordered his memorial brass, he had himself depicted thereon in full abbatial vestments, including a mitre (for Ramsey had a mitred Abbot), but after he had surrendered his own Abbey to Henry VIII and persuaded others to do the same (for which service he received a large pension), he had the brass turned and his figure engraved on the reverse side wearing a simple cap and gown.

Chapter 7

GATHERINGS IN THE PORCH

Most medieval churches are entered by the south door. There may be a corresponding north door, designed originally for processional use, and perhaps also a grand west door in the base of the tower but, unless there is some cogent practical reason for preferring one of these, we shall enter through the south porch. There is almost always a porch, even in very small churches where it is sometimes disproportionately large. There are usually benches along the side walls, which are often pierced by traceried windows, and so it offers us a sheltered, well-lit space, warmed by any sun there may be, even on a chilly day, and tempts us to linger a few minutes before we go into the church, remembering some of the reasons for which people have gathered here in the past. To a medieval community, the porch was almost as important a focal point in their lives as the church itself.

When Chaucer said of the Wife of Bath 'husbands at the church door had she five', he meant what he said. The priest met the couple in the porch, and asked them if they were willing to consent in wedlock, before the party went in to celebrate the nuptial mass. It was this contract at the church door which had to be established in any question about the validity of the marriage. Church porches therefore often contained an altar at which contracts could be sworn. At South Pool (Devon) the stone bench which runs along the east wall of the porch is raised in the centre to form an altar table. Even when the actual altar has vanished we can see proof of its previous existence in the irregular placing of the doors of such late Saxon porches as Bradford-on-Avon and Bishopstone (Sussex); either the outer or inner door being markedly to the west of the axial line of the porch in order to make room for the altar.[1] In some church porches we find a niche (presumably meant to hold a statue) above the stone bench, as at Bampton (Oxon) or Buckland (Berks).[2]

From the 14th century onwards porches with an upper storey

became common and much of the business which had formerly
been transacted in the porch was transferred to the chamber above
it. This secular use of the porch reached its apogee at Cirencester
where the upper floors of the south porch, built *c.* 1400, were for a
long time used as the Town Hall. At Eye (Suffolk) we can see
evidence of the long continuance of the practice of doing business
at the church door. In the attractive 16th-century porch, striped
red and white with an inlay of stone on brick, there is a stone
table attached to the west wall, and above it a battered inscription
which, with some difficulty, may be deciphered as reading:

> Seale not to soone lest thou repent to late
> Yet helpe thy frend, but hinder not thy state.
> If ought thou lende or borrow, truly pay
> Ne give ne take advantage though thou may.
> Let conscience be thy guide, so helpe thy frend,
> With loving peace and concord make thy end.

In smaller towns and villages, where no grammar school was
available, the parson, or a chantry priest, often taught the local
boys in the chamber above the church porch, or in some chapel.
Traces of this past use can be seen in several churches: on the wall
of the vestry at North Cadbury (Somerset) the alphabet is painted
in black letters; at Long Melford (Suffolk) the multiplication table
is painted on the east wall of the Lady Chapel, while the choir
stalls at Blythburgh (Suffolk) have holes for ink-wells in their
desks which tell of previous service in a chapel where school was
taught. The value of such village schools naturally varied with the
intellectual capacity of the priest, who probably aimed at little
more than teaching the boys to understand the forms of worship
which followed directly upon the A B C in their primer, and perhaps the psalms which they might have to sing in church. This
little learning was often literally 'knocked into them'! We might
ascribe to the British working man's taste for grim slap-stick
humour the carvings on misericords at Boston, Norwich and
Sherborne which show the master plying the birch, did we not
remember that a student graduating as Master of Grammar at
Cambridge was handed a birch and a 'palmer' (specially designed
for striking boys on the palm) as the symbols of his new office, and
had forthwith to prove his powers of wielding them upon a boy
who received a groat for his pains.[3]

Many of the chantry foundations, whose chapels have given such a variety of ground plans to English parish churches, included some provision for the education of local children, and appeals against their dissolution in 1547 were often based on the grounds that the chantry priests taught the parochial school. The plea was disallowed and forty-two schools supported by chantry endowments are recorded in the *Calendar of Chantries*,[4] all of which were suppressed, although some of them were later refounded as Edward VI Grammar Schools. We cannot tell how many of the 2,374 guilds, chantries and free chapels suppressed at the same time[5] had previously played a more modest part in the schooling of children. At Farthinghoe (Northants) a chantry chapel was long used as a school.

The pupils of these chantry foundations were often required to pray for the soul of the founder on certain occasions, while the indigent old men who were maintained by his bequest were expected to pray daily beside his tomb. They were called bedesmen (bede = prayer), and are often represented on tombs, wearing their long, hooded gowns, with the badge of the founder on the breast, and holding outsize rosaries. Many medieval wills specify that the Rosary, or 'Our Lady's Psalter', shall be recited to ensure the dead person's rest. At Morley (Derbs) an inscribed brass specifies the prayers to be said for the family of John Stathum (died 1454) who endowed an annual dole of bread.[6]

Charitable provisions for such doles of food, or money, are not infrequently recorded, on painted boards hanging in churches. One can imagine the loaves being handed out in the church porch on the appropriate day, as was done for centuries in many places until the Charity Commissioners diverted the funds to other purposes.[7] At Hilton (Dorset) a short stone shelf, projecting from the south wall of the church, near the porch, is said to have been intended for the distribution of 'widows' loaves'.

Justice was administered in churches from very early times. In the 8th century a Baptistery was added to St. Augustine's church at Canterbury, which was also used for judicial trials and the laws of Edward the Confessor directed that proceedings by the King's Justices should be held in, or near, churches. It has been suggested that a triangular niche on the interior west wall of the tower at Barnack (Northants) and some traces of other seating, suggests that the ground floor of the tower was used for such purposes.[8] Because the church porch was obviously a suitable place for such secular business, it soon became an important part of the building and the Saxon church of Bradford-on-Avon (Wilts) has a disproportionately large stone porch. The tradition of thus using church porches for the ends of justice was long-lived; Manorial Courts were held in the Staffordshire churches of Alrewas and Yoxall in unbroken sequence from the reign of Edward II down to the 19th century.

We find no illustrations of the enduring processes of the Common Law, even in the porches where it may have been administered, but some of the strange ways by which medieval Churchmen sought to test evidence, or mitigate injustice, were clearly recorded by ecclesiastical artists. The most interesting of these were the judicial ordeals which, being considered as a means of securing a verdict of divine justice, were the direct concern of the Church. The Anglo-Saxons conducted trials by ordeal in parish churches, but have left no visual record of them. Under the Normans there were three forms of ordeal: by battle, fire and water. At the foot of a 12th-century wall-painting of the Judgment of Souls, in Stowell church (Glos), there are the figures of two men fighting, painted in thin red line on the masonry. They are dressed in tunics, wearing neither helmets nor body armour, and each carries a square shield and a weapon like a double-headed pick. In Britton, *De Jure Angliae*, fol. 41, we read that those who submitted themselves to the Ordeal by Battle should 'go to combat armed without iron and without the slightest armour, their heads uncovered, their hands and feet bare, with two staves tipped with horn of equal length, and each of them with a target of four corners, without any other arms, whereby either of them might annoy the other'.[9] Two medallions of early 13th-century glass in Canterbury cathedral illustrate the beginning and end of a judicial combat in which the protagonists are thus accoutred.[10] The 14th century has left us a most unusual memorial of a judicial combat in the brass of Bishop Wyvil in the north-east transept of Salisbury cathedral (Fig. 6). This Bishop wished to recover the castle of Sherborne which had been seized by the Crown in 1139 and later given to the Earl of Salisbury. The matter was referred to trial by battle and, at the appointed time, the champions of both parties appeared, clad in white leather next to their skins with surcoats of red sendal painted with arms. They held the shields and double-ended picks prescribed for such combats, and it was hinted that the Bishop's champion was further armed with 'rolls of prayers and witchcrafts' under his coat.[11] At the last moment letters from the King postponed the fight and the matter was settled by a monetary arrangement, but the grateful Bishop wished his champion to be remembered. The brass shows us the half-length figure of the Bishop, framed in a large pointed window on the first floor of a complicated castle, from the portal of which issues the champion accoutred for the trial.

In the St. William window in York Minster we see a woman undergoing the ordeal by fire, and afterwards showing her hand to the judge that he might judge her guilt, or innocence, by the degree of her hurt. The ordeal by water, in which the accused had to pick a stone from a cauldron of boiling water, was much less often used and one of the last cases in which it was applied, before being formally disallowed by the Lateran Council in 1214, is illustrated in the Miracle Windows of Canterbury cathedral where the accused, Eilward of Westoning, is shown being blinded and mutilated after an unjust verdict.[12]

The churches also offered protection to fugitives, whether from justice or from the spite of their enemies. Acknowledgement of the right of sanctuary was included in the laws of King Ina of Wessex in 690 and those of King Alfred in 887, and William the Conqueror introduced a scale of penalties for sanctuary breaking: 100s for taking a fugitive from an abbey; 20s from a parish church and 10s from a chapel.[13] At first only the altar and the inner buildings of the church afforded sanctuary, but this was later extended to cover all the space between the church and its outer walls. This included churchyards and some important shrines spread their protection over a considerable area of surrounding country. Anywhere within a mile of Beverley Minster was considered a sanctuary and the 'Sanctuary Stone' which originally stood in the middle of a path leading to Greystoke church (Cumb) is now set in a recess of the wall in Church Road.

Some churches had a special seat, called the Fridstool, or chair of peace, and that of Beverley Minster originally had a Latin inscription on it telling that the fugitive reaching this chair enjoys

FIG. 6. Bishop Wyvil and his champion
Monumental brass in Salisbury Cathedral

complete safety.[14] A stone seat in Hexham Abbey has also been called a fridstool and the similarity of these two seats to early marble thrones suggests that the sanctuary seeker originally had to take refuge on the throne of the Bishop. Part of a stone seat, thought to have been the throne of the Saxon Bishop, has been excavated at Lichfield and is now in the cathedral. A stone seat at St. Germans (Cornwall), of early date but with later carvings added, and the stone seats at Sprotbrough and Halsham in Yorkshire may all be considered in the same connection.

During the Middle Ages the period of sanctuary was generally forty days, during which the felon was perfectly safe and the officers of the law could only seek by arguments to induce him to 'abjure the realm' and go into banishment. The Rites of Durham give a full account of the procedure by which a fugitive was admitted, and the coroner summoned to hear his confession. If he agreed to abjure the realm he was arrayed in special garments and escorted to a port. In the smaller churches the procedure was simpler, and sometimes only the validity of the felon's oath ensured his taking the required journey overseas.[15] Taking sanctuary in a parish church required no special structural provisions but controversy has raged over the question of whether the decorated closing rings on some church doors were connected with the right of sanctuary.[16] One theory is that the fugitive who had hold of such a ring could not be forced away without breaking sanctuary, and the Constable of Arundel was certainly made to go barefoot to the shrine of St. Richard of Chichester in penance for having taken a thief who had hold of the door handle of Arundel church.[17] Against this it is argued that if the whole of the churchyard was included in the right of sanctuary, the fugitive was already safe when he had reached the door. Truth may lie mid-way and even those who were theoretically in sanctuary may have clung feverishly to the ring with which they hammered on the church door to beg admittance. Some of the more elaborate 'sanctuary knockers', such as those at Adel (Yorks), Norwich, St. Gregory and York, All Saints, show a man's head emerging from the jaws of a beast and may have been designed to illustrate the power of Holy Church to save men both from their worldly oppressors and from the Evil One.

The official notices which are still displayed in the church porches are trivial reminders of the ages when every event of importance to the parish took place in, or near the church, and so any proclamation made there could not be ignored. Here men have gathered to listen to the promulgation of new laws, the reading of Papal Bulls, the administration of oaths, the infliction of penances and for elections, examinations and recantations. It is not surprising that benches were thought necessary for those who gathered here on such widely varying occasions. But we have lingered long enough; it is time that we went into the church.

PART II

The Picture Book of the Churches

Chapter 1

THE ARRANGEMENT OF IMAGERY

THESE few examples of the traces which historic events and social changes have left on our churches must here suffice to lead our imaginations through the centuries which divide a wild island, torn apart by warring races, each with its own pantheon of pagan gods, from the forcibly united kingdom of the Norman rulers, entirely dominated by one supreme Church. Under that all-embracing ecclesiastical organisation every man, woman or child was a parishioner of some church which was not only their place of worship but an important instrument in their education and a focal point in their communal life.

The architectural styles of the churches do not concern us here. Some have come down to us unchanged since the 11th or 12th centuries, while others have been completely rebuilt in later periods. The majority show a medley of styles because they have been enlarged piecemeal, to meet the demands of a growing population.[1] Traces of blocked Saxon windows above nave arcades whose mouldings may reveal a difference of a century, or more, between the dates of the north and south aisles, show us how an early aisleless chapel has been converted into a spacious church. Above one arch of the 14th-century south arcade at Cocking (Sussex) we can see the splay of an 11th-century window, on which a 13th-century painting depicts the Annunciation to the Shepherds. Short chancels with round apses have given place to the characteristically English long chancels with square ends, and majestically solid romanesque arcades have been enclosed by later walls which are little more than screens of glass, lightly framed in stone by the audacious skill of masons who had mastered the Perpendicular style.

This piecemeal rebuilding has often given rise to a difference in orientation between the nave and the chancel, and one of the most widely accepted fallacies about the symbolism of medieval churches is that chancels which are out of alignment with the nave symbolise the head of Christ drooping on the Cross. Inaccurate enthusiasts claim that all such 'weeping chancels' incline to the north, just as Christ's head is always shown drooping towards His right shoulder, but, in fact, a large minority of churches 'weep' to the south and there are several explanations of this feature, ranging from the purely practical reasoning that a north-of-east orientation was common because work usually started in the spring, when the sun is north of the Equator,[2] to a careful analysis of the extent to which the point at which the sun rose on the patronal festival of the church changed over the centuries, owing to the cumulative inaccuracy of the Julian calendar.[3]

Even a commonplace village church becomes interesting as we try to work out the phases of its evolution, but in this book we are looking for problems of a different kind. Medieval churches were primarily places of worship made as beautiful as the skill and resources of their builders would allow, to the greater glory of God and, sometimes, it must be confessed, for the enhanced status of men! But they were something more than that. Medieval imagery was intended to express the teaching of the Church to all who entered, and particularly those who could not read. The figure subjects in windows, wall-paintings and carvings were all so many pages from the Picture Book of the Unlearned and the dignity, as well as the interest, of what remains is greatly enhanced if we understand enough about its composition to be able to interpret what we see.

The principles on which this great Picture Book was planned are not easy to explain simply and briefly. To begin with it depends what period you are discussing and what kind of church. In a great Norman monastery the scholarly monks who designed the imagery of their church sometimes included among its subjects such complexities of symbolism that, even here, written explanations had to be provided. In the library of Canterbury cathedral, there is a scroll inscribed with Latin verses explaining the 'Theological Windows' of the choir aisles (see page 104) and which was probably suspended beneath them.[4] From what remains, or is known to have existed, at Canterbury, we can see that every window in that great church was designed to form part of a majestically coherent statement of Christian teaching.[5] Such scholarly imagery would have been inappropriate in a village church, where the worshippers would certainly not have understood it, and is very rarely found there. Some of its basic principles were, however, generally applied to the choice of subjects and to their placing in appropriate parts of the building.

The French archaeologist, Didron, found an ancient Manual for Painters, incorporating traditions dating back to the 7th century, still being used on Mount Athos in 1839. This not only specified which subjects from the Old and New Testaments should be represented, but also gave the position appropriate to each on the walls and cupolas of a Greek church.[6] The plan of western churches required a different scheme and, unfortunately, we lack an equivalent Manual to codify it for us. The British never have been a consistently logical people, so we need not expect to find one scheme generally applied, but the painted decorations of some early churches, and the stained glass of some later ones, illustrate the main principles which determined the placing of much medieval imagery, particularly in the 12th century. In later periods the over-all planning was often disrupted by the multiplication of chantry chapels and altars.[7] The founders of such chantries usually chose to have their personal patron saints, or those of the guilds to which they belonged, depicted there, or else saints whose special help they wished to invoke—or to acknowledge. The windows of some late medieval churches are therefore more like Bede Rolls, invoking the prayers of the beholder for the souls of past donors, than instructional picture books. The churches of the 12th century show us much more clearly the basic pattern of symbolical arrangement.

All the resources of medieval art were used to stress moral contrasts: Doom and Redemption, Good and Evil, were portrayed in dramatic opposition and the contrast between those safe within the fold of Holy Church, and the hideous fate awaiting all others, meets us, literally, at the doors of our early churches. While most later doors have lost what little figure sculpture they ever possessed, many Norman tympana survive unscathed—perhaps because their symbolism puzzled the iconoclasts as much as it does most people today. It is rare to find a tympanum completely battered out, as at Worth Matravers (Dorset). In his *Rationale divinorum officiorum* Durandus writes 'the door of the church is Christ'[8] and the subject index to C. E. Keyer's *Norman tympana and lintels*[9] makes it clear that this symbolical interpretation of the words of Jesus: 'I am the Way', was generally accepted. Out of 197 examples listed there, 126 allude to Christ in one way or another. The more ambitious sculptors represented Our Lord in Majesty, surrounded by the symbols of the Evangelists, as at Rochester, Elkstone (Glos), Patrixbourne (Kent) and Pedmore (Worcs), or by angels as at Ely cathedral (Plate 13), Water Stratford (Bucks), Essendine (Rutland) or Rowlstone (Herefs). He is shown in the Virgin's arms at Fownhope (Herefs) and Inglesham (Wilts) and Harrowing Hell at Beckford (Worcs), Quenington (Glos) and Shobdon (Herefs). Humbler craftsmen could represent the Agnus Dei (32 examples) and one of the great advantages of medieval symbolism is illustrated by the fact that, however queer a quadruped they produced, the dignity of its symbolism was in no way lessened, provided that the creature was clearly identified by the cross held in its raised forepaw. The merest tyro could scratch out some kind of cross (39 examples). Many of these carvings still convey their message, but the formalised tree which occurs on twenty-eight tympana may confuse those who are not familiar with its symbolical association both with the Tree of Man's Fall and the Cross of his Redemption. Where this Tree of Life is shown between two monsters, as on the fine tympanum at Dinton (Bucks) (Plate 14), the design suggests memories of eastern textiles rather than didactic symbolism, yet this example bears an explanatory inscription: PRAEMIA PRO MERITIS SI QUIS DESPERET HABENDA AUDIAT HIC PRAECEPTA SIBI QUAE SINT RETINENDA. (If any should despair of obtaining reward for his deserts let him attend to the doctrines here preached and keep them in mind.) The carving thus proclaims that the Church is the source of spiritual sustenance to all who enter her gates.

Although the evidence of the Norman tympana is more conclusive, because they are both more numerous and better preserved, the Anglo-Saxon sculptors sometimes expressed the same idea with even greater dignity by placing great carved Rood groups on the walls above their church doors, as we can tell from their battered remains at Headbourne Worthy and Breamore in Hampshire.

The further statement of Durandus, 'the Apostles also are doors', is not borne out by the iconography of Norman tympana. With the possible exception of the figures within an arcade above the doors of Syston (Lincs) and Pampisford (Cambs), the Apostles certainly do not appear in groups, and, even if we rashly identify as Apostles all figures not clearly meant for other saints, they still would be outnumbered by the figures of St. Michael, as at Moreton Valence (Glos) (Plate 18), and Hallaton (Leics), or St. George, at Brinsop (Herefs) or Linton (Roxburgh), whose conflicts with dragons symbolise the eternal conflict between Good and Evil. How far the threshold of the church was considered the physical frontier line of such supernatural warfare it is as impossible to say as it is to interpret the meaning of the gargoyles along the eaves of churches. My own belief is that, if their makers had any intention beyond that of adorning a waterspout, it was to enhance the contrast between the demon-haunted world outside the protection of the Church and the spiritual security within.

The symbolical significance of church doors seems to have lost ground with later church builders in Britain. A plain arch sometimes surmounted by a niche for the statue of the Virgin and Child, or of the patron saint, was considered enough for most parish churches, while the western façades of Wells and Exeter cathedrals and the abbey church of Crowland were entirely covered with a screen of figure-work in which the door was merely a necessary interruption.

The iconographical arrangement of the figure sculpture on the façade of Wells merits careful study.[10] The lowest tier of figures, the foundation upon which rests this great *Te Deum* of sculptured praise, represents the prophets who foretold the coming of Christ. In other niches stand statues of those who testified to His presence upon earth: the saints and confessors, many of them Anglo-Saxon kings and queens, nobles, bishops and abbesses (Plate 5). In quatrefoils within the spandrels of arcades we see angels, and scenes from the Scriptures, while the upper part of the façade illustrates the Second Coming of Christ. Above the Resurrection of the Dead stand the Nine Orders of Angels, the Apostles, and, in the topmost gable, the figure of Christ as the supreme Judge. Instead of the Norman conception of the Church as an austere fortress of refuge against the powers of evil, the west front of Wells offers us a magnificent frontispiece to the Picture Book of the Churches.

Medieval symbolism was all-embracing and the scholarly

disposition of subjects could make the humblest village church portray the entire Universe of space and the ultimate limits of Time. Its roof, and particularly that of the chancel, represented the sky and therefore the glories of Heaven were painted upon it, so long as the plain surfaces of early barrel vaults allowed this to be done effectively.[11] The 12th-century wall-paintings at Kempley (Glos) depict the Apocalyptic Vision of Christ in Majesty with the Cherubim, the Four Beasts and the Golden Candlesticks. The Apostles sit enthroned on the side walls. Although skilful restoration has now rescued these frescoes from the almost impenetrable darkness of 19th-century varnish, the small scale of the chancel makes it impossible for any photograph to do justice to the whole effect. As, in this chapter, we are more concerned with the arrangement of subjects than the merits of individual works of art, I have therefore chosen to illustrate the apse at Copford (Essex) (Plate 19) although these paintings were crudely restored at the end of the 19th century. What their original quality must have been we can see in the unspoilt painting, in the nave, of Jairus' daughter being brought back to life, which was uncovered later.

At Copford the Signs of the Zodiac are painted on the soffit of the arch thus emphasising its symbolism as a division between earthly Time, represented by the nave, and the splendours of Eternity beyond. At Hardham (Sussex) the Labours of the Months are associated with the chancel arch. Because, after the Fall, God had commanded that all men should live by the sweat of their brows, each month was usually illustrated in medieval calendars by the appropriate agricultural occupation.[12] (See Appendix 2.) On the 12th-century lead font at Brookland (Kent) there is a complete calendar showing both the Labours and the Signs of the Zodiac. The Labours alone are carved on a 12th-century stone font at Burnham Deepdale (Norfolk) while some of them are combined with a scene of baptism on a beautiful font at Thorpe Salvin (Yorks). A complete series of Labours is carved on the misericords at Ripple (Worcs), the unique example of consistent imagery on misericords; single subjects copied from calendars are fairly common.

When the greater height and complex vaulting of later churches made roofs unsuitable for large-scale paintings, their association with Heaven was expressed by carving angel musicians on the roof bosses, as in the choir of Gloucester cathedral (Plate 22). Angels spread wide their wings in the spandrels of arches in both Westminster Abbey and Lincoln cathedral, and on the hammer beams of the great timber roofs which are the glory of many East Anglian churches, such as Needham Market and Grundisburgh in Suffolk. Because the Coronation of the Virgin happened in Heaven it is often shown on roof bosses, the most beautiful example being in Lincoln cathedral (Plate 23).

The nave was the domain of the laity and so its windows and wall-paintings illustrated the earthly lives of Christ and His saints, or else moral allegories designed for instruction. On the wall surrounding the chancel arch, or on a tympanum framed within it, was depicted the Last Judgment which should decide whether the soul might pass into the eternal life symbolised by the paintings in the chancel (Plate 45). Most of these painted Dooms are now half-obliterated, but even if we can see no more than the horns and tail of a demon to the north of the chancel arch, we should remember that the whole once presented to the fearful congregation a terrifying forecast of the sinners' fate and added an urgency of significance to the great crucifix, framed within the arch, as the symbol of their only hope of salvation.

The ubiquity of Doom paintings in this position probably accounts for the rarity of the subject in stained glass. The great west window of Fairford (Glos) is a notable exception and its placing, as well as the stylistic character of the designs, suggests foreign influence. The Continental tradition was that the west end of a church was the appropriate place for scenes of death and Judgment, not only because of the obvious association with the setting of the sun, but by a false etymological link between 'occident' and the verb *occidire*, to kill.[13] This tradition was followed by the painters at both Chaldon (Surrey) (Plate 41), and Clayton (Sussex) where the 12th-century paintings are of outstanding, and somewhat mysterious, interest. At Clayton the faded paintings on the walls of the nave show us a simplified adaptation of the Apocalyptic Vision. At the west end of the north wall an angel sounds the Last Trump and the Dead rise. The weighing of the souls has also been identified on this part. The paintings become clearer as a procession of the Blessed advances towards the Heavenly Jerusalem (represented as a hexagonal walled enclosure) and the great figure of Christ in Majesty above the chancel arch. The iconography of the south wall is obscure. An angel who holds a great cross seems to be denying it to the souls of the damned, for his arm is athwart his chest. The rider on a large horse is perhaps dragging a soul by its hair towards the Hell at the west end and beneath the legs of his mount rise a large number of imploring hands.[14]

Perhaps a similar scheme once existed at Stowell (Glos) for a Doom painting, which includes the weighing of souls, remains there in an unusual position, on the north wall of the nave.

At Canterbury the subjects of the windows in various parts of the cathedral seem to have been related to the dedications of the altars immediately beneath them. The windows of the choir of 'Christchurch' were appropriately filled with figures of Christ's earthly ancestors (now in the south transept or in the west window) except for the five eastern windows which illustrated scenes of His earthly life or those of Moses and St. John the Baptist, the first and last prophets of His Coming. The crypt below the Corona, which originally served as a Lady Chapel, has recently recovered some of the glass which there expressed the glorification of the Blessed Virgin, and nine windows illustrating the posthumous miracles of St. Thomas of Canterbury are still in the chapel (now Trinity Chapel) where stood his golden shrine until it was destroyed in 1538. Medallions representing scenes from the lives of SS. Alphege (Plate 20) and Dunstan, now in the triforium of the north choir aisle, are thought to have come from windows near the altar tombs of these canonised archbishops.

The north choir aisle seems to have been considered the most suitable place for windows of a directly educational purpose. At Canterbury there were originally twelve Theological windows illustrating the relation between Old and New Testaments (see page 105), and Thomas Habington tells us that, in the early 17th century, the windows of the north choir aisle at Malvern represented 'the Pater Noster, Ave Maria, the Creede, the Commandments, the Masse, the Sacraments issuing from the wounds of Our Saviour; my memory fainteth. But to conclude all in one, there is the whole Christian doctrine and the fower doctors of the Latin Church.'[15] Unfortunately only scraps of this glass survive to support Habington's description.

The south clerestory windows at Malvern originally contained panels illustrating the lives of Old Testament patriarchs, some of which are now in the south choir aisle. This placing marked a break with the tradition that subjects connected with the Old Law were shown on the sunless north, as in the rose windows of the transepts at Canterbury, where Moses with the Synagogue, the four Cardinal Virtues and the major prophets are still represented on the north side, although only a modern conjectural reconstruction in the south rose shows us Christ, the Church and the four Evangelists. A later, and humbler, example occurs on the stalls in the nave at Astley (Warcs) which are clearly now reversed as their return seats face west. What were originally the south stalls have the haloed figures of apostles painted on the panelled backs of the seats, while the corresponding figures on the north represent the prophets, wearing caps or turbans.[16] At Fairford the windows of the nave clerestory oppose the enemies of the Church, on the north, to the saints in the southern windows.

This mention of Fairford brings me to my last and finest example, for the early 16th-century windows of this magnificent parish church show us one of the most complete schemes of didactic decoration surviving in Britain.[17] Beginning at the north-west corner, the windows of the north aisle represent the twelve prophets who foretold the coming of Christ, each holding a scroll on which is indicated the relevant verse (see page 132 and Appendix 3). The window immediately before we enter the Lady Chapel represents four of the Old Testament subjects which prefigured the Birth of Christ: the Temptation of Eve, who brought sin into the world, while the Virgin brought forth Man's Redemption; Moses and the Bush which burned but was not consumed, a type of the Virgin Birth; Gideon's Fleece on which alone the dew fell, typifying the Incarnation of Christ; and the Queen of Sheba bringing gifts to Solomon as the Magi were to lay their offerings before the Child at Bethlehem. The windows of the Lady Chapel illustrate the birth of the Virgin and the infancy of Christ, the historical sequence being interrupted by the Assumption of the Virgin in the window behind the altar. Across all the upper lights of the great east window is shown the Crucifixion but, below the transom, each light represents one of preceding scenes of the Passion, from the Entry into Jerusalem to the Bearing of the

Cross. The south window of the chancel represents the Entombment. Above the altar in the south chapel, the window shows us
the Transfiguration and post-Resurrection scenes including the rare
apocryphal subject of Christ appearing to His mother in the
house of St. John. The windows of the south aisle contain the
Apostles, each bearing upon a scroll the appropriate phrase from
the Creed (see page 131), and the Doctors of the Latin Church.
The south clerestory windows have figures of saints, kings, an
emperor, cardinals and a pope, each with an attendant angel and
representing the defenders of the Church, while on the north side
the character of such oppressors as Annas, Judas, Caiaphas, Herod
and Herod Antipas is made clear by the flaming background to
each figure and its accompanying demon. The three windows in
the west wall are the climax to the whole scheme. In the centre
we see the Last Judgment, a design of glowing colour whose
dignity is not lessened by the macabre humour which represents
the damned as undergoing tortures akin to the processes of manu-
facturing glass. The flanking windows illustrate the Old Testament types: the Judgment of Solomon, and David and the
Amalekite.

   It would be rash to assume that the more complex schemes of
iconographical arrangement were generally understood in the
Middle Ages. Many parish priests could not even have interpreted
fully such a scheme as that of the Fairford windows, and their
parishioners would have understood even less. Yet even partial
understanding of the teaching thus associated with various parts
of the church must have helped the ignorant in groping towards
worship while, to the better educated members of the congregation, the religious significance of each subject would have gained
a new depth of meaning from being included in such a majestic
conception of the whole.

Chapter 2

CONVENTIONS OF PICTURE-WRITING

THOSE who designed medieval imagery were not afraid to attempt the most cosmic themes and the naive sincerity of their 'picture-writing' enabled them to do so with unself-conscious dignity. They were not only prepared to paint the Last Judgment, in all its terrifying majesty, across the whole width of the nave, as in St. Thomas' church at Salisbury (Plate 45), but they also contrived to carve the subject on a single roof boss, in the porch at West Walton (Norfolk), without omitting any essential detail.

Medieval iconography had two great advantages: its basic symbols were generally recognisable, however poorly they might be executed, and the system was infinitely flexible. The artists, like the writers of the great play cycles, had to meet the needs of a public which ranged from highly educated clergy to illiterate peasants, so the scenes which they represented had to be capable of being interpreted at different levels.[1] To illustrate this, let us take the story of Cain and Abel. Most medieval people would have identified pictures of the first murder, distinguishing it from other scenes of violence by the peculiarly English feature of Cain using a jaw-bone for his weapon.[2] The better educated would have known that the subject was chosen because it prefigured the killing of Christ by his fellow Jews. If the subsequent scene of God questioning Cain was shown, with a small figure apparently buried waist-deep in the ground, as in a wall-painting at Kingsdown, near Sevenoaks (Kent), or in the carvings of the Salisbury Chapter House, the scholarly observer would have been reminded of the contrast between the blood of Abel, which is described in *Genesis* as crying from the ground for vengeance, and the Blood of Christ which calls for God's mercy upon sinful men. In the Cornish Creation Plays[3] the blood of Abel was provided with a voice. This story could thus be interpreted historically, typologically or sacramentally but, not content with these complexities, the medieval preachers also gave it a moral application aimed at recalcitrant parishioners. In sermons and plays Cain is made the type of the grudging, dishonest payer of tithes.[4] Parish priests who had difficulty in collecting their dues no doubt emphasised this comparison when pointing to some illustration of the two brothers sacrificing, like the window in St. Neot (Corn)[5] or the carving in the Salisbury Chapter House (Plate 27), which showed Cain shrinking back from the down-swept smoke which marks God's rejection of his niggardly sacrifice. In the Towneley Plays Cain exclaims that this smoke is choking him.

It is important to remember this flexibility of interpretation, for we shall not then mistakenly reject the whole concept of church imagery serving as the picture book of the unlearned because ignorant men could not have understood its more abstruse symbolism. This was undoubtedly true, but very simple folk could have learned to recognise the commonest symbols as easily as their descendants memorise well-known trade marks or the divisional flashes on soldiers' uniforms.*

The certain interpretation of medieval imagery is, however, sometimes made difficult because the artists did not always restrict their use of a symbol to a single meaning. For instance, lions are generally symbols of good, associated with the Incarnation and Resurrection, but they can also represent the Evil One seizing a soul in his claws. During the past fifty years scholars have established the meaning of many subjects previously obscure, but

---

* The vocabulary of symbolism is somewhat confusing, so it may be wise to state here the sense in which I shall use its principal terms:

A Symbol expresses an abstract idea: *e.g.* the Pelican-in-her-piety is the symbol of Man's redemption through the Atonement of Christ.

An Emblem is used as an alternative to direct portrayal of a person, thus the Agnus Dei is the emblem of Christ, the Lamb of God.

An Attribute identifies the image of a sacred person but has no individual significance. Thus a swan or a pig enable us to identify the figures of St. Hugh of Lincoln or St. Anthony of Egypt when represented with them, but do not embody an allusion to these saints when they occur alone.

Unfortunately for clarity, there are occasions when these meanings overlap. Attribute and symbol merge when a saint is identified by an implement of his martyrdom (such as the gridiron of St. Lawrence) (Plate 44) and does not hold the palm which is the generalised symbol of martyrdom. In late medieval art the heraldic use of some attributes, such as the keys of St. Peter, achieved an independent recognition approximating to that of an emblem.

to compare these interpretations with those of older writers (who were far better qualified to guess aright than the average tourist of today) is to realise some of the risks we run in trying to answer our own questions. To give one example: a misericord in Lincoln cathedral which represents the well-known medieval theme of Tristram and Iseult meeting under the tree from which the head of King Mark is shown peering (see page 168) was interpreted as symbolising the respect paid to the head of St. Hugh, preserved as a precious relic in the cathedral.

Many subjects still defy interpretation, while others suggest a strange variety of possible explanations. The curious composite creature on a misericord in Exeter cathedral (Plate 74) which has the head of a crowned man and the body of a saddled horse, has been explained as alluding either to the story of how Aristotle was inveigled by a revengeful courtesan into serving her as a palfrey,[6] or to Henry III, ridden by his foreign favourites. Comparison with the miniatures of some contemporary manuscripts shows that the creature corresponds closely to the Locusts of the Apocalypse, even to the shape of the saddlecloth and the serpent's head at the end of its tail.

Today our minds are so conditioned by life in a literate world that only a sustained effort of imagination can make us realise the responsibility which rested upon those who directed the adornment of a church in the Middle Ages. When few could read, and even fewer could afford to own a book, the imagery of their parish church offered the only version of the Scriptures which was always available to the laity. It was therefore desirable that the images should express the theological, as well as the historical, aspect of their theme. So scholars designed diagrams expressing matters of doctrine, and symbols which represented the abstract ideas implicit in some Gospel subjects. Sometimes they were successful. It would be difficult to imagine a more concise and effective statement of the triune individuality of the Holy Trinity than the heraldic device (Fig. 7) which appears in many churches, as for instance in the south-east window of Newark (Notts). While the designer has not here entirely dispensed with words, the illiterate person to whom the device had once been explained would have had no more difficulty in recognising its

meaning than *we* have when we see carvings of it from which
the painted letters have worn away, as on the font at Wighton
(Norfolk).

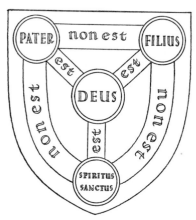

FIG. 7. Arms of the Holy Trinity

Sometimes, however, a device designed to instruct proved to be,
in practice, a stumbling block. In many late medieval Annuncia-
tions we see a small figure of the Christ Child descending on a ray
from Heaven in the wake of the Holy Dove, as on an alabaster
tomb in Ross-on-Wye church (Plate 26). This iconographical
symbol of the Incarnation unfortunately suggested the heretical
belief that the body of Jesus was not formed in the Virgin's womb
and the Church therefore sought to suppress it. It persisted,
however, until it was formally banned by Pope Benedict XIV in
the 18th century.[7]

A few of the more generally accepted conventions of medieval
imagery should be noted. God the Father is rarely shown in
human form in early art, the symbol of His intervention on earth
being then a great Hand reaching down from Heaven to create,
or protect, as we see it on the Castle Frome font (Plate 33). Later
medieval artists often based their designs upon the vision of the
Ancient of Days described in Daniel vii and depicted God as an
old man with flowing beard and long hair.[8] In a window at
Malvern Priory He appears to Abraham, leaning out of a Heaven
which opens in a glory of fire upon a blue sky crowded with the

heads and wings of angels. Sometimes He is shown wearing an early form of the papal tiara, with three crowns of diminishing size mounted upon a steeple-shaped cap. A striking example of such a head is carved on an armrest of the stalls of Lincoln, but whether the carver would have chosen, or been allowed, to represent the Creator in such a humble position must remain one of the problems of the medieval mind.

The clothes in which Christ and His disciples are always represented mark the period at which His physical appearance became traditionally accepted, for the long mantle draped round the body and over the shoulders was the usual garb for teachers, or other persons of dignity, in the 4th century.[9] The bare feet, which distinguish Christ and His Apostles from other figures in a group may have originated in a copyist's misunderstanding of sandals.

The usual manner of presenting the Holy Trinity is that carved upon the tomb at Willoughby-on-the-Wolds (Notts) (Plate 25), or on a beautiful alabaster carving at Kinlet (Salop). God the Father is shown crowned and enthroned, holding the Crucifix between His knees, while the Holy Dove hovers above. On the Suffolk fonts at Snape and Orford the Holy Dove is omitted. On the rare occasions when all Three Persons are represented anthropomorphically, as in windows showing the Coronation of the Virgin at Holy Trinity, Goodramgate, York, East Brent (Somerset) or Doddiscombsleigh (Devon), they all bear the traditional physiognomy of Christ, including the cruciform nimbus.

This representation of the Holy Trinity by three identical figures was denounced by theologians as tending to tri-theism, and some artists attempted to avoid such heretical suggestions by showing the Holy Trinity as partly threefold in form and partly united. On a misericord at Cartmel (Lancs) and on a bench-end at Lansallos (Cornwall) there are carvings of a triple face beneath a single crown, but these triune forms were too grotesque to win approval.[10]

The emblems of the Four Evangelists were often associated with representations of Christ in Majesty, particularly in the 12th and 13th centuries. The identification of these saints with the four beasts described in Revelation iv as standing around the throne,

H

dates back to the 5th century, but the reasons given by various authors for the individual identifications differed. Some were based upon the opening verses of each Gospel. St. Matthew begins with Christ's ancestry (the man), St. Mark with the 'voice crying in the wilderness' (like a lion); St. Luke with the sacrifice of Zacharius (the ox) while St. John takes us directly into the presence of the Divinity, like an eagle soaring up towards the sun. On the other hand a gloss attached to some 13th-century Apocalypses associates the lion with Christ's Resurrection, the ox with His sacrifice, the man with His humanity and the eagle with His divinity, each Evangelist being more particularly concerned with one of these themes. The author of the medieval dialogue between *Dives and Pauper* ignored both these explanations and tells us that the four beasts are often painted on the ends of the Cross because the eagle is king of all fowls, the lion of all wild beasts and the ox of all tame ones, while the man is king of all things visible. In these capacities they attend upon Christ, who is king of all things visible and invisible. Even in the Middle Ages men sometimes had to choose between a puzzling variety of explanations when they sought to interpret the symbolism of ecclesiastical art!

The halo usually shown round the heads of divine persons, or saints, has a long history, beginning as a symbol of supernatural power rather than of sanctity. Both Christ and the Apostles were therefore shown with haloes in scenes of the Last Judgment before it was represented in scenes of their earthly life.[11] While the head halo was a personal attribute, the mandorla, or almond-shaped glory surrounding the whole figure, was associated with certain manifestations of divine power.[12] In British churches it appears chiefly in connection with the Transfiguration, Ascension, or Second Coming of Christ and with the Assumption of the Blessed Virgin. British sculptors were evidently vague as to the nature of this mandorla. On a 12th-century tympanum at Pedmore (Worcs) the carver has made a loop in it through which Christ's hand is extended, and it is frequently shown being hauled up by flying angels, as on the Saxon grave cover at Wirksworth (Derbys) (Plate 24).

The Agnus Dei, or Lamb of God, has remained the familiar emblem of Christ. It can be distinguished from other lambs, realistic or symbolical, by the bannered cross which it holds in an uplifted foot. This cross, or *vexillum*, is usually held by Christ in post-Resurrection scenes and occasionally appears alone, as an emblem of His person. Examples can be seen on the Cornish bench-ends at Launcells (Plate 32), and Poughill.

The fish used in early Christian art as an emblem of Christ was derived from the initial letters of 'Jesus, Christ, Son of God, Saviour' which form the Greek word for a fish. It is rarely seen in British churches, but a late vaulting boss at St. Just-in-Roseland (Corn) has three fishes painted upon it with the word ΙΧΘΥΣ above them.[13]

Sacred monograms occur frequently. The oldest form is the Chi-Rho (see page 25) but the early Church also abbreviated the name of Jesus as IH(ΣΟΥ)Σ. In medieval churches the Greek capital letters were often rendered as IHS and usually, although not invariably, regarded as the initials of *Jesus Hominum Salvator*. Special honours were paid to the Instruments of the Passion from the 13th century onwards and they are illustrated in the windows or carvings of a great many churches. The devotional woodcut shown in Fig. 8 shows how the whole story of the Passion was symbolised by these instruments, and the inscription beneath the Christ of Pity in the centre explains one reason why they were so frequently shown. It promises to all who devoutly beholding these armes of Christ's Passion' say certain prayers, 6,765 years pardon. Rough drawings of these Instruments, accompanied by verses in the vernacular explain the context in which they figured in the private devotions of the ordinary parishioner. If a money bag, or three rows of overlapping coins, as on a bench-end at Kilkhampton (Corn), reminded him of the thirty pieces of silver he might have murmured:

> The pens also that Judas told
> Wherefore Jesu Christ was sold
> Lorde, shield me from treason and covetys
> Therein to sin nowise. . . .

The vessel of vinegar and gall is associated with a prayer not to be poisoned by sin; the sponge on the reed for . . .

> All that I have drunk in gluttony
> Lord forgive me e'er that I die.[14]

FIG. 8. 'Christ of Pity' devotional woodcut

The most elaborate series of carvings of these emblems is on the vaulting bosses of the choir of Winchester cathedral,[15] but the carved bench-ends illustrated on Plates 30–2 show how the scope of their symbolism could be extended. The hand touching the wounded Heart, and the bannered cross, would have been recognised by most parishioners of Launcells as portraying the Incredulity of St. Thomas, but some of them might have been led on to meditate upon the cult of the Sacred Wounds which became more widespread after the 13th century, perhaps stimulated by the stigmatisation of St. Francis in 1224. At North Cadbury (Som) we see the heraldic arrangement of Hands, Feet and Heart (Plate 30) which artists evolved as the coat of arms of Christ. A reference to Isaiah xii. 3 in the Office of the Sacred Heart led to the Wounds being described as 'wells'[16] and on shields depicted in the windows at Sidmouth (Devon) and Froyle (Hants) they are shown as almond-shaped cuts dropping blood, surmounted by crowns, and entitled respectively the Wells of Wisdom, Mercy, Everlasting Life, Grace and Good Comfort.

In the Angel Choir of Lincoln cathedral the great angels, whose outstretched wings fill the spandrels between the triforium arches, hold attributes expressing both the Fall and Judgment of Mankind (the Angel of the Expulsion and the Angel with the scales) and his redemption through the Incarnation (the Virgin and Child) and Passion of Christ (the Spear and Crown of Thorns). The Angel holding the sun and moon in his hands may symbolise the Creation of the World, but these planets are also often included in scenes of the Crucifixion. The remaining angels mostly hold scrolls or musical instruments. Only one figure strikes an apparently discordant note: an angel wearing a falconer's glove and offering to the hawk on his wrist the drumstick of a large bird. It has been suggested that hawking was so important among earthly pleasures that Heavenly bliss would be incomplete without it, but a more relevant explanation is offered by a 15th-century poem preserved in the British Museum[17] and which may record an older tradition. Here Christ is said to win back sinners to grace by showing them His Wounds, as a falconer lures back his wild-flying hawk by offering it raw meat. On the opposite side of the same bay at Lincoln, a figure of Christ wearing the Crown of Thorns points to His wounded side. This feature is, as far as I know, unique, but it illustrates both the strangely concrete similes by which medieval mysticism was sometimes expressed and also how a chance clue can enable us to restore to some apparently incongruous detail the dignity of its true significance.

Chapter 3

THE OLD TESTAMENT

THE MEDIEVAL artists' choice of subjects appears curiously capricious unless we understand their reasons. Some Old Testament subjects recur frequently, while others, which seem to have equal claims, are hardly ever shown. Why was Jonah a favourite figure whilst Joshua was ignored? Why was Noah's Ark preferred to the passage of the Red Sea? Why also, when illustrating a certain episode, did the artist almost invariably chose the same moment in the action, until extreme familiarity has made us accept as normal what is really both surprising and significant?

Since the practical usefulness of iconography depends upon general recognition of its symbols, both the choice and the treatment of these tend to become traditional, and the Old Testament subjects most often seen in British medieval churches are those which also occur among the earliest examples of Christian art, the paintings in the Catacombs of Rome.[1] The close parallel between these subjects and certain early prayers in which God was besought to deliver His servants as he delivered 'Isaac from sacrifice . . . Daniel from the den of lions . . . or the Children of Israel from the fiery furnace . . .' with other examples drawn from the Old Testament, suggests that the artists were directly inspired by these prayers. Several early Christian monuments in Ireland and Scotland show the same range of subjects: the Children of Israel, the sacrifice of Isaac, and Jonah emerging from the whale, are all carved on an 8th-century cross base at Seir Kieran (Offaly) while Daniel in the lions' den occurs on several other early sculptures.[2] These were mostly carved in the period of the Viking raids, when the lives of Christians were as precarious as in the days of pagan Rome, and the emphasis they laid upon the idea of Divine deliverance affected the way in which these subjects were represented throughout the Middle Ages.

The moment illustrated is always that at which God's intervention was made manifest. Abraham's sword is poised above the kneeling figure of Isaac as his arm is checked by the voice of God.

Noah is shown with his arms stretched out to welcome back the dove and, in the early 13th-century glass of Canterbury cathedral (Fig. 9), the Ark is still the *arca*, or shrine, of deliverance, as it was in the Catacombs. Because St. Gregory taught that the Ark had separate decks for animals, birds and men[3] it is carved with three decks superimposed in pyramidal form on the facade of Wells cathedral, and with three towers on a misericord in Ely cathedral.

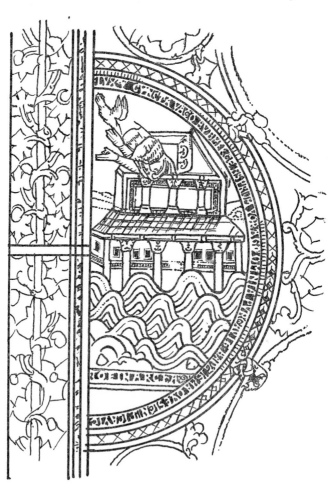

Fig. 9. Noah in the Ark. Canterbury Cathedral

Only two decks are shown in the Salisbury Chapter House (Plate 28), for humanity is here represented by Noah who is shown both embarking, at the stern, and welcoming the dove at the bows, an example of how continuous action was expressed in medieval iconography. The next carving at Salisbury shows the attractive subject of Noah planting the vine, and then we see him lying in a drunken stupor, to the embarrassment of his sons. The reason for the somewhat surprising inclusion of this subject, not only here but in the glass of St. Michael Spurriergate, York, and on the Fitzroy tomb at Framlingham (Suffolk), is that it was thought to prefigure the mocking of Christ.

This prophetic interpretation of certain incidents in the Old Testament was the main factor which determined their inclusion in church imagery. They were not meant to be considered historically, but as proofs that every event in the earthly life of Christ had been preordained by God from the beginning of time. The veil which covers the eyes of Synagogue, carved on the font at Southrop (Glos) (Plate 15) with her spear broken and the crown falling from her head, symbolises this veiled truth of the Old Testament which was to be both revealed and superceded by the clear vision of Holy Church, always shown as a stately queen holding a Gospel book. The finest English examples of such contrasted figures are those which flank the Chapter House door at Rochester.

The balance of the Old Testament types, with their Gospel anti-types, was as carefully planned as the thrust and counterthrust of a Gothic church. The Tree of the Fall of Man was one type of the Crucifixion, when Man's sin was redeemed through Christ's sacrifice on the 'Tree' of the Cross. In the Doom painting at Chaldon (Surrey) (Plate 41), we see the Tree of the Fall contrasted with another symbol of the Cross, the Ladder of Salvation. The words of Jesus, 'For as Jonas was three days and three nights in the whale's belly, so shall the Son of Man be three days and three nights in the heart of the earth' (St. Matthew xii. 40), made the swallowing of Jonah and his miraculous deliverance accepted symbols of the Entombment and Resurrection. They are shown in this context both in the glass of Canterbury and on two misericords in Ripon Minster.

Typological imagery was known in England at least as early

as 685 when Benedict Biscop brought paintings from Rome to adorn his church at Jarrow. These showed 'the agreement of the Old and New Testaments, most cunningly ordered',[4] Isaac carrying the wood for his sacrifice being painted immediately below the Bearing of the Cross. It was in England, in the 12th century, that typology found its fullest expression. Typological paintings once decorated the choir at Peterborough[5] and the Chapter House at Worcester, and, while these have been lost, we still have important remains of the twelve typological windows which were in the choir aisles of Canterbury cathedral,[6] (Fig. 10). In these, each scene from the New Testament was flanked by two types, mostly from the Old Testament, but with a few allegorical subjects.

The same principles applied to the somewhat later east window of the Corona at Canterbury and here the panel showing the Crucifixion is surrounded by four types: Moses striking the rock, the sacrifice of Isaac, the marking of the lintels with the blood of the lamb at the first Passover and the spies bearing the grapes from Canaan. The symbolism of this last subject, which is also shown in glass from the Sainte Chapelle, Paris, now in the east window of Twycross church (Leics), illustrates what variety of teaching could be expressed by a single picture. The spies are always shown carrying an immense bunch of grapes slung from a pole. As the juice of the vine symbolises the Blood of the Redeemer, so the grapes represent His Body. Because the spy walking in front turns his back on the grapes, he symbolised the Jews, while his companion, who is stretching out his hand to touch the grapes at Twycross, symbolised the Christians. The design was formalised by such teaching and appears in just the same way on late medieval misericords at Ripon and Beverley Minster and on a bench-end at Milverton (Som).

The emphasis laid on a single detail can indicate its typological meaning. The association of Isaac bearing the wood, with Christ bearing His Cross, is stressed on a misericord in Worcester cathedral (Plate 9) by the diagonal crossing of the faggots. This was not always possible in the relatively simple designs required for church imagery, so most representations of the Creation of Eve give us no clue as to why they so greatly outnumber those of the Creation of Adam, shown on the font at East Meon (Hants), and

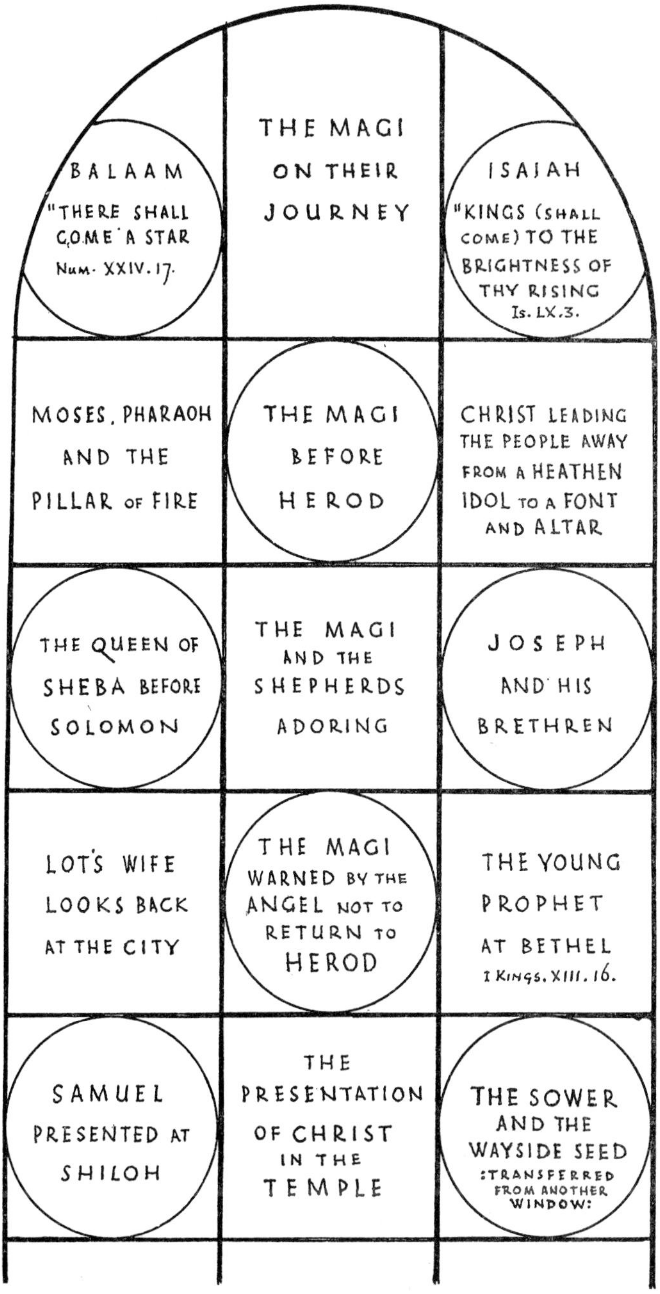

BALAAM "THERE SHALL COME A STAR Num. XXIV.17.	THE MAGI ON THEIR JOURNEY	ISAIAH "KINGS (SHALL COME) TO THE BRIGHTNESS OF THY RISING Is. LX.3.
MOSES, PHARAOH AND THE PILLAR of FIRE	THE MAGI BEFORE HEROD	CHRIST LEADING THE PEOPLE AWAY FROM A HEATHEN IDOL TO A FONT AND ALTAR
THE QUEEN OF SHEBA BEFORE SOLOMON	THE MAGI AND THE SHEPHERDS ADORING	JOSEPH AND HIS BRETHREN
LOT'S WIFE LOOKS BACK AT THE CITY	THE MAGI WARNED BY THE ANGEL NOT TO RETURN TO HEROD	THE YOUNG PROPHET AT BETHEL I KINGS. XIII.16.
SAMUEL PRESENTED AT SHILOH	THE PRESENTATION OF CHRIST IN THE TEMPLE	THE SOWER AND THE WAYSIDE SEED :TRANSFERRED FROM ANOTHER WINDOW:

FIG. 10. Arrangement of one of the theological windows
in Canterbury Cathedral

in the east window of York Minster. Medieval churchmen certainly did not attach higher importance to women. The typological explanation is only illustrated in some complex pictures of the Crucifixion which show the crowned figure of Holy Church emerging from the wounded side of Christ, to symbolise the Sacramental Blood and Water while, at the foot of the Cross, God the Father draws Eve from the side of Adam.[7]

Two books which summarised these prophetic parallels were among the most important sources of medieval art. The *Biblia Pauperum*,[8] of which the earliest manuscripts date from *c.* 1300, included only biblical types, while the slightly later *Speculum Humanae Salvationis*[9] drew also upon secular history, old Jewish legends and the curious lore of the Bestiary. When the invention of paper made possible the printing of blockbooks, these two works were among the first to be produced. The arrangement of pictures and text in the *Biblia Pauperum* is shown on Fig. 11, and the full list of the subjects included, given in Appendix 1, will explain the context in which most Old Testament subjects found in our churches were meant to be considered.

The prophecy of Isaiah xi. 1–2, 'There shall come forth a rod out of the root of Jesse . . . and the spirit of the Lord shall rest upon him', was interpreted from the 3rd century onwards as referring to the Incarnation of Christ. When medieval artists showed the Virgin enthroned, her sceptre often took the form of a budding rod, as on the font at Cowlam (Yorks). On a tomb at Willoughby-on-the-Wolds (Notts) (Plate 48), this rod has grown into a rosebush on which the Holy Dove is alighting. This concept was elaborated into the 'Tree of Jesse', a pictorial statement of the earthly genealogy of Christ which occurs most frequently in stained glass.[10] The 'Tree', mostly shown as a vine, springs from the loins of a sleeping Jesse, and supports the figures of many kings among its coils, while the Virgin and Child are enthroned at its summit. The great Jesse window of Dorchester Abbey (Oxon) expresses this theme in both sculpture and glass, while the monumental wooden figure of Jesse at Abergavenny (Mon) (Plate 93) probably originally formed the base of a lofty reredos. Fine panels from 14th-century Jesse windows can be seen at Lowick (Northants) and Merevale (War). In some later examples the Kings appear as half-length figures emerging from blossoms

Fig. 11. A page from the *Biblia Pauperum* block-book

on the tree, and both full- and half-length kings are included in the superb Jesse window at Llanrhaidr (Denbighs) which is dated 1553.

Moses, receiving the Tables of Stone from God, represented the Old Law which was both fulfilled and superseded by the New Law brought from Heaven by Christ. It is in this context that he appears on the west wall at Trotton (Sussex) (Plate 46). Even if Moses is not shown holding the Tables we can usually recognise him because of two short horns projecting from his forehead (Plate 15). By mistranslation of one Hebrew word in the description of how 'the skin of his face shone' when Moses came down from Mount Sinai, the phrase was rendered in the Vulgate *facie cornuta*, and so the horned Moses became the accepted convention in medieval art.[11] The finest British example is the 12th-century statue from St. Mary's Abbey, York, which is now in the Yorkshire Museum.

Few people can memorise the full development of medieval typology; the 13th-century text *Pictor in Carmine*[12] lists 508 types associated with 138 anti-types. Even the shorter lists of the *Biblia Pauperum* may over-tax our memories, so that we do not immediately recall the context in which one of the rarer Old Testament types occurs in some church, but we shall still see it in truer perspective if we realise that it should be set somewhere within the majestic framework of these prophetic parallels.

Chapter 4

THE NEW TESTAMENT

THE INFANCY AND MINISTRY OF CHRIST

W HEN we turn from the marshalled testimony of the Past to consider the events in the life of Christ which were so prefigured, we soon realise that, here too, the artists' choice of subjects was restricted. Their main concern was to explain, by illustration, the significance of the Church festivals and if we were to catalogue all the subjects referring to the life of Christ, or of His Mother, which are identifiable in church imagery, under the headings of these festivals, there would be very few left out. The events thus celebrated were: the Birth of the Blessed Virgin and (later) her Presentation in the Temple, the annunciation, Nativity, Presentation in the Temple, Epiphany, Transfiguration (late), Entry into Jerusalem, Crucifixion, Resurrection, Ascension, Pentecost, Dormition and Assumption of the Virgin, Exaltation of the Cross. Once this principle of selection has been recognised there is little more that need be said about the choice of New Testament subjects represented in our churches. We may regret the artists' disregard of the pictorial potentialities of many scenes in the adult life of Christ before His Passion, but it will not surprise us.

If to these Gospel subjects we add the painted Dooms, the portrayals of the saints, some formalised representations of the Holy Sacraments (see page 147) and moral allegories (see page 144) we have an almost complete table of contents for the Picture Book of the churches. In their minor decorative sculpture, as on the margins of richly illuminated manuscripts, we shall find a wealth of subjects, some symbolical, some derived from secular literature or popular fables and some purely fantastic, but these we will discuss in another chapter.

What concern us here are the details, not based upon the Gospels, which occur in many New Testament subjects and the interest of which can all too easily be missed, just because they are so familiar to us. Some of these refer back to Old Testament prophecies, others were drawn from the visions of medieval mystics who contemplated the scenes of Christ's earthly life in an ever-enduring Present and described them with the authority of actual participants. The carved alabaster tomb of William Rudhall at Ross-on-Wye (Herefs) (Plate 26), which shows the dead man and his family as kneeling witnesses of the Annunciation, may serve to illustrate a mystical approach to the Gospels which inspired much medieval iconography.

Between the angel and the kneeling Virgin is the traditional lily rising from a small jar, a feature so familiar that it is surprising to discover that scholars disagree as to its origin and precise symbolism. It may have originated in England for it appears on the 12th-century capitals of the crossing of Southwell Minster (Notts) and on the Norman font at Upavon (Wilts) although, according to Émile Mâle[1], it is not known in French art before the 13th-century. In the Anglo-Saxon poem *Solomon and Saturn*[2] Solomon replies to the question, 'which is the happiest of herbs', that 'the lily is that herb for it denoteth Christ', and from the 14th century until the Reformation the lily of the Annunciation was sometimes shown with a tiny figure of the crucified Christ on its stem, as, for instance, on a misericord at Tong (Salop) (Plate 37). An English medieval translation of the *Speculum Humanae Salvationis*[3] explains that the Virgin is the rod from Jesse's root and her Son its flower. Then, after enumerating the healing virtues of the symbolical lily, it adds:

> A man is strengthid noblye
> that he no payne may fele,
> Of this floure, Crist-on-Crosse
> Behalding the coloure.

The Apocryphal Gospels which, since the 2nd century, had partly satisfied men's hunger for further details of the life of Jesus, were supplemented by such works as the 13th-century *Meditationes vitae Christi* of the pseudo-Bonaventura, translated into English *c.* 1410 by Nicholas Love under the title *The Mirrour of the Blessed Lyf of Jesu Christ*,[4] and the *Revelations* of St. Bridget of Sweden who is shown, as a seated nun with an open book, on the painted roodscreen at Horsham St. Faith (Norfolk). The widespread influence of these books is reflected by many details of church imagery based upon them.

How many readers could say with immediate certainty whether the ox and the ass are mentioned in the Gospels? They are not. All we learn there is that the Child was laid in a manger, but the apocryphal Gospel of Pseudo-Matthew[5] describes how Mary left the desert cave in which the Nativity took place, on the third day, and hid from Herod's men in a stable, where she laid the Child in a manger, and the ox and the ass adored Him. Yet, in spite of this historical uncertainty, the two animals were regarded as essential witnesses from the 4th century onwards. On an early sarcophagus in Milan all that the sculptor has considered necessary to convey the message of his work is the swaddled child in the crib and the ox and the ass, one at each end of it,[6] as they appear underneath the Crucifixion on a Saxon cross at Sandbach (Ches). The reason why these apocryphal animals were considered so important is that the text in Isaiah i. 3, 'The ox knoweth his owner and the ass his master's crib; but Israel doth not know, my people doth not consider', was interpreted as foretelling the manger at Bethlehem, and the refusal of the Jews to acknowledge Christ was contrasted with the adoration of the animals. Commentators not only accepted the presence of the ox and the ass but explained it; the sermon of the Pseudo-Augustine, the *Golden Legend* and the *Meditationes,* all tell how they came there. As John Mirk puts it, in his Christmas sermon: 'St. Joseph, for that he had no money, took an ox with him, for to sell there and make him money of. But, for he durst not leave Our Lady behind, for he was nigh time of birth, he set her on an ass and took her with him.'[7] A boss in the north transept of Norwich cathedral shows St. Joseph leading the two beasts with the Virgin Mary following him.

In early Nativities the Virgin is often an impassive, recumbent figure, as on the 12th-century font at West Haddon (Northants), while the Child's crib is sometimes raised so high that He appears to be lying on a sacrificial altar. In the late 14th century there was a sudden change of tradition and henceforth we usually see the Virgin kneeling in adoration of the Babe who lies on the ground surrounded by a glory of light. The growing veneration of the Virgin had introduced the belief that, being without sin, she did

I

not suffer pain in child-birth, but the decisive factor in this change
was the vision seen by St. Bridget of Sweden while she was in
ecstasy at Bethlehem in 1370. She beheld a virgin of extreme
beauty come into a cave, accompanied by an old man leading an
ox and an ass. He tied these to the manger and fastened a lighted
candle to the wall before he withdrew. The Virgin took off her
shoes, veil and mantle and knelt down in prayer. Then, 'suddenly
in a moment, she gave birth to her son from whom radiated such
an ineffable light and splendour that the sun was not comparable
to it, nor did the candle that St. Joseph had put there give any
light at all. . . . When the Virgin felt that she had already borne
her child, she immediately worshipped him . . . saying: "Be
welcome my God, my Lord and my Son." '8 The instantaneous
birth had already been described in the *Meditationes*, but the kneeling Virgin and the glory of light proceeding from the Child were
introduced into Christian art by St. Bridget and it is a vivid
illustration of the international structure of medieval thought that
the vision of a single Swedish mystic should have changed the
traditional iconography of the Nativity. A window in Malvern
Priory (Plate 35) shows St. Joseph kneeling in adoration, shielding
the flame of his candle with his hand.

   The Adoration of the Magi calls to our minds three crowned
figures, one old and bearded, one in the prime of life and often
of African type, and the last a stripling, bringing their offering
to the new-born Saviour. We may even name them, Melchior
Caspar and Balthazar, before we pause to wonder how this
information has been added to the bald statement in St. Matthew's
Gospel that 'there came wise men from the east to Jerusalem' who
when they had worshipped the Child, 'presented unto Him gifts
gold and frankincense and myrrh'. Even their number is left
uncertain!9 It is in a text once attributed to Bede that we first
learn that the oldest of the Magi, Melchior, offered gold, the
symbol of kingship; next Caspar offered frankincense to mark the
divinity of Christ, and lastly Balthazar offered myrrh to the Son
of Man who must die. Artists sometimes indicate the nature of
each offering by the vessel in which they are presented: a ciborium
full of gold coins, an incense boat and the form of spice jar
with a conical top, which is the identifying attribute of Mary
Magdalene. The convention of showing Balthazar as a negro

started in the 14th century, when theologians taught that the Magi had been prefigured by the three sons of Noah who divided the earth between them (they are shown in one of the Theological windows at Canterbury marking out the 'three corners of the world' upon a globe), and that they thus symbolised the three races of men coming to worship their Saviour.[10]

A wooden roof boss at Salle (Norfolk) and a panel of stained glass in the east window of St. Peter Mancroft, Norwich, both show the Virgin giving her breast to the Child as the High Priest leans forward to circumcise Him (Plate 38). This action, typical of the spirit of human tenderness which changed the character of much medieval iconography in the 14th and 15th centuries, was probably inspired by the *Meditationes Vitae Christi* in which we read how the Child wept 'for the sorrow that he felt there through his flesh . . . and then his mother, wiping his face and kissing him, and putting the pap in his mouth, comforted him in all the manners that she might'.[11]

The Massacre of the Innocents was often represented to explain the meaning of Holy Innocents Day and the common medieval tradition of showing it taking place before the throne of Herod (Plate 68), appears as early as the 5th-century mosaics in Sta Maria Maggiore in Rome. Carvings of the scene occur on the 12th-century doorway of the Lady Chapel at Glastonbury.

In the background of the Flight into Egypt we sometimes find motives derived from the apocryphal Gospel of pseudo-Matthew. A palm tree bowing low, as though before a storm, in a window of the Lady Chapel at Fairford, recalls how Mary wished to eat the fruit of a tall tree beneath which the Holy Family rested on their flight, and Jesus commanded the tree to bend down to His Mother's hand. A bent tree is shown in the background of the Flight into Egypt in the 13th-century wall-paintings at Brook (Kent) and the next subject there shows an idol falling from its pedestal. This, and an earlier painting of two falling idols at Hardham (Sussex), illustrate the legend that all the idols in the temple of Sotinen fell to the ground when Mary entered it bearing the Child. The scene of Christ among the Doctors was usually shown with Jesus in the centre, on a high seat, surrounded by learned men who sometimes wear the robes of contemporary doctors. In the windows of Malvern the Jewish sages wear black caps and gowns with fur-edged hoods, as though the debate were taking place in the hall of a medieval University, while at East Harling (Norfolk) an attempt at an Oriental flavour has given the doctors fantastic headgear.

The Baptism of Christ is the one scene of His adult life before the Passion which is often shown (because of its sacramental significance) although not directly related to any Church festival. In some early examples we can trace the influence of ancient ritual. Both the *ampullae* at Monza, *c.* 600, and the ivory throne of Maximian at Ravenna show attendant angels with their hands veiled, a mark of respect correctly reproduced in the Saxon flying angels at Bradford-on-Avon (Wilts). Later Western craftsmen, unfamiliar with eastern ceremonial, transformed this veil into a cloak,[12] or tunic, held by the angel, as on the Norman font at West Haddon (Northants), and the carver of the Castle Frome font (Plate 33), where there are no angels, has given the Baptist a maniple, over his right arm. The fishes in the water at Castle Frome symbolise the souls of Christians (*pisciculi* as they sometimes called themselves) whose spiritual life depends upon the saving waters of baptism as the earthly life of fishes is dependent on their natural element. Here the Baptist only lays his hand on the head of Christ, but he is sometimes shown pouring water from a jug, bottle or shell, following occasional liturgical usages.[1]

The only miracles of Christ normally represented in churches were the Marriage at Cana and the Raising of Lazarus; the former subject being always identified by the prominence given to the waterpots. In the Theological Windows at Canterbury, these pots were equated with the Seven Ages of Man and an inscription tells us that 'The water gives the story, the wine signifies the allegory'[1] a metaphor which may aptly be applied to the whole study of medieval iconography. In the 15th-century glass at East Harling (Norfolk) the Virgin Mary is shown in the foreground, already crowned as Queen of Heaven, directing the servants to fill the waterpots, and opposite her stands a man with a halo, holding the palm of martyrdom. The anonymous 'Ruler of the Feast' has here apparently been transformed into a saint, perhaps following some legend, now lost, of his subsequent conversion and martyrdom.[15]

By far the finest illustrations of the raising of Lazarus are the two panels of early sculpture now in Chichester cathedral, which may once have formed part of a screen. In the first we see Christ arriving at the house of Martha and Mary, who kneel upon the threshold with hands uplifted in entreaty. Here we have a good illustration of the early tradition of hierarchical perspective, for the figure of Christ towers over those of the sisters. On the Norman font at Lenton (Notts) (Plate 42) Lazarus is represented lying in his grave with his body swathed in diagonal folds, and on the second panel at Chichester he stands upright, his hands raised in prayer, while similar bands are being removed from his legs. These swathings recall the earlier convention of representing this scene with a swathed mummy, upright in the entrance to a mausoleum.

The raising of Jairus' daughter, sometimes used as an alternative symbol of resurrection in early Christian art, is very rare in England, but at Copford (Essex) it inspired one of our most important 12th-century wall-paintings. The bold composition has a central feature which suggests the walls and doorways of Jairus' house. On one side of this the mother is shown mourning while, on the other, the father is shown entreating Christ with expressive gestures. The eyes of the great Christ figure gaze into infinite distance but His hand is raised in the gesture of speech as though already pronouncing the words of resurrection.

A medallion in one of the Theological windows at Canterbury which shows the calling of Nathaniel by Peter, as he sat under the fig tree, may be mentioned as introducing the scanty illustrations of Our Lord's teaching which we find in medieval imagery. Upon His description of the Judgment Day (St. Matthew xxv) were based many of the painted Dooms and also the representations of the Seven Works of Mercy (pages 125, 145), but the vivid parables which often inspired later artists were relatively little used by those of the Middle Ages. An exception to this rule is the parable of the Wise and Foolish Virgins, since the image of a gate open only to those who have kept faithful watch was particularly appropriate for the decoration of church doors.[16] Charmingly virginal little figures are set in the mouldings of the 13th-century Judgment Door of Lincoln cathedral, the foolish ones holding their lamps upside down to prove their emptiness, but the theme did not achieve the importance in Britain which was accorded to it on the Continent. Both Wise and Foolish Virgins are shown in the tracery lights at Melbury Bubb (Dorset), with the dialogue between them inscribed upon scrolls.

The parable of Dives and Lazarus is shown in two scenes among the 12th-century carvings on the west front of Lincoln cathedral and a 12th-century tympanum, now in the Yorkshire Museum, may represent the death of Dives. It is rarely shown later but is illustrated in two fragments of 14th-century glass at Great Milton (Oxon).

The other parables occur very rarely. The Sower is shown in two medallions at Canterbury which are among the most beautiful examples of early glass in the country, and we know from the recorded titles of these windows that many other parables were originally shown: the Leaven, the Net, the Tares, the Lost Sheep, the Unjust Debtor, the Wedding Garment and the Good Samaritan, but all these are lost. The single panel of the Prodigal Son in Lincoln cathedral may have formed part of such another series, but, as a general rule, Our Lord's parables did not form an essential part of the Picture Book of the Churches.

Chapter 5

THE NEW TESTAMENT

THE PASSION TO THE LAST JUDGMENT

THE SERIES of subjects connected with Holy Week begins with the Entry into Jerusalem and the iconography of this scene has hardly varied since its first presentation on 4th-century Roman sarcophagi. Christ rides towards the city gates while people spread garments before the ass or throw flowers from the battlements of the gate. In the east window at Malvern the figures on the walls are children, perhaps alluding to the choir boys who greeted the Palm Sunday procession when it entered a church, and at Fairford they hold a scroll inscribed with the words and music of the relevant antiphon.[1] The symbolical association of the church door with this festival is stressed on the Norman tympanum at Aston Eyre (Salop) which shows Christ riding an elongated ass with its colt (rarely included) running behind.

The bread and fish associated with the feeding of the multitude, and with the post-Resurrection appearances of Christ, symbolised the Eucharist in early art and when the Last Supper became an integral part of every cycle of Passion scenes, they almost always replaced the historical lamb of the Passover feast.[2] The moment usually illustrated is that of the identification of the traitor, and Judas often stretches out his hand to seize a fish lying on a plate. Christ's words 'he that dippeth his hand with me in the dish, the same shall betray me' were thus emphasised by showing Judas grasping an accepted emblem of the Saviour.

Roman social conventions influenced the earliest representations of the Last Supper, in which Christ is seated at the dexter point of a horseshoe table, the accepted post of honour. The second most honoured person sat at the opposite point and the rest of the company ranged in order from his right hand, so that the youngest sat next to the principal, who might accord to a favoured friend the privilege of leaning in front of him.[3] Thus St. John by 'leaning

on Jesus' bosom' was only assuming a position normal at a
Roman dinner-table, but misunderstanding of this probably gave
rise to the tradition that he fell asleep. A straight table accommo-
dating all the Apostles along one side could only be represented
on long, narrow panels, as round the font at St. Nicholas,
Brighton, or on the stone reredos at Somerton (Oxon). Where
space was restricted, the Last Supper was shown with a round,
or square, table, as on roof bosses at Salle (Norfolk) or Tewkesbury (Glos). At Madley (Herefs) a 13th-century glazier has solved
a similar problem by showing only three Apostles, including St.
John sleeping on His Master's breast to make identification certain.

The traditional arrangement of the agony in the Garden
shows the Saviour kneeling in the middle distance with the
Apostles asleep in the foreground. The 'Cup' stands on a bank
before Him, or is held by an angel. Sometimes this angel holds
the Cross instead, and on a late carving on the pulpit at Bosbury
(Herefs) both symbols are shown. The Gospels do not speak of an
angel, nor of an actual appearance of the 'Cup' (which is sometimes shown as a chalice with the Host above it), and the convention of representing it thus may have originated in the religious
drama.

In the Betrayal of Christ, the kiss of Judas naturally forms the
central feature, as on the fine alabaster in Hawkley church (Hants),
but the incident of St. Peter striking off the ear of the servant,
Malchus, is almost equally ubiquitous and it is the device of a
drawn sword with an ear upon its blade which represents the
Betrayal on the Cornish bench-ends at Poughill and Launcells.
The modern observer may wonder whether emphasis was being
placed upon the desperate courage of St. Peter or the healing
mercy of Christ, and the ordinary medieval parishioner probably
understood only the historical allusion, but the scholarly medieval
interpretation was quite different. A note appended to a text from
St. Ambrose in Graham's *Decretum* runs thus: 'Peter cut off
Malchus' ear and Christ restored it to him. From this we may see
that if a man hear not (the Church) his ear must be spiritually
smitten off by Peter; for it is Peter who hath the power of binding
and loosing'.[4] Thus this passage, divorced from Christ's own
rebuke 'all they that take the sword shall perish with the sword',
was considered as giving authority for merciless strictness.

The Denial of St. Peter often featured in early art, perhaps bringing a message of hope to those who despaired of forgiveness, and the scene is usually identified by a cock standing at St. Peter's feet, or perched on a column. A porphyry column crowned by a bronze cock, which once stood in the Lateran Palace, was popularly believed to be that from which the cock of the Passion had crowed.[5]

As St. Peter became regarded more exclusively as the Founder of the Church, the Keys rather than the cock became his attribute, but the connection between the cock and the column continued, albeit with a changed significance, among the Emblems of the Passion. Carvings on a bench-end at Sefton (Lancs) and the screen at Llanrwst (Denbighs) (Plate 54), show the bird standing on a short column round which is coiled the rope which proves that the craftsman had in mind the pillar of the Flagellation

The devotional woodcut reproduced in Fig. 8 shows the way in which these emblems expressed the whole story of the Passion, so I shall here confine myself to its less abstract illustrations. In these we shall note a marked difference of outlook between the early Christian artists, who hardly ever represented the Passion scenes, or did so only with austere symbolism, and those of the mid-13th century onwards who included an increasing complexity of realistic or symbolical details often drawn from extra-Biblical sources.

The Flagellation is rare in early art, and the first miniatures representing it show Our Lord fully clothed, but the artistic development of the subject during the 14th and 15th centuries showed an increasing savagery, particularly in northern Europe. The executioners were made hideous, and the artist laid emphasis not so much upon Christ's nobility of expression, as on the multiplication of His wounds. We should, however, be wrong to attribute this treatment to the coarse-fibred imagination of the craftsmen, since the writings of such contemporary mystics as Margery Kempe show us whence they drew their inspiration.

The Crowning with Thorns shows us a similar change in approach. A 2nd-century fresco in the Catacomb of Prestatus in Rome shows Christ crowned with leaves rather than thorns, and a soldier merely touching His head with a long, leafy reed. In 1238 financial straits forced the Emperor of Constantinople to pledge a relic, reputed to be the true Crown of Thorns, to Louis IX of France, and its journey to Paris had an interesting effect on medieval iconography.[6] The relic was not a crown of *thorns* at all, but a wreath of rushes bound together by twisting ties, and, for approximately sixty years after its transit, artists showed Christ wearing a spiral fillet round His brows. It was during this period that the Angel Choir of Lincoln was built and in its western bay we see one angel holding such a Crown and another with a spear, presumably the Holy Lance which had also been brought to Paris. Perhaps later English designers forgot the true appearance of the relic, for they show the Crown of Thorns with the spiral ties exaggerated into a double twisted cable, and, after 1300, the thorns are shown projecting from this with increasing emphasis (Plate 54). From this date also we see, with few exceptions, the crucified Christ wearing the Crown of Thorns, whereas earlier He was often bare-headed or crowned with a royal diadem. Mystics, preachers and playwrights all contributed to an increasing brutality of representation. John Mirk's description in a sermon of how the tormentors beat upon the crown of thorns with staves, until the thorns pierced Christ's brain, is echoed in the *Towneley Plays*. In the glass of St. Peter Mancroft, Norwich, and on alabaster panels and among the carvings over the porch at Tiverton (Devon) we see men pressing the thorns down upon the head of Christ with long staves.

The early iconography of the Bearing of the Cross shows two conflicting traditions, corresponding to the accounts given in the Gospel of St. John, where Christ is described as bearing His Cross, or in the Synoptic Gospels which tell how Simon of Cyrene was charged with it.[7] A 10th-century stone carving in the church at Leek (Staffs) which shows a nimbed figure bending beneath the weight of the Cross is an early example of the tradition which is most frequently represented. The *Meditationes Vitae Christi* developed the theme of how Christ fell beneath the load and the medieval playwrights contributed further incidents to enrich its iconography. On the alabaster reredos at Yarnton (Oxon) (Plate 39) the soldiers press upon the Cross to make it heavier to bear, while a fragmentary alabaster at Blunham (Beds) shows the Virgin trying to share her Son's burden.

The Vera Ikon, or 'true picture', of Christ imprinted upon a kerchief with which He had touched his face, figures in many full series of the Emblems of the Passion (Fig. 8), but it is chiefly in late medieval imagery that we see an anonymous woman, who later became known as St. Veronica, actually handing her kerchief to Christ so that he might wipe the sweat from His brow, as on the Yarnton alabaster. A fine example of the Vernicle, showing the portrait of Christ on the kerchief, is carved on a bench-end at Altarnun (Corn).

The Crucifixion was only represented by abstract symbols so long as the Cross continued to be associated in men's minds with a shameful death. The Saxon grave cover at Wirksworth (Derbs) shows the Agnus Dei in the centre of the Cross (Plate 24), a form of representation forbidden in the Eastern Church in 692, but which was used in Britain until the 10th century, when we find it on the head of the St. Oswald Cross in the cathedral library at Durham.

When Christ crucified was represented in human form the artists faced a difficult choice between showing Him as the Son of God, not subject to death or pain, but glorified through voluntary sacrifice, or as the Son of Man, dying at the hands of sinners, in atonement for men's sins.[8] Until the 11th century artists mostly represented a living, triumphant Saviour, robed and sometimes crowned, standing in front of the Cross rather than suspended from it. One of the two Saxon Roods set on the church porch at Langford (Oxon) shows Christ (now headless) wearing a long straight robe and with His arms spread horizontally, with no suggestion of suspense. It was not until the 13th century that artists adopted the convention of the dead Christ, hanging heavily from his arms. From the invulnerable grandeur of Divinity expressed in abstract symbolism, the mystics of the 14th and 15th centuries turned to contemplate the physical agony of sacrifice, and the artists followed their guidance, showing Christ's body twisted with pain and hanging from almost vertical arms. Any such changes provoked passionate controversies. Luke, Bishop of Tuy in Spain accused those who favoured showing Christ's feet crossed and pierced with a single nail, as seeking to shake men's faith in the Holy Cross and the traditions of the sainted Fathers.[9]

Following the authority of the Gospels the Virgin and St. John are always shown standing beneath the Cross, but during the early Middle Ages they appear rather as statues in a formalised Rood Group, than as living, suffering, actors in the scene of cosmic tragedy. With the increasing emphasis on pathos in the 14th century we see the Virgin swooning amid a group of other women, as on the font at Salle (Norfolk), but the imagery remaining in our churches does not usually lay that emotional stress upon her sufferings which characterises much Continental art.

In all detailed representations of the Crucifixion we see two figures, one holding a lance, the other a reed topped with a sponge. Tradition named the soldier who pierced Christ's side Longinus (from λόγχη, the Greek word for his spear), and the man with the sponge Stephaton. Longinus always stands on the dexter side of the Cross, for although the Gospels give no guidance, and realism would suggest a thrust aimed directly at the heart, the inflexible tradition of the Church dictated that the blood and water, symbols of the Holy Sacraments, issued from the right side of Christ.

Often Longinus points to one of his eyes, an allusion to the legend that he was blind when he aimed his spear at Christ but was healed by the Holy Blood. In a wall-painting at Peakirk (Northants) the eye to which he points is open while the other remains closed.[10] Some artists confused Longinus with the centurion, and an alabaster carving at Drayton Parslow (Bucks) shows both men on horseback.[11]

The difference between the two thieves was clearly indicated. The good thief is always on the right hand of Christ and gazes towards Him; the bad thief averts his head. On the font at Lenton (Notts), in the glass of Hingham (Norfolk) and on a painted panel at Fowlis Easter (Perthshire) an angel is shown bearing the soul of the good thief to Heaven while a demon flies to Hell with that of his companion.

In some representations of the Descent from the Cross actions are depicted which can be traced back to Byzantine iconography. For instance, in the 14th-century wall-painting at Chalgrove (Oxon), Joseph of Arithmathaea supports the body of the Dead Christ in his arms while Nicodemus extracts the nails and the Virgin tenderly clasps the right hand which already hangs free. In the windows of East Harling (Norfolk) the dead Christ lies on the knees of the mourning Virgin with SS. John and Mary

Magdalene standing behind her, and the Cross is in the background, with the scourges, spear and sponge on a reed, formalised about it. Here the group of the two main figures, in the form generally known as a *pietà*, is already becoming detached from its historical setting. It was very often carved in the round, a fact which made British examples particularly vulnerable to iconoclasts. An alabaster figure at Breadsall (Derbs) and a battered wooden one at Battlefield (Salop) survive as free-standing examples, and it is also carved on fonts at Orford (Suffolk) and West Drayton (Midsx).

The Harrowing of Hell was a popular subject based on the apocryphal *Gospel of Nicodemus* which describes how two recently deceased Jews rose from the dead with Christ, and returned home to give their testimony. They told how a great light shone in Hell before Simeon, followed by John the Baptist, came thither to tell of their earthly knowledge of Jesus.[12] On the Norman tympanum at Quenington (Glos) a large sun is shown behind the figure of Christ forcing open the Hell Mouth and represents this 'Dayspring from on high' which pierced even the eternal darkness. Most medieval artists represented Hell in the form of a monstrous head with gaping jaws, a conception possibly derived from the description of Leviathan in Job xli: 'Who can open the doors of his face? His teeth are terrible round about.' The Harrowing of Hell occurs on Norman tympana at Beckford (Worcs) and Shobdon (Herefs) and in early carvings at South Cerney (Glos), Jevington (Sussex) and Bristol cathedral.

The first Christian artists shrank from portraying the sublime mystery of the Resurrection realistically and only indicated it by showing the three Maries and the angel at the Sepulchre. On the Norman font at Lenton (Notts) (Plate 42) we see the Resurrection both prefigured by the raising of Lazarus and attested by the appearance of the angel to the three women. The Sepulchre is here shown with a domed roof supported on columns, recalling a classical mausoleum or perhaps the actual appearance of the tomb chamber in the Church of the Holy Sepulchre at Jerusalem as it was restored by the Crusaders. From the 13th century onwards the artists more often showed the Sepulchre as a Gothic altar tomb, even though the Gospels prove that it was a chamber large enough to contain several people. This may have been due to the fact that such tombs were often used as Easter Sepulchres (see page 158). At Fairford the glazier compromised by placing an altar tomb in the entrance to a cave.

The post-Resurrection appearances of Christ are relatively rare. In the Fairford windows we see His appearance to His Mother in the 'chapel' mentioned by Margery Kempe as the scene of this event.[13] The greeting inscribed on a scroll in this panel *Salve sancta parens* (Hail, Holy Parent) is the introit of the Mass of Our Lady from Easter to Pentecost. The appearance to Mary Magdalene appears more often: in the windows of Fairford and Bledington (Glos), on an alabaster in the Victoria and Albert Museum and on the supporters of a misericord at Lincoln (Plate 63).

The Incredulity of St. Thomas was introduced into composite alabaster retables but does not often occur as a separate subject. It is shown in a window in All Saints, North Street, York, and a 13th-century wall-painting at Rotherfield (Sussex). On the bench-end at Launcells (Cornwall) (Plate 32) it is symbolised by a hand touching the wounded Heart which is supported on the *vexillum*.

There were two different traditions in the early iconography of the Ascension.[14] In one Christ is shown striding up a mountain peak to grasp the Hand of God stretched down to receive Him, in the other he floats upwards in a mandorla supported by angels (Plate 24).

In the 11th century a new type of Ascension picture shows Christ disappearing into a cloud so that only His feet and the hem of His garment remain visible. We know that in some churches on Ascension Day an image of Christ was drawn up into the vaulting where it disappeared into a ring of curtains[15] and the highly conventionalised 'clouds' in some later British examples, as on a misericord in Lincoln cathedral, suggest that the craftsman was visualising the event in terms of such dramatised ritual. Sometimes two footprints are shown upon the rock beneath the feet of the ascending Christ, as on the bench-end at Launcells (Plate 31) and these refer to the footprints shown to pilgrims in the Church of the Ascension on the Mount of Olives.

Pentecost is represented in the glass of the Corona at Canterbury with Christ seated upon the rainbow throne and rays of fire proceeding from the clouds under His feet to touch the heads of the

Apostles. Usually the Apostles are shown grouped together, with either the Virgin Mary or St. Peter in the centre, while the Holy Dove hovers above them in a downward darting glory of fire.[16]

Single subjects from the Apocalypse rarely figure in parish churches but in some cathedrals we still see full series of illustrations. The paintings in the Chapter House at Westminster are somewhat naive including one scene which is a good example of the literal accuracy of the medieval imagination. Because St. John addressed the Book of Revelation to 'the Seven churches which are in Asia' the artist has depicted him sitting in a meadow surrounded by seven miniature churches, each having an angel standing within its doorway. The Apocalypse subjects shown in the east window of York Minster and on the cloister bosses at Norwich are of finer quality artistically (Plate 70). The window was made *c*. 1405 and the bosses are a little earlier. Norwich has the wider range of subjects, since the many bosses of a lierne roof offered greater freedom to the carver, while the glazier concentrated chiefly on subjects of didactic importance, such as the Judgment of the Dead. There may be about a hundred bosses at Norwich illustrating the Apocalypse but the identification of some of these depends only upon their context. Thus a carving of an angel with a trumpet, seen elsewhere, would have no special significance, but here it may recall the 'great voice as of a trumpet' (Revelation i. 10).

The Picture Book of the Churches ends with the Last Judgment. In the wall-paintings at Hardham and Clayton the artists visualised this scene in terms of the Apocalypse but later Churchmen seem to have realised that apocalyptic symbolism was too obscure for the instruction of an uneducated congregation, and also perhaps less authoritative than Our Lord's own prophetic description in St. Matthew xxv. Most 14th- and 15th-century Doom paintings therefore follow the arrangement which we see in St. Thomas' church, Salisbury (Plate 45). Christ is enthroned on the rainbow; displaying the Wounds of His Passion; to His right, the blessed are admitted to Heaven, which is shown as a fortified city, while, to His left, demons drive damned souls into the jaws of Hell. Occasionally artists follow the Apocalypse in showing Christ with a sword issuing from His mouth, as, for instance, in a painting at Widford (Herts).

The minor variations in such paintings need not concern us but to see how far-flung were the sources from which medieval artists derived some of the details they included, let us look at the 12th-century Doom painting on the west wall of Chaldon (Surrey) (Plate 41).[17] The design is divided horizontally by a band painted with the wavy lines which usually symbolise clouds, and vertically by the Ladder of Salvation which extends from deepest Hell to highest Heaven, here indicated by the head and shoulders of Christ appearing in a circular glory. This Ladder, which is included among the symbols mentioned in the Byzantine Manual for Painters, symbolises the Cross of Christ by which alone sinners may climb to Heaven. Its typological contrast with the Tree of the Fall is illustrated by placing this Tree on the right of the painting with the Serpent entwined among its branches. Above the level of the clouds, naked souls are successfully climbing upwards towards Christ, but, from the lower rungs, most of them are being clawed off, and pitchforked into the eternal fires, by a gigantic demon. The Christian mystical writers who described this Ladder, and the various temptations which caused men to fall from it, may have based their concept upon Jacob's vision, or it may have been another of the many pagan traditions adapted to Christian usage. The early Memphites believed that Heaven was reached by a ladder standing on the western edge of the world and model ladders continued to be buried with the Egyptian dead long after this primitive belief had been abandoned.[18] The mystic ladder was also a Mithraic symbol.

To the left of the ladder other demons are pitchforking souls into a boiling cauldron. This cauldron occurs in many representations of Hell including the 12th-century Doom Stone in York Minster, and a vision described in the *Gesta Romanorum* tells us that it is full of 'hot, welling, brass'.[19] A large dog standing on its hindlegs to bite at the hand of a soul, may refer to the damnation of those who lavish on their pet animals the food which they should have given to the poor as described in one of Herolt's sermons.[20] The soul being held down amid flames by two flying demons, between the Ladder and the Tree, is identified as a miser by the money-bag hung round his neck. This attribute figures in several Dooms and is described in Dante's *Inferno*. At each side of this group stand larger demons supporting between them a saw, or beam set with spikes. The idea of a bridge, narrow, slippery, sharp-edged or set with spikes, over which the spirits of the dead must cross, occurs in many religions. The Zoroastrians knew of the strait bridge Chinavar, and from them it passed into Mohammedan traditions of the bridge al-Sirât, sharp as a scimitar, fine as a hair, and Jewish writings also tell of a bridge in Hell no broader than a thread. There are other eastern variants some of which must have reached England to inspire, not only this painting, but the famous Whinney-Moor Dirge with its grim description of the 'Brig o' Dread na brader than a thread'. In the *Vision of Tundale, c.* 1149, we are told that the bridge is two miles long and scarcely a handswidth across, set with 'sharp spikes of iron and steel'. Tundale sees a man who particularly dreads the crossing he must attempt, because he is burdened with the sheaves which he stole from Holy Church, so perhaps the objects held by the souls at Chaldon, a smith's hammer and tongs and a bowl of some liquid, may refer to similar dishonesties in respect of tithes.

In the upper righthand section Christ harrows Hell and a prostrate Satan lies within the lower jaw of the Hell-mouth with his hands manacled in the curious manner we have already noted (see page 57) and which may symbolise eternal bondage. On the opposite side of the Ladder St. Michael is weighing souls.[21] The idea of judgment by weighing is universal, but this popular Christian theme may have been more directly based upon the weighing of souls before Osiris which appears in the Egyptian 'Book of the Dead' for, when Christianity became established in Egypt, the Church there paid high reverence to St. Michael as the escort of departed souls and the Holder of the Balance. The weighing of souls is carved on the 10th-century High Cross of Muiredach at Monasterboice (Louth), probably copied from some Coptic manuscript[22] and this already shows the devil trying to pull down the scale of sin. At Chaldon, as in many later Dooms, this trickery proves unavailing and the innocent souls are being led, or carried, by angels towards the final rungs of the Ladder.

In later medieval art the weighing of souls often occurs as a separate subject and, some English examples show the Blessed Virgin intervening to tip the scales towards mercy by laying her rosary beside the shivering soul whose sins outweigh his merits but who has been assiduous in devotions to her. Paintings at

K

Ruislip (Middlesex), Lenham (Kent) and South Leigh (Oxon) are examples of this subject which also occurs on alabasters.[23] On a tomb at Harewood (Yorks) it is epitomised by showing a rosary hanging on the scales.

The craftsmen who decorated our churches may not have understood the theological science which underlay the choice and treatment of their subjects. Not every parish priest would have been able to explain to his parishioners the deeper meanings of some of the details we have been considering, and, in some cases, misunderstandings even gave rise to dangerous heresies. Still, in spite of all its obscurities and distortions, medieval iconography was nobly planned and combined flexibility of interpretation with an impressive affirmation of belief.

Chapter 6

THE VIRGIN MARY AND THE SAINTS

THE ICONOCLASTS fell with particular fury upon images of the Madonna; carvings were burnt or smashed and few of the thousands of windows in which she must once have been represented remain intact. Natural decay, as well as deliberate damage, have obliterated many wall-paintings but the exquisite 13th-century roundel in the Bishop's Palace at Chichester escaped and is one of the masterpieces of British painting. A few early carvings survived, on Saxon crosses at Shelford (Notts) and Nunburnhome (Yorks), and an 11th-century fragment, at Inglesham (Wilts) shows the Virgin and Child under the Hand of God. Occasionally we find later figures of the Virgin in unexpected places, such as the heart of a flaunting Tudor rose on the west wall of King's College Chapel, Cambridge, or between the devoutly folded hands of the effigy of Lady Alicia de Mohun at Axminster (Devon).[1]

Some Lords of the Manor must have protected the imagery of their family tombs for carved Virgins were left unharmed on tombs at Warkworth (Northants) and Willoughby-on-the-Wolds (Notts) (Plate 48). The exquisite Madonna of the Rosebush on the tomb of Sir Hugh Willoughby (died 1448) is characteristic of the later medieval conception of the Blessed Virgin. She is no longer the humble maiden of the Gospels and early Christian art; after the Council of Ephesus had condemned the Nestorian heresy, which maintained a distinction between the divine and human natures in Christ and denied her the title 'Mother of God', she was represented enthroned and crowned. In Western churches such regal honours were first accorded to her in scenes of the Adoration of the Magi, and the Norman tympanum at Fownhope (Herefs) is an unusually early example of the Virgin and Child appearing alone in such a position. The Fownhope Virgin appears remote and austere, inspiring awe rather than love, but at Willoughby-on-the-Wolds the sculptor shows us the supremely beautiful Queen of Heaven, whom men reverenced with warm, romantic devotion and who inspired innumerable poems, legends and paintings of tender loveliness.

While theologians thus exalted the meek Virgin, the simple folk longed to learn more of her earthly life and benevolent intervention on behalf of sinners who truly honoured her. Artists drew largely upon the *Liber de Infantia B.V. Mariae et Salvatoris,* compiled in the 5th or 7th century from earlier texts, and legends multiplied. The fullest representation of miracle stories is contained in the wall-paintings in Eton College Chapel[2] while the richest series of illustrations to a single legend is found on the roof bosses of the Bauchun Chapel in Norwich cathedral.[3]

Only a few scenes from her life normally appear in church imagery. The meeting of her parents, Joachim and Anna, outside the Golden Gate, after the birth of Mary had been foretold to them, was made popular by the belief that this was the moment of her conception. Her Birth is rarely shown but the institution of the Feast of the Presentation of Mary in 1372 made this subject increasingly popular. There is a fine example in foreign glass at Elford (Staffs). The Child Virgin is usually shown climbing an impressive flight of steps to the Temple because one version of the Gospel of pseudo-Matthew told how she climbed them without aid and recited one of the gradual psalms on each step.

The cult of St. Anne became widespread in the later Middle Ages and, as the only way to identify her images was to show her with the Child Virgin, the subject of her teaching Mary to read became a theme of touching beauty, still to be seen in windows at Stanford-on-Avon (Northants), Queenhill (Worcs), and All Saints church, North Street, York.

The Betrothal and Marriage of Mary are shown in the faded paintings at Croughton (Northants)[4] but are less common than the subjects associated with the festival by which the Church celebrated her death and Assumption. The legend of the impious Jew who tried to arrest the funeral procession occurs exceptionally early in England, on the 8th-century grave cover at Wirksworth (Derbs) (Plate 24), which also shows angels appearing in clouds above the bier, as described by the pseudo-Mellito.[5] Here we also see St. John leading the cortège bearing the palm branch brought by an angel to Mary in order to announce her imminent death and which she had given to this Apostle. This is why St. John is often shown holding a palm branch, the usual sign of martyrdom as on a tomb chest at Harewood (Yorks) (Plate 44), although he died a natural death. The funeral of the Virgin is represented in windows at Gresford (Denbighs), North Moreton (Berks) and Stoke d'Abernon (Surrey), and in a wall-painting at Chalgrove (Oxon). Some representations of the Assumption show the Virgin casting down to St. Thomas the girdle which is honoured as a precious relic in the cathedral at Prato.[6] This is shown in a wall-painting at Broughton (Oxon) and on a roof boss in the porch of Peterborough cathedral.

The theme of the Coronation of the Virgin (Plate 23) seems to have developed in western Europe during the 12th century and England can perhaps claim the earliest surviving example in monumental art, a capital from Reading Abbey now in the Victoria and Albert Museum. Another early example is on a Norman tympanum at Quenington (Glos). At first Mary was shown being crowned by Christ alone but, in the 15th century, all Three Persons of the Holy Trinity are shown participating, as in the east window of Holy Trinity Goodramgate, York.

There are many books dealing with the legends of the saints commonly found in the imagery of churches and the attributes by which we recognise them, so the small space available here shall be devoted to the context in which medieval parishioners regarded those most commonly represented and the reasons which determined their choice. Some framework of precedence is needed and so, while we picture a medieval church, its windows glowing with the figures of saints in richly coloured robes, its walls painted with scenes from their lives, and images of them in the now empty niches, all reminding beholders that their acts of worship were one with the eternal homage of the saints in Heaven, let us follow the sequence of the *Te Deum* which has been sung in all Christian churches since the 4th century.

'The glorious company of the Apostles' is rarely represented as a group, except in such Gospel scenes as the Last Supper or Pentecost, but in stained glass we very often find a series of single figures, each breathing forth a scroll on which appears a phrase of the Apostles' Creed. The tradition that all the Apostles combined to compose the Creed is mentioned *c.* 400, but it is in a sermon attributed to St. Augustine of Hippo, although probably later, that each article of that Creed is associated with a particular Apostle.[7] 'Creed Windows' were once common in British churches, to judge by the remaining fragments,[8] and the Fairford windows have shown us how each Apostle was associated with a member of 'the goodly fellowship of Prophets'. To St. Peter, whose figure in the south aisle windows proclaims: 'I believe in God the Father Almighty, maker of Heaven and Earth', Jeremiah answers from the north, with two quotations merged into a single prophecy, 'Thou shalt call me, My father' (iii. 19) and 'Ah Lord God! behold thou hast made the heaven and the earth by thy great power' (xxxii. 17). St. Andrew's phrase, 'and in Jesus Christ, His only Son, Our Lord', is foreshadowed by the verses from the second Psalm of David, 'The Lord hath said unto me, thou art my son; this day have I begotten thee'. The texts allotted to the prophets are not always correctly assigned; a verse from Zephaniah iii. 9 is attributed to Micah, not only in the Fairford windows and on the 15th-century painted screen at Thornham (Norfolk), but also in Queen Mary's Psalter.[9] (The full Creed sequence is given in Appendix 3.)

These great figures of the Old and New Testaments seem to march abreast in their testimony, like the parallel piers of a great arcade, and in some places they are associated with the Sibyls, expressing the belief that classical antiquity had also known fore-shadowings of Christ. A 15th-century Dominican, Filippo Bar-bieri, wrote a treatise in which he assigned such prophecies, and also attributes referring to them, to each of twelve sibyls, and all these are painted on the Devon screens at Ugborough, Heavitree, Exeter and Bradninch. Isolated figures, the remains of similar series, occur on the screen at Ipplepen (Devon) and in the east window at Coughton (Warcs). The allocation of attributes to the sibyls is variable, which makes identification difficult, where their names are not given. The Sibylla Persica generally holds a lantern in which the light glimmers feebly, because she foretold the Saviour, albeit obscurely, while Samia has a cradle because she prophesied that a child should be born of a poor maiden, and the beasts of the earth should adore Him.[10] Plate 43 shows three of the Sibyls at Bradninch: Tiburtina with a hand, because she fore-told the mocking and scourging of Christ, and Hellespontina with a Cross, for her prophecy of the Crucifixion. The middle figure may be the Sibylla Libica, who foretold the manifestation of Christ to the Gentiles, although her attributes are mysterious.

Although we sometimes see an incomplete series of the Apostles painted on screens or carved on bench-ends, they are rarely shown singly and their noble, bearded figures are only distinguishable by their attributes (see Appendix 3). The spectacles given to St. Matthew on a statue in Henry VII's Chapel, Westminster, are an unusual reference to his clerical occupation before his calling. There are three exceptions to this rule.

The physical appearance of both St. Peter and St. Paul seems to have been determined by ancient tradition. St. Peter always has a square bushy beard, and a ring of thick hair surrounding a bald crown, like the Roman tonsure. In the *Golden Legend* (iii. 52) we read that 'when St. Peter preached the first time in the city of Antioch, the paynims sheared him upon his head above, like a fool, in despising Christian law. And because this was done to St. Peter to do him despite and shame, it was sith established that the clergy should have his crown shaven in sign of right great honour and authority.' St. Paul always has a bald forehead and a long pointed beard, and holds the sword of his martyrdom. These two saints very often appear in association, a link forged in the earliest days of the Church in Rome. In the wall-paintings at Clayton (Sussex) and on the Norman tympanum of Siddington (Glos) Christ delivers the Keys to St. Peter and the book of the Law to St. Paul. St. Paul is rarely represented apart from St. Peter, either in church dedications or in imagery, this rule of rarity being proved by a most magnificent exception in the 12th-century painting of 'St. Paul and the Viper' in Canterbury cathedral.

St. John is distinguished by his youthful appearance and the 15th-century dialogue between *Dives and Pauper* explains correctly why the saint is shown 'with a cup in his hand and an adder therein, in token that he drank deadly venom and through virtue of the cross it lost its malice and did him none harm', but it rationalises a misinterpreted symbol (see page 130) when it goes on, 'And in his other hand he beareth a palm in token that he was a martyr, and had the palm of martyrdom, although he was not slain; for his will was to die for God's sake'.[11] The 'adder' is usually shown as a small black dragon emerging from the chalice (Plate 44).

Because of the immense fame of his shrine at Compostela as a place of pilgrimage, St. James Major is usually shown in the dress of a pilgrim (see page 201).

St. Andrew, holding the cross saltire which, curiously enough, is not mentioned in his 'Acts' as the instrument of his martyrdom, is often seen in imagery, and he was among the most popular dedication saints. His special connection with Scotland dates from the 8th century when some of his bones are said to have been secretly transferred from Greece to St. Andrews.

The position of St. John the Baptist, being unique, makes it appropriate to consider him directly after the Apostles, and, as a patron saint, he was preferred to all save St. Peter and St. Andrew. Since his feast, on June 24th, coincided with the celebrations of Midsummer, the Baptist probably took over both the sites and customs associated with the pagan solar festival. Dr. Hildburgh has suggested that the choice of the saints shown flanking the head of St. John on the charger, a frequent subject in alabaster, was determined by the coincidence of their feast days with the solstices.[12] Another reason for the extreme popularity of such carvings, of which there is a fine example in Amport church (Hants), (Plate 86) was perhaps an association with the feast of Corpus Christi. In some York service books the fourth lesson for the feast of the Decollation of St. John states that the saint's head symbolises the body of Christ.[13]

Most of these alabasters show a wound on the saint's brow because a frontal bone, claimed as that of St. John, in Amiens cathedral had a hole at this point. To reconcile this with the Biblical account of his death, the legend was told that Herodias, when presented with the head on a charger, pierced its tongue with a pin and stabbed at its brow with a knife.[14] This incident is illustrated in a window at Gresford (Denbighs) (Plate 69) (see also page 162).

St John the Baptist was one of the most popular patron saints among guilds and craft associations, and the reasons why he was thus chosen may serve to illustrate the general principles of such choice.[15] Because his images are identified by the Agnus Dei lying on the book in his hand, all those connected with the wool trade, also all domestic animals and those in charge of them, were held to be under his special protection. Because he wore a garment of camel hair girt with a leather girdle, he was the patron of those who worked in cloth, leather or pelts; because his head was struck off with an axe, all those who made, or used, incisive instruments, such as cutlers or carpenters, claimed his patronage. Those who worked with needles or awls remembered the legend of Herodias and the pin; the chandlers recalled the fact that the word *lucerna* was applied to the Baptist in the liturgy, while his incarceration may perhaps have endeared him to the bird-catchers. In order that there should be no mistake as to the material from which his shaggy robe is made, figures of St. John are often shown draped in the whole skin of a camel with its head hanging down in front. This motive is chiefly confined to northern Europe, the main area of the wool trade, and appears first in 14th-century glass, as in St. Denys, York, or at Grappenhall (Ches). Stone images which show the camel's skin very clearly are preserved in Hereford cathedral and Tewkesbury (Glos).

'The noble Army of Martyrs' is the most numerous group of saints represented in imagery, for men revered these as the most powerful intercessors before the Throne of God, and divine assurance that their intercession would be effective is often recorded in their legends. St. Catherine, before she was beheaded, prayed to God that any who should 'remember my passion, be it at his death, or in any other necessity, and call me . . . shall have by thy mercy the effect of his request and prayer', and a voice from Heaven answered: 'to them that shall hallow thy passion, I promise the comfort of Heaven' (*Golden Legend*, vii. 25). The same celestial assurance is recorded in the legends of three other virgin martyrs familiar in medieval imagery: SS. Barbara, Dorothy and Margaret of Antioch, and also in that of St. George. St. Dorothy's dying prayer, as told in the *Golden Legend* (vii. 46–7), was that any household in which her life was read should be protected from storms, fire and sudden death, and similar powers were exercised by St. Barbara. St. Margaret of Antioch (who appears more often than any female saint except St. Catherine) was granted the request that any woman who invoked her name in childbirth should be safely delivered (*Golden Legend*, iv. 71). Liturgical invocations, and hymns celebrating her power to protect, show that this belief was widely accepted,[16] and some of her surviving images may have been thank-offerings for a safe confinement.

Historically St. Margaret, like St. Catherine, is a shadowy figure, but her legend tells how a dragon appeared in her prison cell and swallowed her. She made the sign of the Cross and immediately burst through its side. On an early Norman tympanum at Long Marton (Westmorland) she is being swallowed, and only a cross shown beyond the dragon's tail promises deliverance but on a capital at Bretforton (Worcs) and a bench-end at North Cadbury (Somerset) the tail of her robe is still disappearing into the dragon's jaws, as she rises again from its side. On a misericord at Sherborne (Plate 61), she seems to be comfortably seated upon the vanquished dragon.

St. Dorothy is identified by the basket of roses, or apples, sent from Heaven after her martyrdom to convert a scribe who had mocked her hope of entering Paradise. She appears in paintings on East Anglian rood-screens, such as Eye (Suffolk) or Walpole St. Peter (Norfolk), in carving on a bench-end at Fressingfield (Suffolk) and in glass at Langport, Mark and Middlezoy in Somerset. St. Barbara carries a small tower and appears in many windows, including one at Awliscombe (Devon), and on painted screens as at Ranworth (Norfolk) and Whimple (Devon).

In what remains of our medieval imagery it is rare to find a series of subjects illustrating the life and miracles of a single saint. The outstanding exception is in the Chapel of St. Thomas in Canterbury cathedral, although only the windows showing his posthumous miracles have survived (Plate 21). A window in the nave of York Minster shows us nine scenes from the life of St. Catherine, including her conversion of the pagan philosophers and their subsequent martyrdom, her ordeal by the spiked wheels and eventual beheading. The Nottingham alabaster panels in the Roman Catholic Chapel at Lydiate (Lancs) add to these subjects the rarer scene of her burial on the summit of Mount Sinai by angels, with the miraculous springs of oil gushing from the tomb. Two early scenes from the life of St. Margaret remain in the glass of North Tuddenham (Norfolk) and several later episodes at Combs (Suffolk). Far more often we see only single figures of the saints, each with some attribute referring to their martyrdom which is often fantastically formalised. Thus, on a cusp of the Percy tomb in Beverley Minster, St. Catherine holds a small spiked wheel at the end of a stick, like the modern firework.

Such formalised attributes were probably familiar to many humble worshippers who had never seen the legend of the saint fully illustrated, or even heard it told. Like the Cross of Christ, these gruesome instruments of torture became symbols of victory, a transformation which justifies the otherwise curious medieval reasoning that, because St. Blaise holds the iron comb with which his flesh was torn in his martyrdom, he would regard with special favour those who used similar implements in their daily toil. The wool-combers claimed him as their patron and a wooden statuette of him still stands on the Spring chantry at Lavenham (Suffolk). He also appears on the painted screen at Eye (Suffolk) and in a window at Payhembury (Devon).

By the same reasoning St. Bartholomew, who, because he was flayed, holds a skinning knife and sometimes his own skin over his arm (as on the statue in Henry VII's Chapel, Westminster), was the patron of all tanners. St. Erasmus was invoked by sufferers from internal complaints because his entrails are shown wound round a windlass, and the tooth which St. Apollonia holds up in a pair of pincers, as on the painted screen at Ashton (Devon), led to her invocation for toothache. Because St. Lawrence was identified by the gridiron on which he was roasted, as on the font at Cottam (Yorks) and a tomb chest at Harewood (Plate 44), men invoked his protection against the flames of Purgatory or Hell. His single figure often appears in windows, and the glass in his church at Ludlow shows many scenes from his life.

Martyrdom by shooting with arrows was held to confer powers of protection against disease and sudden death, which, according to primitive belief, were caused by the shafts of angry spirits. Saints who had been miraculously healed from arrow-wounds, like St. Sebastian, or shielded from them, like St. Christopher, were credited with the power of protecting those who did them honour from infection and sudden death. In medieval Britain this belief seems more particularly to have referred to St. Christopher, and the inscription on the wall-painting at Wood Eaton (Oxon), KI CEST IMAGE VERRA LE JUR DE MALE MORT NE MURRA (who looks upon this image, that day shall not die an ill death, *i.e.* without the rites of the Church), explains why every church in Britain probably once had some representation of him. C. E. Keyser lists 186 wall-paintings of St Christopher,[17] far more than those of any

other saint, and almost all of them placed where they could b
seen from the threshold of the main door. Many of these painting
are so much alike in general design that they suggest a commo
original. One of the earliest known woodcuts (Fig. 12), datin
from 1423, shows the holy giant who sought to serve the mightie
of all Lords by carrying travellers across the stream. He grasps th
staff which miraculously sprouted as he reached land. Man
artists indicated the depth of the water by showing ships sailin
past the giant's calves, and added mermaids, perhaps to represen
the powers of evil opposing him, as at Hayes (Middlesex). Suc
woodcuts, widely distributed by those who wished to carry a
image of their protector always with them, helped to crystallis
the tradition of his representation.[18] Scenes from the passion o
St. Christopher are rare but appear in small panels flanking th
large central scene at Shorwell (Isle of Wight) and may have bee
represented at St. Keverne (Cornwall), where an allusion to th
legend that St. Christopher was originally dog-headed, of the rac
of Cynocephali, has been tentatively identified.[19]

'The Holy Church throughout the World' is most often repre
sented by the four Doctors of the Latin Church: SS. Gregory
Jerome, Ambrose and Augustine of Hippo. They are carved upo
the pulpit at Trull (Somerset) (Plate 47) wearing the robes of
Pope, Cardinal, Bishop and Doctor respectively. They also appea
on the painted pulpits at Burnham Norton and Castle Acre i
Norfolk, presumably, because their teaching opened men's mind
to the meaning of Holy Scripture. At Castle Acre each figure i
accompanied by a Latin inscription referring to such teaching.[20]
On the Bruce Cenotaph at Guisborough (Yorks) St. Ambrose i
shown with a beehive, to recall the legend that, when he was
baby in his cradle, a swarm of bees flew in and out of his mout
and then ascended to Heaven (*Golden Legend*, iii. 111).

Of the founders of the great monastic Orders, St. Benedict i
the only one often represented; he appears on screens at Burling
ham St. Andrew, North Elmham, Great Plumstead and Small
burgh, all in Norfolk. A 12th-century panel of glass in St. Deny
at York shows him beating the devil with rods. St. Bernard is rar
despite the great influence of the Cistercian Order. The window i
St. Mary's, Shrewsbury, which illustrates his miraculous exter
mination of the flies infesting a new church, is of German o

FIG. 12. St. Christopher

Flemish origin and belongs to the same series as those in Marsto
Bigot (Somerset).[21] The Stigmatisation of St. Francis is shown o
the screens at Bradninch (Devon) and Hempstead (Norfolk) an
his preaching to the birds in a much faded wall-painting at Littl
Kimble (Bucks).[22]

St. Nicholas of Myra comes seventh in order of popularity fo
the dedication of English churches. He was considered the patro
of both seamen and children, and the miracle which may hav
given rise to his association with children is represented on th
Tournai marble font in Winchester cathedral (Plate 34). Th
legend of how St. Nicholas brought back to life three childre
who had been murdered, and their bodies cut up in a pickling tu
by a wicked innkeeper, probably originated in the conventions o
early imagery. Because the saint was famed for the number of hi
converts, he was shown with three of these standing in a baptisma
font. Obeying the laws of hierarchical perspective, the artist
made them so small by comparison with the saint that they wer
later mistaken for children. The second miracle shown on th
font refers to the man who vowed to give a great gold cup to th
altar of St. Nicholas, but later defaulted and gave a smaller on
instead. Travelling by ship with his son, he bade the boy fill th
great cup with water, but the child overbalanced and was drowned
The carver has shown the boy lying on the seabed with the cuj
still in his hand. Lively illustrations of other miracles performe
by St. Nicholas are shown in 15th-century glass at Hillesde
(Bucks).

Of the English saints I can mention only a few. King Edwar
the Confessor can be recognised by his attribute of the ring which
he gave in alms to St. John, in the guise of a beggar, and which
the saint gave to some pilgrims in the Holy Land, bidding then
return it to the King and tell him that his death was near. Thi
legend is fully illustrated in the Pilgrims' Window in Ludlov
church and the King appears among other saints on a tomb-ches
at Harewood (Yorks) (Plate 44). Great churchmen such as St
Wilfrid of Ripon or St. John of Beverley were mostly honoure
in the districts where they served, and ruled, but almost ever
church in the country probably had some image of St. Thomas o
Canterbury until the deliberate campaign waged against hi
cult by Henry VIII destroyed most of them. A boss in Exete

cathedral, wall-paintings at South Newington (Oxon) and Brookland (Kent) and two alabaster panels at Elham (Kent) (Plate 40) are among the more interesting survivals. The chief female saint was the Saxon queen, Etheldreda, who became Abbess of Ely and whose life is illustrated on carved capitals beneath the lantern of that cathedral. Her statue also stands on the west front of Wells cathedral.

The reasons why a church was dedicated to a particular saint are rarely recorded except in cases like St. Bartholomew the Great in London, when we know that the saint appeared to its founder, Rahere, and commanded him to build it. The reasons for choosing the saints represented in imagery are still more conjectural. Memorials of St. Nicholas, who protected sailors, occur chiefly in coastal areas and may express supplication or gratitude. Some representations of St. Leonard with his attribute of fetters may be thank-offerings for safe deliverance from captivity,[23] while images of St. Roch, who laboured among the sick, probably multiplied in times of pestilence. St. Sitha, the holy waiting-maid of Lucca, had the power of finding lost articles, and her image appears, with keys at her belt, in a window at Mells (Somerset) and carved on a tomb-chest at Croft Castle (Herefs). The choice of saints represented in our churches may have been determined by any one of a wide variety of factors, but we can do little more than guess at them.

Occasionally historical records will confirm a lucky guess. On the Kirkham Chantry chapel in Paignton church (Devon) there are numerous small figures of the saints invoked for protection against illness and sudden death. There are also larger carvings illustrating scenes from the lives of Isaac, Samson and SS. Anne and Elizabeth.[24] The choice of these themes seemed curious until I remembered that one factor is common to all the stories—the birth of a child being divinely foretold after all hope had been well-nigh abandoned. Following up this clue it was satisfactory to discover that Sir John Kirkham, who probably built the chantry screen, had a son by his third wife, after his two previous marriages had been fruitless.

Chapter 7

THE PREACHERS

IN THE FOREGOING chapters we have seen how the austerely formalised conventions of early Christian art, still followed in some Norman churches, gradually became relaxed, so that the same lessons were expressed in more easily comprehensible terms of human drama. Simultaneously the minor decorative carvings of the churches, which had hitherto consisted chiefly of abstract ornament, began to show, on capitals, bosses, bench-ends and —most of all—on misericords, a variety of figure subjects, derived from secular as well as religious sources, which is unparalleled in other European countries. What brought about these changes? Obviously there can be no one comprehensive answer to such a question, but in this chapter, and the next, we will consider two contributory factors: the influence of the preaching Friars and of those who staged religious dramas.

Sermons had been the one form of public speech for which English was still used by educated men during the centuries when Latin and French were the two dominant languages, but the coming of the Friars in the 13th century changed their character.[1] These Friars were able and highly educated men, but when they preached to the common people they recognised the limitations of their audiences. Not only did they speak in English, but they used as similes things familiar in the experience of their listeners. It would be foolish to suggest that all the scenes of sport and labour, homespun domesticity and popular fables which we see illustrated on misericords were directly inspired by sermon stories, but very few of these carvings could not be matched by some simile in a sermon manuscript.[2] If the preachers described an incident in the Gospel story, they did so in terms which were topical as well as reverent, just as the artists introduced details of contemporary costume and usage into their renderings of such subjects, without in any way lessening their dignity.

One practical result of more frequent preaching was that seating was introduced into the churches; benches dating from the 14th

3 The Baptism of Christ, Castle Frome font
4 Miracles of St Nicholas, Winchester Cathedral font

36 The Sacrament of Ordination, Melbury Bubb

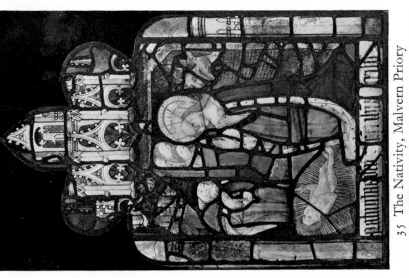

35 The Nativity, Malvern Priory

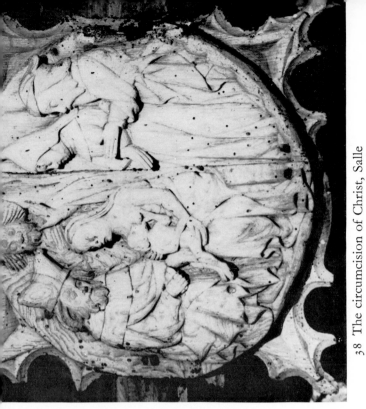

38 The circumcision of Christ, Salle

37 The Annunciation with Lily Crucifix, Tong

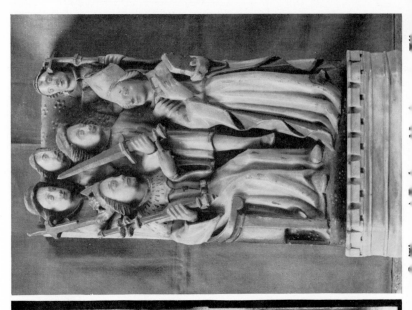

41 Doom painting, Chaldon

42 The raising of Lazarus and the women at the sepulchre, Lenton font

49 Hart eating a snake, Ely
Cathedral

50 Basilisk, Stonham Aspall

1 Tigress deceived by a mirror,
Lakenheath

52 Camel, Boston

53 Virtues and Vices, Salisbury
Chapter House door

54 Rood screen at Llanrwst

5 Warning to blasphemers, Broughton

56 Gluttony, Norwich Cathedral
57 The Bigorne, Carlisle Cathedral

58 The preaching fox,
East Brent

59 The execution of Reynard the Fox, Bristol Cathedral

60 St James, Yarcombe

61 St Margaret, Sherborne

and 15th centuries are often to be found but hardly ever do we see anything older. Less obvious, but more interesting, are the reflections of the preachers' oratory in the imagery of our churches. Some wall-paintings and windows were clearly designed to reiterate the lessons expressed in surviving sermons, while many sermon stories and similes were illustrated on misericords, bench-ends and bosses.

To start with a certainty, let us look at a late 14th-century wall-painting at Broughton (Bucks) (Plate 55), which unquestionably illustrates two themes of medieval preaching. It shows the dead Christ lying across His Mother's knees, His right hand and foot amputated and the flesh cut back to show the bones. Round the central figure stand richly dressed gallants who hold the severed hand and foot, a heart and bones. At the foot of the picture two men are fighting over a gaming board. A medieval sermon quoted by Dr. Owst as being in St. Albans cathedral[3] denounces those who swear blasphemously by parts of the Lord's Body. 'They think the cursed Jews did not torment him enough so they, with their grisly oaths, draw Him limb from limb as crows pluck carrion.' This was apparently a generally accepted theme for Chaucer uses almost the same words in *The Pardoner's Tale* where he associates such blasphemous oaths with the deadly quarrelling of gamblers. A similar wall-painting at Walsham-le-Willows (Suffolk) has been destroyed, but another, at Corby (Lincs),[4] shows a demon in attendance on each blaspheming youth. Both here, and at Broughton, the young men wear those forms of fashionable dress which were particularly obnoxious to the preachers. Robert Rypon, sub-Prior of Durham, described the very short tunic worn by the youth in the upper left-hand corner at Broughton in terms as forceful as those with which Chaucer, in *The Parson's Tale*, denounced such 'horrible, disordinate scantiness of clothing', while the waste of material and labour involved by its scalloped hem would also have drawn down the wrath of the St. Albans' preacher. The exaggeratedly long-toed shoes, the parti-coloured hose and the very full sleeves, falling almost to the ground but gathered in at the wrist, are all made the objects of vitriolic abuse in surviving sermons, the sleeves being called 'devil's receptacles'. In a sermon on the Magdalene, Robert Rypon summarises the history of clothing and concludes that the purpose of fashionable

L

dress is no longer 'necessity of nature' but 'to excite lust in men
as in women'.⁵ The painter at Corby has made the same point by
including in his subject a naked woman riding a horned beast.
The Vice *Luxuria* (Lechery) is often represented in medieval art
as a naked girl either riding a goat, stag or ram, or else holding its
skin about her.⁶ A misericord at Stratford-upon-Avon (Plate 66),
which might have been copied from a similar painting to that at
Corby, clearly reflects a process of the medieval imagination, often
apparent in sermons and literature, whereby pagan gods personify
evil. Diana, supposed to lead human witches to ride through the
woods on strange beasts, appears in these two churches as the
personification of lust.

Extravagant preoccupation with fashion in men's dress was
characteristic of the Court of Richard II and some painted allegories suggest a political, as well as a moral, satire. At Hoxne
(Suffolk) Pride is represented as an over-dressed youth, crowned
and with a sceptre in one hand, while in the other he holds a
mirror in which he gazes at his own reflection.

Whilst men's finery was thus deplored, it was upon women's
fashions that the full flood of pulpit invective was poured and
on minor carvings we find many sly allusions to these strictures.
The preachers considered the tall, twin-peaked headdresses a
truly devilish fashion, and on a misericord at Minster-in-Thanet
(Kent) a demon peers between a lady's 'horns'. Another misericord, at Ludlow (Plate 65), shows the Dishonest Ale-Wife being
carried to Hell, naked save for this headgear, and in the windows
of Malvern Priory the Serpent of the Temptation is given a
woman's head similarly attired.

The preaching Friars were concerned with giving practical
moral instruction rather than attempting to explain abstruse
theology. Such lessons, if they were to be effective, had to be
expressed dramatically, and the way in which medieval artists
represented the conflict between Virtues and Vices at various
periods illustrates the change thus brought about. The poem on
the *Psychomachia*, written by Prudentius in the 4th century
described how the Virtues, in the shape of armed virgins, each
engaged in single combat with the appropriate Vice, employing
symbolical arms, but British artists in the 12th century preferred
to show the Virtues already triumphant and trampling on their

foes.[8] The Psychomachia was represented on the south porch of Malmesbury Abbey, but the carvings are now almost indecipherably weathered, and it is more clearly shown upon the 12th-century fonts at Southrop (Glos) and Stanton Fitzwarren (Wilts) (Plate 16). The carvers of these fonts were obviously directed by literate employers, for the Latin names of the Vices and Virtues are incised upon the backgrounds, or round the arches which frame each pair of figures. Above this arcade at Southrop there is a decorative design of small domed buildings, perhaps alluding to the Heavenly City which, according to Prudentius, was built by the united efforts of the Virtues after their several victories.

On the late 13th-century doorway to the Chapter House at Salisbury (Plate 53) this dignified, but static, allegory has been popularised. The Virtues are still noble ladies, as they were often described by the preachers, but the methods which they use to chastise their vanquished opponents have an element of grim comedy that foreshadows some of the later morality plays. The figures shown in the photograph are Liberality choking Avarice by ladling coins down his throat (at the bottom), then comes Chastity scourging Lust, and Falsehood having his tongue pulled out by Truth with an outsize pair of pincers. At the top we see the Vice dangling from a miniature gallows; probably Doubt being despatched by Faith, for the suicide, by hanging, of Judas made this form of death a symbol of the ultimate sin—despair of God's forgiveness.

A late 14th-century painting on the west wall of Trotton church (Sussex) (Plate 46), illustrates the next form taken by this allegory and this painting could have illustrated a great many sermons. At the top, Christ is enthroned upon the rainbow and below him stands Moses with the Tables of the Law. On Christ's left is a figure of the good man surrounded by medallions each showing one of the Seven Works of Mercy derived from the words which Christ put into the mouth of the Supreme Judge: 'For I was an hungred, and ye gave me meat: I was thirsty, and ye gave me drink: I was a stranger, and ye took me in: naked, and ye clothed me: I was sick, and ye visited me: I was in prison, and ye came unto me' (St. Matthew xxv. 35–6). To these six manifestations of mercy was added the Burying of the Dead, which is mentioned as a work of piety in Tobit i. 17–18. This last work is omitted from the 15th-century window of All Saints, North Street, York, which is our finest surviving illustration of the Seven Works of Mercy.

On Christ's right is a nude giant from whose body emerge small dragons, each holding within its gaping jaws small human figures which enact the Seven Deadly Sins: Pride, Envy, Gluttony, Avarice, Anger, Lust and Sloth. Paintings of the Sins in this form, which corresponds to the lively personifications of sin in contemporary sermons, must have figured in a great many churches for we still have recognisable remains, or reliable records, of twenty examples.[9] Nor is it only in paintings that we find them so portrayed. On the bench-ends of Wiggenhall St. Germans (Norfolk) Lust is represented by a couple embracing and Gluttony by a man pouring out a cup of wine, and in each case the figures stand within a dragon's mouth, as do similar figures on arm-rests of the stalls of Norwich cathedral. Preachers sometimes used animals as typifying Vices and one of the misericords in Norwich cathedral (Plate 56) shows:

> Loathsome Gluttony, deformed creature on a filthy swine,
> His belly was up-blowne with luxury
> and eke with fatness swollen were his eyne
>
> .   .   .   .   .
>
> And in his hand did beare a bouzing can
> Of which he supt so oft that on his seat,
> His dronken corse he scarse upholden can.
> *Faerie Queen*, Canto iii.

The close parallel between Spenser's words and the carving made several generations earlier, shows how the preacher's vivid similes affected every aspect of medieval culture and became part of a national tradition. Other misericords in Norwich cathedral show Anger mounted on a wild boar, with sword half-drawn and Lechery riding a stag.

The allegorical wall-paintings of the Sins take various forms. At Alveley (Salop) and Raunds (Northants) Pride, shown as a crowned woman, is made the source of the other sins; at Hoxne (Suffolk) there is a Tree of the Sins and at Ruislip (Middlesex) the central form is a dragon; at South Leigh (Oxon) the minor dragons rise direct from a Hell-Mouth. At Arundel, and formerly at Ingatestone (Essex), the sins were shown in a wheel pattern

A significant feature of these allegories is that Gluttony is almost always shown drinking. The only exception I remember is the bench-end at Blythburgh (Suffolk) where this Sin hugs a distended paunch. This drunkard seen at Trotton, Little Horwood (Bucks), Cranborne (Dorset), Crostwight (Norfolk) and Ruislip, links the paintings with a form of instruction on the Lord's Prayer which is expressed in at least three surviving sermons. In *Mirk's Festial*[10] we are told that all curates are bound by law to expound the Paternoster once or twice a year and he then goes on to explain that this prayer includes seven petitions which put away the Seven Deadly Sins. To say 'Our Father' is to acknowledge that all men are brothers and therefore to cast away the sin of Pride, and the words 'Thy Kingdom come' indicate a disregard of worldly wealth which can overcome covetousness. The association of each petition with a particular sin was not standardised; the writer of a sermon in MS Royal 18, B. xxiii in the British Museum, says that it is the envious who cannot pray 'Thy kingdom come'. The preachers associated Gluttony with the plea 'Lead us not into temptation' because, in the form of drunkenness, it tempts men to commit all other sins.[11]

Although we cannot prove that these paintings were specifically designed to illustrate such teaching on the Pater Noster, the probability that this was so is of interest because of the light that it may shed on the mysterious nature of the lost *Pater Noster Plays* given in York, Beverley and Lincoln at about the time when these paintings were being executed and of which all we know is that they dealt with the Seven Deadly Sins. If the paintings are not Pater Noster allegories, then it seems strange that no other imagery referring to the Lord's Prayer exists (although the words are inscribed in a window in Ludlow church) when we consider that almost all other frequent themes of popular instruction were so illustrated. We have already seen how the Apostles' Creed was represented in windows and on painted screens (see page 131). The many Seven Sacrament fonts in East Anglia (Plate 85) are the carved equivalents of the window at Doddiscombleigh (Devon) which shows blood-red lines, symbolising divine authority, radiating from a central figure of Christ to touch the hands of the priests who administer the sacraments in each of the surrounding panels. At Doddiscombleigh the Christ is a modern interpolation, but the original one remains at Crudwell (Wilts) and detached panels from such windows can be seen at Melbury Bubb (Dorset) (Plate 36), Tattershall (Lincs) and Buckland (Glos).[12]

In St. Lawrence's church, Ludlow, there is the only surviving window illustrating the Ten Commandments. Each panel shows Moses displaying, to a group of people, the Tables of Stone on which is written one of the Commandments while, below him, smaller figures enact an example of its disregard. Thus a pickpocket is at work beneath 'thou shalt not steal', and armed men attack a castle in defiance of the commandment 'thou shalt not covet thy neighbour's house'.[13] This use of familiar sins to emphasise the teaching of virtue, and the lively topicality of their presentation, both window and wall-paintings, are characteristics of many sermons.

The inevitability of death and the contrast between worldly pomp and future corruption was a constant theme of preaching and it is also expressed by the ghastly cadavers shown on the lower stages of some tombs, such as that of the Duchess of Suffolk at Ewelme (Oxon), while the effigy above shows the dead person in idealised beauty and splendid array. Long before the *Dance of Death* had become a favoured theme with late medieval artists, the Austin Friar, John Waldeby, had anticipated Shakespeare by speaking of how 'Death, who is God's Bailiff, shall come to arrest'.[14] We have lost all the full series of paintings on this theme recorded in England, but four panels in Hexham Abbey survive and the summoning of the Gallant is painted on a chantry chapel at Newark (Notts). On a misericord in St. George's Chapel, Windsor, Death calls a rich man from his laden table and two labourers from their toil.[15]

Another reminder of mortality once seen in many churches is that of The Three Living and the Three Dead.[16] Some thirty examples have been identified and recorded in British churches but of these only about a dozen can still be recognised. The fable may have had an eastern origin but the medieval artists knew it chiefly through a French 13th-century poem by Baudoin de Condé which describes the meeting of three gay young courtiers with three Deaths.[17] The animated cadavers remind them that even as they now are so shall all courtiers be. The first youth flees, the second hails the Deaths as sent from God, and the third discants upon the horrors of decay. Some of the remaining wall-paintings also differentiate the reaction of the Living. In the little chapel of Widford, near Burford (Oxon), the youth is intent upon his hunting and does not see the Dead, the middle-aged man tries to draw his attention to them and the old man shields his eyes from the horrible sight. At Charlwood (Surrey) the Kings were shown on horseback, a feature commoner in France than England. A pictorial tradition, independent of literary authority, associated the meeting of the Living and the Dead with a hunting scene, although neither this fact, nor the royal status accorded to the Living, are mentioned in the poems. A forest setting is suggested, if only by one tree, and the only King who survives at Paston (Norfolk) has two small huntsmen in attendance. At Peakirk (Northants) the horror of the vision is enhanced by a background covered with flies, beetles and other insects that feed upon corruption.[18] Other examples can be seen at Tarrant Crawford (Dorset) and Hurstbourne Tarrant (Hants).

The painting of the Three Living and the Three Dead at Raunds (Northants)[19] is on the same wall as that of the Deadly Sins, and we can thus imagine the sequence of admonitions which these paintings were meant to express. At the west end of the wall, above the nave arcade, the little group of sins in the dragons' mouths portray acts whose extreme familiarity inclines men to condone them, yet, as the eye travels down those branching dragons' bodies into the giant form of Pride, and through her limbs to their true place of origin, in Hell, these petty vices are seen in the awful perspective of eternity. A few paces eastwards and our glance falls upon the second allegory, seizing first upon the rabbit and the hunting dogs, still clearly visible, and then discovering upon the darkened plaster above them, first the Kings, in their careless enjoyment of the chase, and lastly their horrible vision of the Deaths, unheralded and inescapable! The figure of St. Christopher, also painted on this wall, offers a limited protection against unshriven death, but even his legendary power extends only to the day in which we have gazed upon his image, and only the vanished Rood, which has left a pale scar above the chancel arch, brought to medieval parishioners a hope of escaping from the terrors of damnation.

The finest preachers were fearless in their denunciations of the rich and powerful who oppressed the poor and such sermons are reflected in church imagery. The subject of Adam digging, as we see it in the early 13th-century glass of Canterbury cathedral and the carvings of the Salisbury Chapter House (Plate 27), merely illustrated the earthly descent of Christ, and the doom of labour laid upon Mankind at the Fall but, by the late 14th century, representations of Adam digging and Eve spinning had become associated with pulpit condemnations of unjustifiably arrogant nobles, and the theme song of the Peasants' Revolt was the jingle:

> When Adam delved and Eve span
> Who was then the gentleman?

The preachers not only attacked tyrannical kings and proud landowners, who stole the livelihood of the poor, but they did not spare the unworthy priests who were more inclined to fleece their flocks than to feed them. The fox in clerical garb, preaching to a congregation of geese, so as to lure them within reach of his teeth, is a common subject in the detail carvings of churches, and a fine example on a bench-end at East Brent (Som) shows Reynard vested as a mitred abbot (Plate 58). The general theme of the sermons was that all such evil-doers would receive their just punishment at the Last Day, and the Dominican preacher, John of Bromyard, gave a most dramatic forecast of how the oppressors will then be denounced by their victims.[20] The playwrights took up the theme and a Pope, Emperor, King and Queen figure among the damned in *The Chester Plays*. Similar dignitaries, identified by their tiaras, mitres or crowns, appear among the naked souls being hurried to Hell in many Doom paintings, including those in St. Thomas' church, Salisbury (Plate 45), and South Leigh (Oxon).

Perhaps a political slant, given to a subject originally designed as a moral allegory, may account for the varying interpretations given to a design generally known as 'the Christ of the Trades'. This can be seen distinctly in wall-paintings at Breage (Corn) and West Chiltington (Sussex) and more dimly discerned in several other churches.[21] Christ is represented wearing only a loincloth and bleeding from many wounds, while around His figure are displayed the implements of daily toil or amusement: axes, hammers, saws, wheels, scales, playing cards and dice. A similar painting in San Miniato, Florence, has an inscription at the base warning those who do not keep holy the Sabbath of their future damnation. The preachers frequently denounced Sabbath-breakers but I know of no sermon which corresponds exactly with the paintings.

The alternative interpretation, that the tools are symbols of honest labour offered to God, was supported by the inscription, bidding us 'in all labour remember the end' which could once be read above a Christ of the Trades at Fingrinhoe (Essex). Langland's description of Piers Plowman 'painted all bloody', coming in with a cross before the common people may have been partly inspired by such paintings and it expresses the theme which the Mendicant Friars proclaimed up and down the country, that God would eventually punish the pride and corruption of the mighty and would exalt the humble and oppressed. The parish priest may have pointed to one of these paintings as showing the sinfulness of working, or playing, on the Sabbath, but peasants who had listened to the Friars preaching on the green, probably saw in it an assurance that Christ Himself was their champion in poverty and pain.

So far we have only considered cases in which the artists had clearly been commissioned to illustrate themes also expressed by the preachers. The identification of isolated subjects, which may have been suggested to the carvers of misericords or roof bosses by the similes used in sermons, is much more difficult and needs a great deal of further research. Listening to sermons was perhaps the only form of adult education which would have been available to an ordinary craftsman, so it is only natural that what he heard should sometimes be reflected in his work. The clearest indication of this is to be found in the frequent carvings of exotic, or mythical, animals and a list of those which can be recognised in church imagery is given in Appendix 4.

Animals of all kinds were popular subjects for sermon moralisations and the carvers found the stories of fantastic creatures, which the Friars culled from Bestiaries, far more stimulating to their creative imaginations than real life. Griffins, half-eagle and half-lion, are far more plentiful in detail carvings than sheep and the naturalistic cock is rare compared with the basilisk, a cock with a snake's tail, whose very glance is lethal. A particularly ferocious example of this monster occurs at Stonham Aspall (Suffolk) (Plate 50).

It was from the pulpit that the carvers probably learned how the hunter who rides off with a tiger cub, in the absence of its parents, baffles pursuit. In the words of the 13th-century English Franciscan, Bartholomew Glanville, 'he leaveth in the way great mirrors, and the mother findeth the mirrors and seeth her own image therein and weeneth that she seeth her children therein and is long occupied therefore to deliver the children out of the glass'.[22] This warning against the decoys which enable the devil to steal men's souls is carved in detail on a roof-boss at Queen Camel (Som) and a misericord in Chester cathedral. The latter has a fine design which might have been copied from some illuminated Bestiary, but when we find the story epitomised by showing only the tigress with the mirror, as on bench-ends at Lakenheath (Suffolk) (Plate 51), Wendens Ambo (Essex) and Wiggenhall St. Germans (Norfolk), we realise that it must have been widely known.

Many strange tales were told about elephants, but these included no information about their appearance, beyond the fact that they had long noses and carried wooden towers on their backs, from which Indians and Persians fought with javelins. With the exception of a misericord in Exeter cathedral which is so naturalistic that its carver may have seen the African elephant given to Henry III, these two attributes are enough to identify as elephants some very strange creatures! In the same way a hump, usually covered with tufts of long hair, identifies a camel, but the carver of a misericord at Boston (Lincs) may have heard the Bestiary story of how the camel kneels to accept its load, used as a simile for Christ who, in His humility, stooped to take up the burden of men's sins (Plate 52). Another very popular subject, both with preachers and carvers, was the pelican which first slays its rebellious young and then brings them back to life with its own blood, symbolising the Fall and Redemption of Mankind. Usually the carvers only show the pelican reviving its young, but on the supporter of a misericord in Lincoln cathedral the mother bird is literally 'biting the head off' an importunate fledgling. The ostrich is said in the Bestiary to have feet like a camel, and, since this comparison was no help to an English carver, they are often shown with cloven hoofs. They were said to digest stones (which they do) and even cold iron. On a misericord at Stratford-upon-Avon an ostrich is shown holding a horseshoe in its beak and on another, in Worcester cathedral (Plate 11), it balances horseshoes on its head.

If we look through the collection of sermon stories compiled by such medieval writers as Odo of Cheriton, Nicholas Bozon or Richard Glanville, we find many subjects familiar in carvings. The fierce unicorn laying its head meekly in the lap of a pure maiden, and thus falling victim to the hunter, usually exemplified the Incarnation of Christ, although Mirk also used the story as a simile for the conversion of St. Paul. It is shown on misericords at Chester, Lincoln, Stratford-upon-Avon, Tewkesbury and Nantwich (Ches). The mermaid is shown luring seamen in a boat, at Boston (Lincs), but usually appears alone, with comb and mirror, as at Norwich, Nantwich and Ludlow. In these three last examples the supporters show dolphins, presumably because these animals were said to be attracted by the human voice. The fox shamming dead to attract birds is carved on a misericord at Whalley (Lancs) and the story figures in Odo of Cheriton's *exempla* where we are also told of the panther's sweet breath attracting other animals, a subject seen on a roof boss in Tewkesbury Abbey and which symbolised Christ drawing souls to Him.

On a fine misericord in Norwich cathedral (Plate 62) we see the owl mobbed by small birds when it ventures out in daylight. This is one of the few Bestiary stories which conform to reality and it was used to typify the Jews who preferred to remain in the darkness of their disbelief. Neither preachers nor carvers cared whether familiar animals ever performed the actions which they moralised. Because the Bestiary, quoting Pliny, told how stags force serpents from their holes by the power of their breath, and subsequently eat them, both the artist of Queen Mary's Psalter and the carver of a misericord in Ely cathedral (Plate 49) show a stag placidly munching a snake, although anyone living in medieval England must have known that this was very improbable!

There are surprisingly few allusions in sermons to the famous beast epic of Reynard the Fox, perhaps because, while the literary versions were enjoyed by the Anglo-Norman aristocracy, their stories were not current among the common people.[23] The carvers show us many satirical subjects of animals performing human actions, some of which must be related to the *Roman de Renard*[24] but the only carvings which correspond exactly with the text are some 16th-century misericords in Bristol cathedral (Plate 59) (see page 216).

Many of the genre subjects on misericords which find parallels in the sermon stories, might also have been based upon the carver's own observation, but when trying to identify a mysterious subject which occurs too often to be dismissed as mere fantasy, it is sometimes useful to consider the context in which such a theme might have been used in sermons. A monster holding in its mouth the head and shoulders of a man while the victim's legs kick helplessly in the air, occurs on misericords in the cathedrals of Carlisle (Plate 57), Gloucester and St. Davids; on a bench-end at Cawston (Norfolk) and a roof boss in Southwark cathedral. It is usually described as 'Judas in the jaws of Satan' following the description in Dante's *Inferno*, but this motive does not appear in English Doom paintings (the west window at Fairford probably follows a Continental design) nor have I met it in any sermon, although the preachers often mention other features of Hell, such as the Cauldron and the Gallows, which are familiar in our infernal imagery. Moreover the man is always fully dressed, which makes it unlikely that he is meant to be a disembodied spirit. A more probable explanation was suggested to me by a wall-painting of a similar subject at Villeneuve-Lembron, Puy de Dôme,[25] where the monster is identified by an inscription as the 'Bigorne' which waxes fat on a diet of obedient husbands while its mate, Chichevache, almost starves because she can only digest obedient wives! The origin of these monsters is uncertain but they are mentioned in French poems from the 14th century onwards and an English poem, intended to explain some painted hangings devised by John Lydgate, expresses both the dietary preferences of the beasts and the warnings of their victims.[26] Chaucer refers to Chichevache in the Clerk's Tale.

I have not yet found a mention of the Bigorne in any sermon but there seems little doubt that the fable about the two beasts was generally current. Among the poets Chichevache was more often mentioned, but her mate would have appealed to the preachers who so often denounced masterful wives. The description of womankind given in the *Speculum Laicorum* as 'an incessant warfare, a daily ruin, a house of tempest and a hindrance to devotion' finds its counterpart on many misericords, including one in Bristol cathedral (Plate 90), which show women belabouring their husbands. In such a context the carvers might well have heard tell of the Bigorne and been inspired to represent it in their work.

One of the rare carvings which can be identified with absolute certainty as illustrating a sermon story is the misericord in Ely cathedral (Plate 64), which shows the demon Tutivillus at his work. His special function was to gather up the idle chatter of people in church, or the words slurred or misspoken by drowsy clerks, and to record them on scrolls, to be read out at the Day of Judgment. On one of the supporters he is stretching out an over-filled scroll by pulling at it with his teeth, just as Jacques de Vitry described him in one of his *Exempla*. This eavesdropping demon also occurs on misericords in New College Chapel, Oxford, Enville (Staffs) and Gayton (Northants) and in wallpaintings at Peakirk (Northants), Colton, Seething and Little Melton in Norfolk and Melbourne (Derbs). An allusion to his activities is inscribed along the wallplate at Churchtown, near Garstang (Lancs). Such frequent warnings are perhaps an indication of how difficult it was for medieval preachers to hold the attention of their congregations and why they had to include such dramatic stories in their sermons. Many of these stories were actual dramas in embryo and we will follow their further development on the medieval stage in the next chapter.

Chapter 8

THE PLAYERS

THE PROBLEM of how far medieval drama inspired the artists working in our churches is as frustrating as it is fascinating.[1] There are plenty of obvious parallels in both media, but we can very rarely prove a direct connection because the sources of the dramatists' material, such as the apocryphal Gospels and the vernacular texts which supplemented their paraphrases of the Scriptures with colourful legends, might also have been known to the artists through sermon stories and readings in church. For instance, *The Northern Passion*,[2] which was translated into English from a French original in the 14th century, includes a description of how the executioners stretched Our Lord's arms on the Cross because the holes were bored too far apart. The dramatists expanded this into a sadistically jocular scene, perhaps in order to account for the practical necessity of *tying* the actor playing Jesus onto the Cross before this was lifted up, and their action is shown on English alabaster panels at Afferden in Holland and in the Victoria and Albert Museum, on a roof boss in the nave of Norwich cathedral and in a fragment of stained glass at Stockerston (Leics). Had the craftsmen in each case listened to readings, or looked at plays? We can only guess, and the type of imagery in which we find such parallels is one of the factors which must be considered.

By the late 14th century many glaziers and workers in alabaster had established their own workshops, from which they sent out their products to clients at home or (in the case of the alabasterers) abroad. They were not therefore in such close touch as their forebears, employed in monastic workshops, with artists who had the scholarship, as well as the skill, to produce fresh designs for unusual subjects. Some glaziers went on working from the same cartoons of familiar themes for several generations[3] but, if they were called upon to produce an unusually lavish series of illustrations of some story which they had previously seen staged, it was natural that they should have based their designs upon their memories of the play.⁴ What I must, anachronistically, call the theatrical 'producer' for lack of an exact term, had already faced the problem of how to make a few figures, crowded into a small space, express the deeper meaning of each episode. It is precisely in such 'shop-work' that we find the most unmistakable illustrations of stage effects, with the notable exception of Norwich cathedral where the immense number of designs needed for all the bosses of its late medieval vaults must have confronted the carvers with the same problem.

Minor details often hint at such copying of stage effects. We know that medieval actors used heavy make-up and sometimes wore masks, so the exaggerated ugliness of the executioners in some forms of imagery representing the Passion of Christ, or the martyrdoms of saints, may record their appearance. In the glass of St. Peter Mancroft, Norwich, St. John is led to prison by a gaoler who wears what is obviously a mask in the shape of a pig's snout. On some alabasters, as also on the Norwich bosses, the apostles are shown carrying their identifying attributes even in Gospel scenes where individual identification is unnecessary. Was this a stage convention which eliminated the need for self-identifying speeches? Details of costume, staging and scenic effects can often be guessed at from church imagery, and, if we are not over-confident about the validity of our guesses, such comparisons will widen our interest in both drama and art.

The attitude of the early Church towards the stage was one of uncompromising hostility, and any actor who wished to be baptised had first to renounce his profession. The legends of several saints illustrate this phase. A jester with a tragic face, carved on a bench-end at Combe-in-Teignhead (Devon), has been identified as St. Genest, a famous comedian of the time of Diocletian who was baptised during a burlesque of Christian rites. The Holy Sacrament proved effective, nevertheless, and Genest died a Christian martyr.

By a curious paradox, the drama which the Church almost succeeded in abolishing, sprang up anew as part of her most solemn ritual, with priests accompanying their singing of certain parts of the liturgy with appropriate actions, in order to increase their impact upon the imaginations of the worshippers. In England, at least as early as the 10th century, priests enacted on Easter morning the scene between the Women and the Angel, beside a 'Sepulchre' in which the crucifix from the High Altar had been laid on Good Friday, after which it was triumphantly restored to its place. At first this 'Easter Sepulchre' was only some temporary arrangement, but, later, wooden structures were specially made for the ritual drama. What is perhaps an example of a wooden Sepulchre is preserved in Cowthorpe church (Yorks). In the 14th century some English churches were provided with elaborately carved stone Sepulchres,[5] which varied from a modest niche on the north wall of the chancel to the splendid examples at Hawton (Notts) (Plate 67), Heckington (Lincs), Northwold (Norfolk) and Lincoln cathedral. A Renaissance example at Tarrant Hinton (Dorset) is inscribed, in Latin, with the words of the Angel: 'Come, see the place where the Lord was laid.' On the base of some Sepulchres are carved the sleeping soldiers of Pilate's guard and a panel of 14th-century glass in York Minster shows the Resurrection with similar figures in niches on the tomb-chest, a clear example of an artist visualising a historical event in terms of its dramatic presentation.

Similar acted scenes were also introduced into the Christmas services and as both cycles gradually developed into full liturgical plays, involving more actors, the action was spread over various parts of the churches, and some effects of costume were introduced.[6] It was probably during this phase that the tradition arose of showing Christ in medieval dress only in the scenes of His Post-Resurrection appearances to Mary Magdalene and the pilgrims at Emmaus. In the 13th-century Fleury *Resurrection Play*, Christ first appears in the guise of a gardener and then withdraws to come again as the risen Lord, carrying a processional cross and Gospel Book. The misericord of the Dean's stall in Lincoln cathedral (Plate 63) shows the risen Christ dressed in a loose robe and wearing a large hat. He holds a spade, as he does also on a fine alabaster panel in the Victoria and Albert Museum where he is shown similarly disguised. The central carving of the Lincoln misericord shows the Resurrection, with Jesus resting His foot on the shoulder of one of the sleeping soldiers as he leaves the Sepulchre. This is a peculiarly English feature and the text of the *Chester Plays* proves that it was also a dramatic convention. The action had obvious advantages for an actor who wished to step out of a deep tomb chest with dignity, and so the artistic tradition may well have originated on the stage.

Copying of stage effects is relatively rare in 12th-century imagery but an early example of shop-work, the black marble font, imported from Tournai, in East Meon church (Hants), represents the Expulsion taking place in front of a great Romanesque cathedral. In the Anglo-Norman play of Adam the *Figura* of God re-entered the church after giving orders to Adam, and then the Temptation was enacted with an artificial Serpent which rose up by the trunk of the Tree. On the font, a conventionalised snake is twisted amid the branches. Although the origin of the human-headed Serpent of the Temptation is ancient and complex,[7] its increasingly frequent appearance in later medieval art, together with growing bushiness of the Tree, suggest that stage managers found it useful when the longer texts of the Corpus Christi Plays demanded that the Serpent should speak. In a window at St. Neot (Corn) the Serpent of the Temptation not only has a male head, instead of the usual virgin's face, but its curiously bulgy body suggests a human form concealed within an elongated sack.

As the liturgical plays overflowed into the nave, full use was made of its architectural features. The entrance to the crypt served as 'Hell' and the triforium of a large church, or the roodloft of a smaller one, as 'Heaven', unless special structures were available. One can imagine the 'angels' making their Annunciation to the Shepherds from the charming little gallery in Exeter cathedral, carved with angel musicians, which also served when anthems, sung from a high place, greeted the entry of the Palm Sunday procession. Simpler galleries, perhaps primarily intended for use on Palm Sunday, can be seen in the south porch at Congresbury (Som) and inside the south door at Bildeston (Suffolk). The action of a full Easter play demanded many settings and the *mansiones* of Pilate or Caiaphas were represented by booths set against the piers and probably containing a chair, on which the principal actor could sit when not involved in the scene being played. We do not know what these booths looked like, but their appearance may have inspired the convention by which buildings are often repre-sented in imagery. In the panel showing the Massacre of the Innocents in the glass of St. Peter Mancroft at Norwich (Plate 68) Herod sits in something more than just a throne, but not quite a

M

building, and a rich fabric thrown over the front of it might have been the curtain used to shut him off from later scenes in which he did not figure. Such curtains are recorded as being used in some later plays.[8]

In order to fill out the action of the plays apocryphal incidents were introduced and anonymous participants in Gospel scenes were given individuality and function. The minor figures shown in some imagery illustrating such scenes often seem to repeat the actions of the players. Thus a soldier in the Massacre of the Innocents (Plate 68) holds high a baby spitted on his sword, reminding us of the grim jests of a soldier in the *Chester Plays* who told a mother that her son 'must hop . . . upon my speare end' while he probably shook a dummy into some ghastly semblance of life. The faded 14th-century paintings at Croughton (Northants) depart from the traditional presentation of the early life of the Virgin Mary in exactly the same way as does the *Ludus Coventriae*, by making Joachim take Mary from her parents' home to her wedding. Had the painter seen one of the much earlier plays which are incorporated in this part of the 15th-century cycle, or merely used the same source book—now lost? We shall never know, but the fact that both the author of the *Ludus Coventriae* and the designer of a Brussels tapestry now in the Metropolitan Museum, use this New York rare scene to exemplify Mary's observance of the Law probably also explains the Croughton painter's choice.

Scenic effects also became more elaborate as the plays emerged from the churches into the open air, although the very limited scope of medieval stage machinery must have made many of these ludicrously inadequate. The strongest evidence that the craftsmen did sometimes copy what they had seen on the stage is to be found when a carver has laboriously reproduced some absurd effect, which only makes sense if we translate it into a primitive stage device, when he could quite easily have illustrated his subject more realistically in his own medium. For example, an alabaster Presentation of the Virgin in Kinwarton church (War) instead of showing Mary as a child of three, ascending unaided the long flight of steps up to the Temple, represents her as a half-grown girl (or probably a boy) firmly supported by St. Anne as she prepares to climb a rickety step ladder propped against the altar table behind which the High Priest is seated. A small child obviously could not be trusted to play this part, and the Temple steps would have been hard to stage, so this is what a medieval audience may have seen, a probability increased by the fact that there are five veiled figures in the background, corresponding to the 'maidens five' who are mentioned in the *Ludus Coventriae* as being with Mary in the Temple.

On a roof boss in the cloister at Norwich, showing the Supper at Emmaus, a curtain, suspended by rings from a pole behind the table, is carved in the fullest detail. In a sculptural design this is irrelevant, but it explains exactly how Christ managed to 'vanish' on a small raised stage at the breaking of the bread. The nave bosses at Norwich offer many similar indications of probable stage effects. The carved Tree of Knowledge would stand up steadily on stage because its trunk is set in a solid circular base, like a toy tree. One of Noah's sons struggles to carry two sheep on to the Ark, and Pharoah's host is clearly being 'overwhelmed' by cloths painted with waves, which explains the intriguing payment of sixpence for 'half a yard of Red Sea' recorded elsewhere. But it is on the bosses of the transept roof, rebuilt after a fire in 1509, that we find the most certain evidence of the carvers having copied stage effects. There are some 150 of these bosses, all representing subjects illustrating the early life of Christ and that of St. John the Baptist and all different. With such a wealth of illustrations it is natural that we should find many scenes not included in more restricted series; the illuminator of a very rich Gospel Book would have done as much. What is significant is that, whenever the bosses show us some very unusual subject, this can be matched by either the rubrics, or the texts, of some medieval play. Unfortunately the only play from the Norwich Cycle which has survived deals with the Fall of Man, so no exact comparison can be made between the transept bosses and their most probable source of inspiration.

Some of these bosses show successive moments in the action of a scene, like a strip cartoon.[9] We see Gabriel receiving his orders in Heaven, with God the Father appearing in a 'glory' of light but standing on a solid round base, beneath which the rays are markedly out of alignment, as though some of them were the legs of a stool. Gabriel is then shown *walking* out of Heaven's gate and into that of Nazareth, as the actor must have done. He enters the house of Mary, he greets her, and then kneels before her, after her speech of humble acceptance has already made her the Mother of God—each scene on a separate boss. Then he is shown leaving the house, the outer wall of which is represented by a vertical line (Plate 88) while Joseph appears outside it. As a rubric of the Towneley Cycle directs: *Gabriel retires, Joseph advances*.

If we accept that these bosses are a record of the lost Norwich plays, then they tell us of two perfectly natural developments in English religious drama at this date, of which we have no textual record. The inclusion of a full series of scenes from the life and death of the Baptist in a cycle of mystery plays certainly happened in some French and German play cycles, and was very likely to have been repeated in Norwich which had important trade links with these areas. The prosperity of the city also depended upon the wool trade of which St. John was the patron, and there were many guilds dedicated to him in the area.

A small group of three bosses illustrates the death of Herod who has been shown on earlier bosses gesticulating with an exaggerated fury that reminds us of Shakespeare's reference to the bad actor who 'out-Herods Herod'. On the first boss a bottle nosed doctor is shown feeling Herod's pulse (Plate 89). In the *Croxton Play of the Sacrament*, a comic doctor scene has clearly been introduced into an earlier, and wholly serious, miracle play, and the same thing seems to have happened in the Corpus Christi Cycle at Norwich. Next we see Herod on his death bed, surrounded by mourning courtiers, and finally he is left alone to face the fiends, come to fetch his soul to Hell, to which he refers in the *Chester Plays*.

On all these bosses, Herod is shown wearing a pointed cap within his crown, the top of which ends in a demon's face. This demon-headdress is often given to tyrants on alabasters and in stained glass, where there are other indications of dramatic inspiration. For instance, in a window at Gresford (Denbighs) (Plate 69) Herod wears a dragonlike crest within his crown as he sits at his feast, while Herodias stabs a dagger into the head of the Baptist as the charger on which it lies is presented to her, a macabre incident, which figured in two French play cycles before it was represented in art.[10] Several payments for a hat for Herod were recorded in the accounts of the Coventry guilds and this demon-cap was, I suspect, a stage device invented to replace the little black devils often shown whispering evil suggestions in a tyrant's ear in illuminated manuscripts, to symbolise the satanic origin of his wicked thoughts.

Two stage characters, sometimes found in imagery, shall bring down the curtain on this carved and painted puppet show. The first is our Old Enemy of the sermon stories, Tutivillus, who appears on one supporter of a misericord at Ludlow (Plate 65) reading out his scroll at the Last Day. His head is disproportionately large and he wears a fringed hood over his shoulders which would have concealed the junction of a complete false head, such as we know that some medieval actors used. In the Towneley Doom Play, Tutivillus plays what is perhaps the first sick comedy role in English drama; in this, as in the sermon stories, he carries a sack for his scrolls, but I have only seen this represented on a bench-end at Charlton Mackrell (Som). In the centre of the Ludlow misericord another fiend carries off the naked soul of the Dishonest Ale Wife, her short-measuring tankard in hand, towards the Hell Mouth which must have been an essential accessory for all Doom plays. In the Chester Cycle the Dishonest Ale Wife is the only soul left in Hell after Christ has harrowed it, and Secundus Demon offers to wed her. In this context it is interesting to see her standing, beside a horned devil at the entrance to Hell, in the painting in St. Thomas' church, Salisbury (Plate 45). She is richly dressed and waves her tankard in a gesture of humorous defiance at the forces of good on the other side of the chancel arch, as the other damned souls are being herded, naked, into the Hell Mouth behind her. To a preacher denouncing the results of drunkenness, an ale-wife was the mother of many sins and a dishonest one worthy even to be the bride of a demon!

Chapter 9

HOW THE CRAFTSMEN GOT
THEIR DESIGNS

WHEN STUDYING the picture-book aspect of medieval churches one is constantly confronted by the problem of how did uneducated craftsmen achieve such a wide diversity of designs? This applies particularly to the subjects taken from secular literature which occur on misericords for, with the single exception of the Labours of the Months at Ripple (Worcs), which were all presumably copied from the calendar illustrations of the same psalter, there is no indication that misericords were planned to express any consistent scheme of iconography. The grander the church, the more varied and haphazard are the subjects of its misericords.[1] It seems therefore unlikely that the woodcarvers were closely supervised by their clerical employers although these may have reserved the right of vetoing unsuitable subjects. What models were given them, or did they make their own designs? We have no records of the normal procedure but sometimes individual carvings suggest what may have happened in that instance and, since we are so poor in proofs, we cannot afford to despise inferences.[2]

The crudely primitive figure subjects on some Norman tympana, such as Little Paxton (Hunts) or Danby Wiske (Yorks), show how greatly these carvers needed guidance when something beyond geometric ornament was required of them. At first it seems to have been the painters who came to their aid. Not only the plain surfaces, but also the capitals of Norman churches were decorated with painted designs and on some detached capitals in Hereford cathedral, and in the triforium of Westminster Abbey, we see figure subjects carved in such flat planes that their maker may only have enhanced the effect of a painted design by cutting away the background and marking the folds of drapery with incised lines. Even such a comparatively sophisticated work as the tympanum of the Prior's door at Ely cathedral (Plate 13) is so markedly calligraphic in its design as to suggest some such co-operation between painter and carver, and the latter has clearly misunderstood the foreshortened drawing of the angels' arms, as they support the mandorla, and produced a curious distortion. On the late 12th-century font at Coleshill (War) the carver has reproduced the contour lines of a drawing without realising that the three-dimensional nature of his own medium made these superfluous, and the lines of shading by which the draughtsman indicated the modelling of the figures have become meaningless incisions, which contradict, rather than emphasise, the curve of the stone.

In some cases the carver's model was apparently a drawing dating from an earlier period. The demi-angel on a Norman tympanum at Halford (War) recalls an Anglo-Saxon drawing of at least a century earlier, and some Norman reliefs at Barton-le-Street (Yorks) also look like copies of drawings of the Winchester School.[3] Foreign characteristics may imply that the original model had been imported. The Saxon angel at Breedon-on-the-Hill (Leics) raises his hand to greet, or bless, with the gesture of the Eastern Church, the fourth finger bent over to meet the thumb and three fingers held erect, rather than the old Roman gesture of speech, used by the Western Church, with only the first two fingers raised. The eastern legend of SS. Paul and Anthony breaking bread in the desert appears on the late 7th-century cross at Ruthwell (Dumfries), other details of which suggest a Syrian origin.[4] The vine scrolls, familiar in much Mediterranean decorative art, which appear on Saxon cross shafts, were perhaps copied from Byzantine carvings in ivory or bone, and the carvings of confronted animals on some Norman capitals may repeat the designs of eastern silks which once decked the sanctuaries of great churches. A few precious scraps of such silks survive in the library of Canterbury cathedral, preserved by their use as seal-bags.

As the carvers progressed in technical skill, they adapted designs from other media[5] borrowing from the workers in metal the ornament resembling plaited wire which surrounds the font at Castle Frome (Plate 33), and the moulding of linked medallions on the famous doorway of Kilpeck (Herefs). A drawing of the ornament round the font at Stottesdon (Salop) which did not indicate the material, might be taken for some rich necklace of gold, and the draperies of the Virgin's robes, on the tympanum at

Fownhope (Herefs), are outlined with fine parallel grooves, following the example of the goldsmiths or ivory carvers.

In the 12th century, wall-paintings are sometimes so closely allied in style to the miniatures of contemporary manuscripts as to suggest that the same artists were concerned with their design.[6] The small round drawings of the Guthlac Roll, in the British Museum, could so aptly have been translated into stained glass, wall-paintings or roundels of enamel, that they may have been made for some such purpose. Roundels linked together by foliate ornaments were popular in all forms of ecclesiastical art in the 13th century. We need only compare the painted roundels on the roof of Salisbury cathedral, or on the walls of Brook (Kent) and Romsey Abbey, with the similar designs on the tympana of Higham Ferrers (Northants) and Crowland Abbey (Lincs) to see that the character of designs was not determined by the medium in which they were meant to be executed.

The misericords of Worcester cathedral, dating from 1390, include several Old Testament subjects and my chance recognition that the one showing Isaac bearing the faggots for his own sacrifice (Plate 9), closely resembled the 12th-century enamel medallion of this subject on the Warwick Ciborium, now in the Victoria and Albert Museum, brought to light several interesting examples of this transposition of designs from one medium to another.[7] Despite a gap of two centuries the carvers were clearly copying the same designs, almost certainly those of the 12th-century typological wall-paintings which once decorated in the walls of the Worcester Chapter House. As at Canterbury, verses explaining these paintings have been preserved and titles drawn from them appear both on the Ciborium and on some pages of 13th-century decorative designs bound up with another manuscript in the library of Eton College.[8] On these pages the central subject, taken from the life of Christ, is surrounded by medallions illustrating its Old Testament types, just as, to judge from the verses, the painter arranged his subjects on the Chapter House walls. In the margin beside the drawing of the Circumcision of Isaac in the Eton MS. a note has been written in a later hand referring to the alternative type of Zipporah circumcising her son in front of Moses, and the carver of a corresponding misericord evidently worked from a design which had been incorrectly adapted to this subject, for he has given the officiating High Priest the horns which always identify Moses (see page 108). Thus these carvings give us an impression of the way in which designs were handed down in the workshops of religious houses, adapted to illustrate different subjects, and used by craftsmen working in various media over a long period of time.

Some of the other misericords at Worcester seem to have been copied from calendar pictures in rich psalters (Plates 11 and 91), and a fine basilisk flanked by weasels eating the rue which protects these creatures alone from the monster's lethal glance, has characteristics which recall some 12th-century Bestiaries. Yet other misericords seem to have been copied from the marginal ornaments of manuscripts. We find the same haphazard copying of isolated subjects on the earlier stalls of Exeter cathedral. Here one subject has been taken from an Apocalypse, the Locust (Plate 74), and another from the Romance of the Knight of the Swan (Plate 72), better known to most of us in its operatic form of *Lohengrin*. This detachment of single subjects from their literary context is characteristic of misericords and adds greatly to the difficulty of identifying them. At both Exeter and Worcester one gets the impression that the carvers making the new choir stalls were given drawings by artists working on illuminated manuscripts, perhaps rough sketches, or pages that had been accidentally spoilt, and the fact that none of these designs recurs on stalls elsewhere probably indicates that the carvers were permanently employed there.

By contrast, the stalls of Lincoln cathedral, made *c.* 1377, were clearly the work of men who also produced stalls at Chester, Holy Trinity, Coventry, and the misericords from Roche Abbey which are now in the church of Loversall (Yorks). They must either have been a band of craftsmen who travelled from place to place, as work offered, or else were established at some centre from which they despatched stalls in sections, to be assembled in their destined position. In their work we see designs repeated, sometimes by different hands, as though the carvers shared a book of patterns, and varied these with assured freedom. For instance, the misericord of Tristan and Iseult meeting beneath the tree in which King Mark has concealed himself at Chester (Plate 76), is both more sophisticated and correct than that at Lincoln, the difference being greater than the probable improvement made by the same man on a second attempt. The subject of a wodewose, or wild man, bestriding a lion and controlling it by means of a chain round its neck is rare elsewhere but appears several times on the stalls made by these carvers, with unmistakable differences of handling.

Why certain subjects from secular literature were popular among carvers of misericords while others, with apparently higher claims, were ignored, is a tantalising question. A French compilation of moralised stories, *Cy nous dit*, may explain the presence of Tristan and Iseult at Lincoln and Chester, for it says that men, knowing that God knows all we do, should avoid sin, as the guilty lovers, seeing King Mark's face reflected in a pool of water, kept their conversation innocent. The same text uses the story of how Alexander was borne up into the heavens by hungry griffins, lured upwards by lumps of meat impaled on spears just out of their reach, to illustrate man's hunger for the beauty of Heaven, but other authors made it an example of pride. The subject is correctly shown on misericords at Wells, Gloucester (Plate 75) and Darlington (Durham) while in several other places we see carvings of kings and monsters arranged in a way that suggests a craftsman's recollection of a picture which he did not fully understand. Were such moralised stories, matched with drawings, produced in some rough form and widely distributed? Since no examples have survived, we cannot tell, but such a supposition would explain why there are five misericords (at Enville (Staffs) (Plate 77), Chester, Lincoln, Boston (Lincs) and New College (Oxford)) which show Sir Yvain pursuing an enemy into his castle and being trapped by the portcullis which fell on the hindquarters of his horse. In each case the supporters represent the wholly unimportant soldiers who tried to seize Sir Yvain when he was thus trapped, instead of either the lion, or the damsel, who played much more prominent parts in the romance.

In all these cases we do, at least, know the story behind the design, though not its moralised context, but where did the carvers find their model for the mermaid suckling a lion which occurs at Edlesborough (Bucks) (Plate 73) and in the cathedrals of Hereford and Norwich? And what did it mean? There are many other single subjects which suggest a literary source, as yet unidentified, and which may have been suggested to the carvers by a chance sight of some long series of illustrations to a romance. The Falling Knight at Lincoln is typical of these challenging subjects.

The subjects of misericords did not have to be consistent, so any good design, from whatever source it came, could be used on them. It was a very different matter when the monks of Norwich wished to have many subjects from the Apocalypse carved on the roof bosses of their cloister and it seems certain that they must have shown the carvers the miniatures from some illuminated manuscript. A boss at the west end of the south alley shows St. John describing his vision to a group of five men, and Dr. M. R. James considered that this scene related the carvings to a group of East Anglian Apocalypse manuscripts of which an outstanding example is in the British Museum (Royal MS 15.D.ii).[9] To show what use the craftsmen could make of such a model we can compare the drawing of the Angel with the Second Trumpet (Fig. 13) in a manuscript belonging to Trinity College, Cambridge[10] with the boss illustrated on Plate 70. The Angel is blowing his trumpet over a rough sea, heaped high in one place to indicate the fall of the flaming mountain; ships in the foreground sink vertically, their occupants falling out, while those of ships still afloat make gestures of despair. All these elements have been fitted into the restricted space of the boss without either overcrowding or weakening the design.

We can rarely say with any certainty what the carvers copied, and I know of only one case in which we know how it probably came to be copied.[11] Some of the late 15th-century paintings on the stalls of Carlisle cathedral illustrate the life of St. Cuthbert, and Richard Bell, who was Bishop of Carlisle when they were made, had previously been Prior of Durham. In the library of Durham there was then a 12th-century Life of St. Cuthbert (now in the British Museum) and, out of the seventeen panels of the Carlisle paintings, thirteen correspond so closely to the miniatures of this manuscript that they were probably based upon them. We know that in 1426 the monks of Durham had lent this manuscript to York, perhaps in connection with the making of the St. Cuthbert window in the Minster, although only one panel of this window shows any similarity with the miniatures, and it seems

FIG. 13. The Angel with the Second Trumpet. Trinity Apocalypse

most likely that Bishop Bell arranged for the painter at Carlisle to use it as his model.

For the later medieval periods the glaziers provide us with the best evidence of how designs were conveyed.[12] Until the mid-15th century cartoons for windows were drawn upon plastered boards which were supported on trestles. These 'tables' served both as model and work-bench, for the craftsman cut and leaded his material upon the blank end of the board. Since their bulk made difficult the storage of many 'tables', the same designs were constantly repeated, slight alterations in their details increasing the range of their subject-matter. The identification of most saints depended only upon an attribute, so that, by varying the attributes, one cartoon could easily do service for all saints within a given group, identified by their clothing as apostles, Popes, bishops or deacons. This repetition was particularly easy when all the windows of a cathedral clerestory had to be filled, for then the subjects would be far above the eye-level of carping critics. In the clerestory of the western choir of York Minster a five-light window showing a central pope flanked by a king and an ecclesiastic on each side is repeated six times with slight variations, and at Malvern the same cartoon served for both Edward the Confessor and William the Conqueror. The late medieval practice of filling each light of a window with a single figure made their balance most important, and many glaziers achieved symmetry by the lazy process of reversing the cartoon for use in the corresponding light. Thus, in a window in North Cerney (Glos), we can see three female saints worked from one cartoon. In one case this has been reversed and in the other two a change of attribute, or the introduction of the Child Virgin beside St. Anne, was all that was needed. A single cartoon of a shield-bearing angel could serve to fill the tracery lights of many windows and, when the family of a donor were shown kneeling behind him, the same child could be repeated in descending scale as often as was required.

The introduction of paper, or parchment, to replace the boards increased this repetition, for it was easier to store such 'scrolls' over long periods of time. The wills of medieval master glaziers record bequests of 'scrowles' as well as of tools to their heirs or partners. In St. Michael-le-Belfrey, York, there is a St. Christopher in a window probably put up after the rebuilding of the church in

1528–36 which is identical in design with one in All Saints, North Street, supposed to be the work of John Chamber the younger, who died in 1451. The scroll bearing this design had therefore been handed on from one master glazier to another, and used, as need arose, over a period of eighty years at least. Had more churches retained their ancient glass we should probably have seen other windows taken from this cartoon in districts served by the glaziers of York. At Bolton Percy (Yorks) the saints represented in the east window include a bishop taken from the cartoon used for the figures of St. John of Beverley and St. William of York in the Parker window, and an archbishop repeating the figure of St. Paulinus in the Wolveden window in York Minster.

Even groups and subject pictures were sometimes composed from cartoons already drawn for a different purpose. Miraculous cures at the shrine of a saint often had a similarity of which the glaziers were quick to take advantage, and in the St. William window at York two cartoons have been repeated without change while two others have been varied by a mutual interchange of the blind and the crippled coming to the shrines. It is thus obvious that very little clerical supervision would have been thought necessary in the glazing of a later church, even if cartoons for the subjects chosen were not already in stock. An important master glazier probably had some list of the attributes of outstanding saints in his workshop, so that the cartoons could be correctly adapted, and the co-operation of an ecclesiastical adviser would only have been necessary when rare subjects were required.

The same process of repetition characterises the later shop-work of the carvers, particularly those who made alabaster panels, but the unusual imagery of some panels, such as the 'St. Boniface overthrowing the Tree of Thor' in the Victoria and Albert Museum, suggest that a cleric may have designed them.

The invention of paper, followed by that of printing, made possible the wide distribution of single woodcuts, and of illustrated books which were not too precious to be used directly as models. The designs of the block-book *Biblia Pauperum* (Fig. 11) appear in glass and carving in many churches, and the glaziers of Malvern made such frequent use of the woodcuts of the *Speculum Humanae Salvationis* that these have been used as the basis for restoring scattered panels. The windows of Tattershall church

(Lincs) were originally filled with glass which followed such designs and some panels remain there while others have been moved to St. Martin's church, Stamford. Here we can see the Deposition, Entombment and Resurrection, together with Moses striking the rock, Samson with the gates of Gaza and David and Goliath. How closely a carver would sometimes follow a drawing can be illustrated by comparing the misericord at Ripon of Samson carrying away the gates (Plate 10) with the woodcut reproduced in Fig. 11.

It was not only figure subjects which the carvers copied from books; they also made use of the grotesques found in the margins of early printed Books of Hours, but these we will consider in a different context (see page 215). The romantic conception of the medieval craftsman glorying in his own freedom to create endless original designs, is thus shown to be a nostalgic illusion. He was no more averse to saving himself trouble by copying other men's ideas than are many of his descendants. All the same, the identification of his models, and the study of how he used them, is a fascinating pursuit, worthy of more attention than is usually given to it.

PART III

The Record of Social History

Chapter 1

PRINCES OF CHURCH AND STATE

A CHURCH was the place to which all men came, the great as well as the small, the living and the dead. Some of them contributed largely to its embellishment and expected to be remembered there far longer than they were. Others served God with the skill of their hands and, through their art, sometimes enable us to distinguish faintly the figures of thousands more who had nothing to give but their worship and who would have been surprised to learn that they would be remembered at all. In the last chapters of this book we will consider some memorials which these different types of people have left in the churches and, since they lived in an age of rigid social hierarchies, we will begin with the great of the land and end with the common people.

Although the iconoclastic fury of the Reformation destroyed most of the imagery which once made English churches veritable treasure houses of sculpture, stained glass and goldsmiths' work, the monuments of the great families suffered little deliberate damage, beyond, perhaps, having the heads knocked off some saints carved on the tomb chests. These monuments therefore constitute a richly illustrated record of the history of many periods. The fine church of Norbury, on the borders of Derbyshire and Staffordshire (Plate 80), contains many fine medieval monuments. On the south of the chancel aisle is the altar tomb of Sir Nicholas Fitzherbert, Lord of Norbury, who died in 1473. The finely cut details of his alabaster effigy include a Yorkist collar of suns and roses. His two wives are represented on the west end of the tomb chest, and his seventeen children, as weepers, down its sides. On the tomb to the north of the chancel lie the effigies of Sir Ralph Fitzherbert, died 1483, and his wife. A lion serves him as a footrest and, on its back, crouches a little bedesman, rosary in hand, probably meant to remind us of some charitable foundation by the dead man. This combination of lion and bedesman can also be seen at Harewood (Yorks,) Lowick (Northants), Strelley (Notts) and Godshill (Isle of Wight). Norbury has kept much of its original glass and there are large shields at the top of the lights. In many other churches armorial glass survived in the tracery heads when the religious imagery of the main lights was smashed and the sunlight streaming through these shields sometimes restores to the effigies of those who once bore them, the richness of heraldic tinctures which time has worn away.

The Kings of England have not been great church builders, apart from the royal foundations of Westminster, Windsor, Eton and King's College, Cambridge. Little is left of Battle Abbey (Sussex), built by William the Conqueror on the site of King Harold's last stand, but at Battlefield (Salop) the church built by King Henry IV in 1406 still stands, with a statue of the King upon its tower. Eight chaplains were attached to it by the original foundation, to pray for the souls of those who fell in the bloody victory at Shrewsbury which had won the King his throne.

From a distance the church of Fotheringhay (Northants) appears disproportionately tall, for it consists of the nave and western tower only of a magnificent collegiate church planned as a chantry chapel and mausoleum for the House of York. Here were buried Edward of York, founder of the college, who fell at Agincourt, Richard, Duke of York who rebuilt the nave, and his son Edmund, both of whom fell at Wakefield in 1460, and Ciceley, Duchess of York. Two identical monuments, to the second and third Dukes of York, were erected there, in 1573, by Queen Elizabeth.[1]

Most English royalties are buried in Westminster Abbey and it would be absurd to include such famous tombs in this book, but there are a few others in various cathedrals. King John is buried at Worcester, where we also see the elaborate chantry chapel of Prince Arthur, eldest son of Henry VII. Edward II lies at Gloucester with a beautiful effigy (Plate 81), and there also is an interesting 13th-century wooden effigy marking the tomb of Robert 'Courthouse', the son of William the Conqueror. Henry IV and Edward, the Black Prince, have their monuments in Canterbury cathedral and William of Hatfield, son of Edward III is buried in York Minster. Katherine Parr, Henry VIII's last queen, is buried at Sudeley (Glos).[2]

Even in parish churches we may find memorials of royal persons, or those in some way connected with them. In Wimborne Abbey,

John Beaufort, Duke of Somerset, who was the grandson of John of Gaunt and grandfather of Henry VII, has a splendid tomb. The right hand of his effigy is extended to take that of his wife, who lies beside him. At Framlingham (Suffolk) Henry Fitzroy, the bastard son of Henry VIII, has a tomb of royal splendour. The most unexpected monument is in the little church of Bacton (Herefs) where a statue of Queen Elizabeth is placed on the tomb of Blanche Parry, a member of her household, who is represented kneeling at the side of her royal mistress. Windows from this church, transferred to Atcham (Salop) in 1811, show Blanche Parry offering a book to the queen. Another statue of Queen Elizabeth, said to have been erected by the Earl of Leicester in the garden of Dean Court, is now in Cumnor church (Berks).

Portrait heads of Charles I and his queen are carved on a boss under the tower of Winchester cathedral, but only careful comparison with contemporary coinage could prove whether the many crowned heads shown on earlier bosses and capitals bore any resemblance to the then reigning monarch.[3] We are on safer ground when looking for references to royal personages in parish churches if we confine our search to heraldry. In the east window of Etchingham (Sussex) are four Plantagenet shields, those of John of Gaunt, Edward III and his two sons, the Black Prince and John, Duke of Brittany. In the glass now at Radley (Berks) we see the arms of Henry VI, Richard III, Henry VII and Henry VIII, and a figure which is said to be a portrait of Henry VII. Figures representing Henry VII and Elizabeth of York have been restored to the east window of Stanford-on-Avon (Northants) where there is also a fine display of armorial glass. Much easier for the ordinary traveller to identify are the royal badges. The most famous of these is the Prince of Wales' badge of the ostrich feathers, which can be seen on the Black Prince's shield for peace, above his tomb, in Canterbury cathedral. The Prince of Wales' feathers appear on misericords at Abergavenny (Mon) and Ludlow and on the font at Elmley Castle (Worcs) where other panels show the rose and portcullis of the Tudors, the latter device being a rebus on their name—'two-doors'. The falcon and fetterlock badge of the House of York, which figures largely in Henry VII's Chapel in Westminster Abbey, is also carved on one of the misericords at Ludlow. The sun-burst badge of Edward IV appears in windows at Bishops Hull and Huish Episcopi in Somerset and is carved on the corbels of the Great Hospital Chapel, Norwich. Prince Arthur's personal badge of a rose surrounded by many arrows appears in the glass at Yarnton (Oxon). Sometimes the variations of these royal badges help to date the work on which they appear. For instance, when the Tudor rose is shown dimidiated with the pomegranate of Aragon, as on the font at Prittlewell (Essex), the bosses of the south aisle at Thaxted (Essex) or the screen at Holbeton (Devon), it is evident that the carving was done during the period of Henry VIII's marriage to Katherine of Aragon.

Sometimes the imagery of a building reflects the fluctuating fortunes of the Wars of the Roses, or the political sympathies of those who built it. A reminder of these wars can be seen in the east window of Little Malvern (Worcs) where the figures of Elizabeth Woodville and her four children, together with that of Bishop Alcock who rebuilt this church, recall that the queen took sanctuary in Westminster Abbey, where Alcock was then Dean, after Edward IV had fled the country. Quarries of 15th-century glass at Chewton Mendip (Somerset) and Langley Marish (Bucks), which show a crown in a bush together with the initials H. R., or H. E., for Henry VII and Elizabeth of York, remind us of the dramatic episode when the crown of England was found in a hawthorn tree after the Battle of Bosworth. The device was a favourite badge of Henry VII and also appears in his chapel in Westminster Abbey.

Although no partisan enthusiasm disturbs the carved faces of the effigies of men who fought in the Wars of the Roses, we can sometimes discover, by a single detail of their dress, to which side they adhered. This evidence is to be sought in the livery collars which became fashionable in the late 14th century.[4] At first the collar merely displayed the heraldic devices of its owner; Thomas, Lord Berkeley (died 1417), wears a collar of the Berkeley mermaids on his brass at Wotton-under-Edge (Glos), while the effigy of Thomas Markenfield, in Ripon cathedral, wears a collar in the form of a very spiky paling. The most famous of all these livery collars is the SS collar which distinguished the adherents of the House of Lancaster, but, oddly enough, its origin and the significance of the initial are unknown. Many solutions have been advanced. The 'S' may stand for Sanctus, since vestments are known to have been embroidered with the letter used in this sense. The most usual interpretation is that 'S' stands for 'Soverayne' or 'Souvegnez', both words being used in connection with collars given to his supporters by Henry IV, but this theory does not explain the appearance of the SS collar on the effigy of Sir John Swinfield (died 1371) at Spratton (Northants), so it has been suggested that John of Gaunt may have introduced the collar and that the 'S' stands for his office of Seneschal of England. Whatever its meaning may have been, the SS collar was certainly a mark of Lancastrian sympathies which was worn by persons of every degree from the King to the humble esquire, by women as well as men, and by civilians as well as soldiers. Shortly after his accession Henry IV bestowed the SS collar upon William Bagot and both he and his wife are shown wearing the collars upon their brass at Baginton (Warcs). Less often seen on effigies than the SS collar is that designed for the House of York, with the blazing sun of Edward IV alternating with the white rose of York. The pendant is often the lion badge of March, until after the accession of Richard III when it is usually his white boar. Examples of the Yorkist collar can be seen on effigies at Abergavenny (Mon), Aston (Birmingham), Holme Pierrepont (Notts) (Plate 82) and Stanton Harcourt (Oxon). In Aston church, an effigy, supposed to be that of Sir Thomas de Erdington (died 1433), wears a collar from which the SS have been effaced. Perhaps a change of allegiance in the next generation made such an alteration politic, but, if so, why did they leave his wife's collar intact? The Tudors brought back the use of the SS collar, with a rose or portcullis as its pendant, as on the effigy of Sir George Forster at Aldermaston (Berks). After the reign of Henry VIII the use of the collar became restricted to judges and other officials. The only example of a medieval collar surviving is that presented to the City of London by Sir John Alleyn, Lord Mayor in 1525, and still used by his successors in that office. The statue of Sir Robert Clayton (died 1707) at Blechingley (Surrey) shows him wearing this chain.

The stability of England during the Middle Ages depended largely upon the King's ability to win the loyalty, or force the obedience, of his most powerful subjects. When Edward III founded the Order of the Garter in 1349 he added to the ties of fealty between sovereign and subject the new bond of loyalty between brothers-in-arms which forbade a knight to betray the Head of his Order. Originally the Knights wore the cross of St. George encircled by the Garter, embroidered upon their cloaks. Only the Primate was allowed to substitute his own arms, impaled with those of his see, within the Garter, as we see those of Bishop William Waynflete in the windows taken from Tattershall to St. Martin's church, Stamford. The fame of St. George's Chapel, Windsor, makes any description unnecessary, but the Garter Church at Stamford (Lincs) is relatively little known.[5] In 1449, Sir William Bruges, first Garter King at Arms, completed the rebuilding of St. George's church, Stamford, and the windows then included portraits of the twenty-five original Knights of the Order, including Edward III, the Black Prince and Henry, Duke of Lancaster. These windows have perished except for the head of a single knight, which has gained a misleading semblance of a halo in modern resetting, and a window filled with background quarries, each showing the Garter with its motto in its original spelling: 'Hony soyt qui mal y pence'. The early representations of the Knights of the Order, such as the brasses of Lord Thomas Camoys (1419) at Trotton (Sussex) and Sir Simon de Felbrygge (1416) at Felbrigg (Norfolk), or the effigy of the Duke of Somerset (died 1444) at Wimborne (Dorset), show them in full armour with the Garter on the left leg. A little later we see figures wearing the mantle also, on the brasses of two Lords Treasurer of England, Henry Bourchier, Earl of Essex (1483), at Little Easton (Essex) and Ralph Cromwell (1455), at Tattershall (Lincs) or on the effigy of the Duke of Suffolk at Wingfield, but it is not until the Tudor period that we find the full insignia represented on the brass of Sir Thomas Bullen (1538) at Hever (Kent) (Fig. 14). On the rare occasions when the Order was bestowed on a woman, the Garter was worn on the left arm, as shown on the effigies of the Duchess of Suffolk at Ewelme or Lady Harcourt at Stanton Harcourt (Oxon).[6]

Like the King, the great nobles moved from one residence to another. John of Gaunt had a score of castles and his arms appear in windows at St. Albans cathedral, West Tanfield (Yorks) and Carlisle cathedral, and used to be discernible carved on the tower

1 Foot

FIG. 14. **Sir Thomas Bullen wearing the robes of the Order of the Garter**

of Tickhill (Yorks) where he had a minor stronghold.[7] His claim to the kingdoms of Leon and Castile, on the grounds of his marriage to Constance of Castile, is recalled by a window in the antechapel of All Souls College, Oxford, where a kingly figure is entitled *Johe's Rex Ispanie dux Lancastre*, and by his quarterings of 1 and 4 Castile, 2 and 3 Leon impaling France ancient and England quarterly, in the window at Carlisle. His nearest rival, the Earl of March, had ten castles, the Earls of Stafford and Warwick two or three apiece, and we find frequent reminders of their power in churches where are represented the white lion of March, the Stafford knot, and the bear and ragged staff of Warwick.

The student of heraldry will recognise many coats of arms, or badges, in the windows or on the minor carvings in churches, which tell of the widely dispersed spheres of influence of the great medieval nobles. It was an important factor in the history of the period for, although the wealth and power which they derived from their scattered estates was very great in some cases, it was not such a danger to the stability of the Crown as it would have been if all these estates had been in one area. This even applied to the Anglo-Norman Marcher Lords. Although they carved out little kingdoms for themselves on the Welsh and Scottish Borders by the valour of their private armies, and administered them according to their own interpretation of feudal laws, the arms of de Clare, Mortimer (Fig. 16), Bohun, Valence and Fitzalan may be seen in many other areas, for their wealth was drawn largely from their English estates. Richard de Clare took his name from Clare in Suffolk, the most important of the 176 fiefs granted to him by William the Conqueror. These included lands in Kent and Surrey where the red chevrons of the de Clare arms can be seen in the churches of Chartham and Selling in Kent and Shere in Surrey.[8]

The Marcher Lords built castles rather than churches and, since peace was never secure on the Marches, even churches in these areas sometimes have a fortified appearance. At Newton Nottage (Glam) a range of massive corbels, projecting from the face of the tower, supported a covered wooden gallery from which missiles could be more effectively discharged than from the battlements, and it is possible that Cheriton church (Glam) once had a similar arrangement. The church of Newton Arlosh (Cumb) looks like a fortress guarding a point at which the Solway Firth can be crossed at certain states of the tide, for its windows are seven feet from the ground and only a foot wide. The door also is very narrow. The windows of the church at Burgh-on-Sands (Cumb) are almost equally high up and narrow and the walls of this tower are seven feet thick. [9]

With the exception of Westminster Abbey, there is probably no church in England which offers us a finer record of monumental history than Tewkesbury, for the manor belonged to five great families of Marcher Lords, and the traveller, who lingers there long enough to unravel their record of succession from the tombs which surround the choir, will thus gain a clearer understanding of a tangled skein of English history. [10] Robert Fitzhamon, who first enriched Tewkesbury Abbey with the spoils of Llantwit Major, lies in a late 14th-century chantry chapel, and both he and his son-in-law, Robert Fitzroy, are represented in the choir windows. Four of the de Clare Earls of Gloucester also figure in these windows, but their tombs have been destroyed. A statue dug up during restorations may represent Gilbert III de Clare, for it holds an inverted torch to mark the extinction of the family by his death at Bannockburn. The windows also show Robert Fitzhamon and Hugh Despenser whose wife, Elizabeth, rebuilt the choir in the 14th century. Their effigies lie on a tomb near the High Altar. The Warwick Chantry marks how Tewkesbury was brought into the Beauchamp estates by the two marriages of Lady Isabella Despenser, first to Richard Beauchamp, Earl of Abergavenny and Worcester, and then to another Richard Beauchamp, Earl of Warwick, whose grand-daughter lies at Tewkesbury beside her ill-fated husband, the Duke of Clarence. The chantry chapel of Edward, Lord Despenser (died 1375), recalls one whom Froissart described as 'the most honourable, gallant and valiant knight in all England, much beloved of the ladies'. He was one of the original Knights of the Garter. The slender mullions and delicate tracery of this chantry chapel give it charm, but its unique distinction is the canopied niche which rises from the centre of the roof to shelter the kneeling figure of Lord Despenser, which faces the High Altar. Lifted high above the reach of the vandals who destroyed so much of beauty at Tewkesbury, and with its colour and gilding recently restored, this statue can be chosen to illustrate all that was best in the Marcher Lords (Plate 83).

The northern counties of England, like the Welsh Marches, were dominated by feudal Lords so powerful as to be virtually independent of the Crown. The Percies and Nevilles raised magnificent castles, and the personal loyalties of the warlike farmers who fought under them represented the law in the Border lands. The lofty tomb of Lady Eleanor Percy in Beverley Minster, with little figures of knights holding shields blazoned with the Percy lion, in the cusps of its exuberant canopy, is a monument which might have been raised for a queen, and the splendid tombs of the Earls of Westmorland at Staindrop and Brancepeth in Durham, bespeak their wealth and power.

In the church at Guisborough (Yorks) the panels from a richly carved 16th-century tomb show us an unusual illustration of the tangled loyalties which linked the feudal lords on each side of the Scottish border (Plate 79).[11] Each of the side panels is decorated with figures of knights in armour, standing within niches, alternating with smaller figures representing the Doctors of the Church. On one side the figures hold shields which identify them as members of the Skelton branch of the Bruce family, which remained in England, while the slightly larger figures on the other side represent the Bruces of Annandale. The central figure on the Scottish side, who bears on his shield a saltire in chief and a lion passant to the dexter, represents Robert the Bruce III of Annandale who married Princess Margaret. One end panel shows a Prior surrounded by his monks, the other has been lost. An engraving in Dugdale's *Monasticon Anglicanum*, 1661, shows that the lost panel was carved with the figure of a crowned king, with the lion rampant of Scotland on his shield, presumably King Robert the Bruce, and two smaller crowned figures who may have represented his father and grandfather, both unsuccessful claimants to the Scottish throne. The tomb can be ascribed to the period 1519–34, when James Cockerell was Prior of Guisborough, for the scallop-shell of St. James and a device of a cock standing upon a reel recur several times. There is no record to tell us who, in the period of bitter hatred that followed Flodden Field, would have erected such a monument in an English church, but it has been suggested that the most likely person was Margaret Tudor, daughter of Henry VII and widow of James IV of Scotland who fell in that battle.

Another unexpected memorial of Scottish royalty is the monument, in the north aisle at Conington (Hunts), which commemorates King David I, who was also Earl of Huntingdon. A crown, in the central niche, is flanked by the unicorns of Scotland, facing outwards. A simpler memorial, in the same church, commemorates his son, Henry of Scotland. Both were erected *c.* 1600 by Sir Robert Cotton who claimed descent from Prince Henry.

In most cases it is only the leaders in these Border wars who are commemorated, but at Middleton (Lancs) we find an unusual memorial to the archers whose superior skill was the determining

FIG. 15. The archers of Flodden Field

feature in many battles between the Scots and the English. In 1524 a window was placed there by Sir Richard Assheton, who had commanded the archers sent from Middleton to join Sir Edward Stanley's contingent at Flodden, and acquitted himself so well that he was knighted on the field of battle. In the window now fragmentary, we can see Sir Richard and his wife kneeling in prayer, together with seventeen archers, headed by their chaplain, Henry Tayler. Each man wears a blue jerkin and has a sheaf of arrows at his back, while his name appears beside the stave of his bow.[12] When he returned from Flodden, Sir Richard dedicated his arms to St. Leonard, patron of Middleton church, and a flag, helmet, sword and spurs, traditionally supposed to be his, are still preserved there. His commander, Sir Edward Stanley, built a new tower to Hornby church (Lancs) as a thank-offering for his safe return from the battle, and we can also see his badge of an eagle's claw, together with the arms of the Kingdom of Man (which the Stanleys also ruled), carved on the chancel of this church.

In carvings it is the badges of the great nobles, rather than their arms, that we find represented, although there is an interesting collection of heraldic bosses in the cloisters of Canterbury.[13] In an age when most men were illiterate, the badge, as the emblem of individual ownership, had an importance which can be paralleled today by the Divisional flashes of the Army. This was, in fact, the original purpose of many badges, for most of them came into use during the 15th century, to distinguish men serving in the private armies of the great feudal Lords.[14] They are, therefore, a picturesque allusion to the then most unhappy state of the country. The growing supremacy of the Tudor monarchs is reflected in the way in which their badges supersede all others in the later churches. A badge had the great advantage of simplicity as a mark of identification. While the correct blazon of the King-maker's arms was probably known to comparatively few (as witness its curious rendering upon the font at Holt (Denbighs)), his bear and ragged staff would have been instantly recognised by most of his contemporaries. A late example, which occurs on the tower of St. Sampson's church, Cricklade (Wilts) reminds us that its builder was John Dudley, Earl of Warwick, and later Duke of Northumberland, who was beheaded for his share in the rebellion of Lady Jane Grey. We can also see it carved on bosses in the north aisle of Northleach (Glos) and the porch of Burford (Oxon) and on a bench-end at Rettendon (Essex) where we also find the Stanley badge of the swaddled baby in the eagle's nest.[15] The identification of the badges carved or painted in churches is made more difficult by the fact that one person might have several badges, sometimes referring to different aspects of his career.[16] Over the west window of Castle Hedingham church (Essex) can be seen the various badges of John de Vere, Earl of Oxford, in the 16th century.[17] A whistle and chain denote him High Admiral of England and a chair of estate refers to his office as Hereditary Great Chamberlain. An ox in a ford and a boar (old French *ver*) are puns on his name, as is also, perhaps, the jack, or cranket, used to wind up crossbows, which also appears, with the boar, on the south door of Lavenham (Suffolk). The molet, or five-pointed star, badge of the de Veres, can be seen in many places in Essex and Suffolk, where their influence was strong.

The effigies on tombs are among the best examples of medieval figure sculpture but, with the possible exception of some royal tombs, they should not be considered as portraits. The medieval belief was that all men should rise from the dead of the same age as Christ rose, about 33, and so many a battle-scarred old veteran is shown on his tomb in the idealised beauty of young manhood. This ideal is well represented by the effigy of Sir Henry Pierrepont at Holme Pierrepont (Notts) (Plate 82). What the tombs do show us is a wealth of illustrations of dress, arms and accoutrements, faithfully rendered, but these also may have been made finer by the image-maker than they would have been in life, just as the 18th-century journeyman painter sometimes provided his female sitters with far grander dresses and jewels than they had ever possessed. Another trap for the unwary student is that the year of death given in the inscription on a tomb may not provide a correct date for a detail of costume, since tombs were sometimes made several years before, or after, the death of their occupants. Sometimes a space, intended for the date of death, had not been filled in, as, for instance, on one of the Feilding tombs at Monks Kirby (Warcs).

A few churches show us, not only carved replicas of arms, but the actual helms, swords and coats of arms which were carried

in the funeral processions and afterwards hung up over the tombs.[1]
The most complete early achievement which has survived robbery
decay and neglect, is that which hangs over the tomb of the Black
Prince at Canterbury, for though sword, dagger and spurs have
been lost, the helm with its crest, and cap of maintenance, tabard
targe, gauntlets and scabbard are still there. Fairly complete
achievements of later date can be found in St. Mary Redcliffe
Bristol, Kingston and Chevening in Kent, and Kimbolton (Hunts)
while single specimens of medieval armour, surviving from such
achievements, are quite often to be seen. The custom of decorat
ing the tombs of the great with their armorial trophies fell into
disuse in the 17th century, though its tradition lingered on in the
armorial hatchments which, almost within living memory, were
hung up in front of houses after the master of the house had died
and afterwards placed in the parish church. Large numbers of
these lozenge-shaped boards painted with coats of arms can still
be seen hanging in parish churches, amongst others at Heacham
(Norfolk), where the Rolfe hatchments recall the introduction of
an exotic royalty, the Princess Pocahontas, into English village
life.

Occasionally one can measure some of the forces which shaped
English history by following the rise and fall of a single family
on their tombs in various churches. Among the first of the great
merchant princes of England was William de la Pole whose effigy,
with that of his wife Katherine, can be seen in Holy Trinity church
at Hull, where he made that vast fortune which enabled him to
finance the wars of Edward III and thus to win the title of knight
banneret and baron of the Exchequer. His son, Sir Michael, served
as Admiral of the Fleet and was created Earl of Suffolk but died in
exile. The second Earl died of fever at the siege of Harfleur in
1415 but his body was brought back to Wingfield (Suffolk) where
his tomb bears wooden effigies of the earl and his wife. The widow
of William de la Pole, first Duke of Suffolk, lies in one of the most
beautiful medieval tombs in England, at Ewelme (Oxon), where
she and her husband founded the little hospital. Returning to
Wingfield we see the superb effigies of John de la Pole, second
Duke of Suffolk, and his wife Elizabeth Plantagenet, sister of
Edward IV, marking at once the apogee of the fortunes of this
merchant dynasty and the cause of their decline. When the

Tudors came to the throne they systematically suppressed all descendants of the Plantagenets, including the de la Poles.[19]

The Lords Spiritual had considerable influence upon church-building. As it was not considered necessary for a man to be in priest's orders before holding ecclesiastical preferments, provided that these did not involve the cure of souls, many Clerks of the King's Works were rewarded for their purely secular services by being appointed to benefices. William of Wykeham was not the only bishop of whom it might have been said that he was literally the architect of his own fortunes. It used to be thought that this great administrator was also a practising architect and, although most of the artistic credit has now been transferred to his Master Mason, William of Winford, we should not therefore underestimate the importance in architectural history of the appointment, as Chancellor of England, of a man whose enlightened taste in matters of design and widespread contacts probably influenced patronage in all parts of the country, and may have contributed to the rapid spread of the Perpendicular style. One of the first parish churches to show Perpendicular features is Edington (Wilts), built by Bishop Edington, Wykeham's early employer, and it is sometimes said that Wykeham designed this church, which was begun in 1352. Even if we suppose that this tradition only meant that Wykeham brought to the Bishop sketches made by a Royal Mason when he visited Hampshire in the King's service, it may still serve as an example of the part played by bishops in architectural development.

A case in which the movements of an individual can definitely be connected with the migration of a stylistic peculiarity is that of Walter Skirlaw, who was Bishop of Bath and Wells from 1386–8 and who, in 1403, built a chapel in his native village of Skirlaugh (Yorks, E.R.) on which his arms are prominently displayed.* The tower of Skirlaugh church is clearly derived from the Somerset towers, although details of construction show that it was built by local men.[20] It became the model for a group of Yorkshire towers which show western influence. Sometimes the bishops imported their new ideas from the Continent whither they went on

---

* Skirlaw's arms (which also appear on the tower of Howden (Yorks, E.R.) towards the building of which he left a legacy of £40) show six wands bent in the fashion of a sieve, perhaps an allusion to his father's trade of sieve-maker.

O

pilgrimage, on diplomatic missions, if they stood high in the King's favour, or into exile if they did not. It seems more than co-incidental that in several cases where English churches resemble those on the Continent the bishop concerned should have known the foreign original. The early use of the pointed arch and cross vault at Durham has been associated by M. Rivoira[21] with Bishop William of Carilef's journey to Rome, during which he may have seen similar vaulting at Montefiascone. Three foreign cathedrals which have transeptal towers were known to Bishop Grandisson who not only spared the Norman towers of Exeter cathedral in his rebuilding but reproduced this unusual feature in his church at Ottery St. Mary (Devon).[22] When the famous Judgment Porch at Lincoln was built in 1260, Bishop Richard of Gravesend had recently been to France and had probably seen the wonderful new portals of Amiens cathedral,[23] while the taste for profuse ornament which characterises Bishop Alcock's chantry chapel at Ely cathedral may have been formed when he was ambassador to the Court of Castile in 1470.

The influence of this last-named bishop upon the architectural schemes of his diocese is a matter of record and he acted as Comptroller of the King's Works for some years during the reign of Henry VII. His badge appears in the windows at Little Malvern (Worcs), All Saints', York and Madingley (Cambs), and is carved on a corbel in Great St. Mary's church, Cambridge, and on the woodwork of Wilburton church (Cambs) as well as on his chantry chapel in Ely cathedral. This badge, a cock standing on a globe, is typical of the punning devices by which we can often recognise an allusion to a bishop's share in building churches. The hart-lying-down of Bishop Lyhart at Norwich, the beacon-on-a-tun of Bishop Beckington at Wells and the large eye, beside a man falling from a tree, of Abbot Islip in Westminster Abbey, are some of the most famous examples. Occasionally a rebus may throw light on the provenance of objects removed from their original church.[24] The rebus of Abbot Heslington (a hazel twig fixed in a tun) on one of two fine bench-ends in Aysgarth church (Yorks) suggests that they came from Jervaulx Abbey, and another pair in Leake (Yorks) probably came from the Augustinian house at Bridlington for they bear the rebuses of Prior John Hompton (a figure of St. John the Baptist holding a book, on which lies a lamb, standing on a tun tabelled Homp) and Sub-Prior Peter Hardy (crossed keys on a shield labelled Harde).

The heads of bishops appear on corbels and capitals in many churches. One on the screen at Ottery St. Mary may represent Bishop Grandisson; in the choir of Adderbury (Oxon) the allusion is perhaps to William of Wykeham, for the living belonged to New College, but in most cases no identification is possible. The enigmatic eyes of wood or stone which look down upon us may have studied the plans for the building in which we stand and contributed to its beauty by their constructive criticism, but ignorance prevents us from expressing the gratitude we owe.

It would be an incoherent study of medieval life which took no account of the gradually increasing force of the Common Law to whose rule the brilliant personages whom we have been considering grew progressively more obedient. From the beginning of the 15th century onwards we find monuments to eminent judges, the most sumptuous being perhaps that to Sir Richard Choke, *c.* 1483, in Long Ashton church (Somerset), which has a canopy composed of angels' wings. I think the most striking memorial to medieval Law is the effigy of Chief Justice Gascoigne (died 1419) at Harewood (Yorks). The close-fitting hood and long robes make a severe pattern of lines from which the stern face, a little battered by time, looks out with as much dignity surely as on the day when its original bade the Heir Apparent to the Throne submit his wild will to the Common Law. Let us remember here the words which Shakespeare puts into the mouth of the newly crowned Henry V:

> You did commit me:
> For which, I do commit into your hand
> The unstained sword that you have us'd to bear;
> With this remembrance, that you use the same
> With the like bold, just and impartial spirit
> As you have done 'gainst me.
>
> (*Henry IV*, Pt. II, Act V, Scene ii.)

The battle between force and law is unending, its participants are innumerable, and the long retrospect of English history, shown in our churches, should fill us, not only with pride, but with a sense of trusteeship for the future.

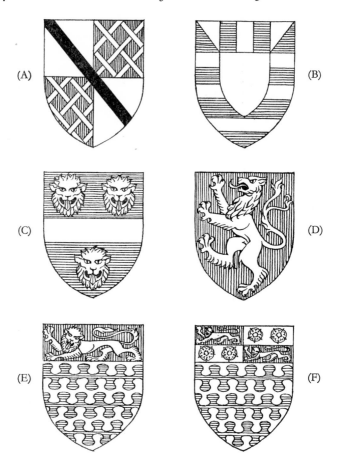

FIG. 16. Coats of arms

(A)—LE DESPENSER: Quarterly argent, and gules fretty or, over all a bend sable.
(B)—MORTIMER: Barry, a chief paly and corners gyronny, or and azure, an escutcheon argent.
(C)—DE LA POLE: Azure a fess between three leopards' faces or.
(D)—SIMON DE MONTFORT: Gules, a lion rampant queue fourchée argent.
(E)—MERCHANTS OF THE STAPLE: Barry nebuly of six argent and azure, chief gules a lion passant, guardant or.
(F)—MERCHANT ADVENTURERS: Barry nebuly of six argent and azure, a chief quarterly gules and or; 1 and 4 a lion passant, guardant or, 2 and 3 two roses gules, barbed vert.

Chapter 2

THE CRUSADERS

THE ENGLISH have always been inveterate globe-trotters, and at all periods the motives for their journeys have been mixed. In the Middle Ages, curiosity and love of adventure mingled with the piety which sent men on pilgrimages, or to the Crusades. As navigation and commerce became more developed, they went further afield and brought back more exotic reminders of their travels. The growth of the British Empire, and of the naval power on which it was founded, is reflected in the many monuments which commemorate men who worked, and often died, in remote places, and the long, biographical epitaphs of some 19th-century monuments can be read as chapters of history. A complete change in the style of church architecture was brought about in the 18th century, largely through the influence of those who had made the Grand Tour of Europe. So, in the next few chapters we will consider the traces which these returning travellers have left in our churches.

During the period of the Crusades, increased contact with the countries of the Mediterranean influenced English art. The domains of Henry II stretched from the Cheviots to the Pyrenees and the carvers of Poitiers and Bordeaux had more influence upon English sculpture than those of Normandy.[1] An ornamental motif, half-bird, half-leaf, which occurs both at Rochester cathedral and Poitiers is an example of this. Although the First Crusade received little support from England it included the only episode directly illustrated on any English church. A carving over the south door of Fordington church in Dorchester, shows the miraculous appearance of St. George during the siege of Antioch in 1098 (Plate 17). The saint is shown on horseback, thrusting down his enemies with his lance while other Seljuks are shown kneeling in his wake. The subject is probably repeated on a Norman tympanum at Damerham (Hants) and perhaps on the capitals of the chancel arch at Wakerley (Northants). With the possible exception of a wall-painting of St. George at Hardham (Sussex), in which it has been thought possible to discern prostrate figures, these carvings are the only memorials of a miracle which made such a lasting impression upon the English in the 14th century that St. George replaced Edward the Confessor as the national patron saint.

The most important outcome of the Crusades for our present purpose was the foundation of the two great Military Orders, the Knights Hospitallers and the Knights Templars, although these have left fewer traces upon English churches than might have been expected from the extent of their possessions when their power was at its zenith. Both Orders set up Houses in London. The western bays of the crypt of St. John's church, Clerkenwell, may have been part of the Hospitallers' first church, founded about 1140, while its eastern bays, with their side chapels, are probably part of the later building consecrated by Heraclius, Patriarch of Jerusalem, in 1185. The foundations of the original round nave are marked on the ground at the west end of the present church. The finest remaining relic of the Priory is St. John's Gate, built in the beginning of the 16th century, under Prior Docwra whose arms appear on a shield on the south front and on the bosses under the arch.

The circular foundations of the Templars' first church in London were temporarily uncovered during building operations in Holborn, and their second church, in the Strand, was bombed in the Second World War but afterwards reconstructed. One of the most widely believed fallacies about English architecture is that all round churches were built by the Knights Templar. Actually, out of five surviving examples, three, those at Cambridge, Northampton and in Ludlow Castle, had no connection with either Order, and the 14th-century church at Little Maplestead (Essex) was built by the Hospitallers. They were, however, all inspired by the Church of the Holy Sepulchre at Jerusalem, and the church at Northampton was founded, *c.* 1100, by Earl Simon de Senlis, perhaps as a thank-offering for his safe return from the First Crusade.[2] All Templar churches originally had small chancels, since the Knights were often unlettered and did not take part in the services.[3] Several circular churches which were built by one or other of the Military Orders are known to have existed, although only their foundations remain. Amongst these we may mention

Dover (Kent), West Thurrock (Essex),* Aslackby and Temple Bruer in Lincolnshire, Garway (Herefs) and Orphir in the Orkneys. The circular plan eventually went out of fashion, and the Commanderies of Swingfield and Sutton-at-Hone in Kent had 13th-century rectangular chapels, as had also that at Yeaveley (Derbs), amongst whose ruins can still be seen a gravestone inscribed with a cross and a sword. The much restored chapel of Temple Balsall (Warcs) is also rectangular.

After the dramatic trial of the Templars in the early 14th century most of their English preceptories passed into the hands of the Hospitallers who, although even wealthier than their rivals, had maintained a justification for their existence by their occupation of the island of Rhodes, whence their ships attacked Moslem vessels and rescued Christian galley slaves. They also cared for the sick and wounded. This tradition of helpfulness also applied to the English Houses of the Hospitallers. When Bishop Henry de Blois founded the Hospital of St. Cross at Winchester in 1136 he placed it under the direction of the Knights of St. John and their connection with it lasted for about a hundred years.[4] The old men who are cared for today in that enduring monument of human kindness wear the black cloak with the cross of the Hospitallers on the left breast, and any travellers may ask there for a dole of bread and ale.

At Garway (Herefs) the fine Norman chancel arch of the parish church does not immediately suggest any association with the Templars, although the transverse moulding carved across each voussoir, an unusual feature which also occurs at Winchfield (Hants), may have been copied from the decoration of the Bab el Foutouh at Cairo, built *c.* 1090.[5] Close inspection will show that, on the south side, the bases and capitals curve markedly outwards, following the original line of the round nave, although those on the north side have been cut back into alignment with the later wall. Several stone grave-slabs of the 13th century, which may have marked the graves of Templars, have been re-used as steps in various parts of the church. Such tombs are often the only traces we shall find of a lost preceptory. A coffin lid with the insignia of the Templars in the church at Selborne (Hants) marks

---

* Uncovered in 1912. The west tower covers most of the site of the original round nave.

their former possession of this manor, and the cross of the Hospitallers also appears on tombs here and at St. Mary Bourne and Michelmersh. The Hospitallers were extensive landlords, and some of the churches connected with them may only have been built for their tenants. Thus the chapel at North Baddesley (Hants) was built on lands granted to their House at Godsfield, where remains of the chapel can be seen. A tomb marked with the cross of the Hospitallers stands in the chancel at North Baddesley.[6]

Scotland has preserved an interesting memorial of the Hospitallers at Torphichen (Linlithgowshire) where their church looks, appropriately enough, more like a fortress than a shrine. A 17th-century parish church has been built over the nave, but the long narrow choir and transepts and the massive central tower remain. The upper storeys of the tower and some rooms over the transepts are said to have formed part of the Hospital.[7]

There is a romantic glamour about the memory of the Crusades which seems to inspire picturesque, but inaccurate, theories with regard to their traces. Just as all round churches are supposed to have been built by the Templars, so all cross-legged effigies are often said to represent men who went to the Crusades, while the straight-legged ones stayed at home. Actually, this fashion, which is peculiarly English, did not become popular until the mid-13th century, when the great period of Crusading was almost over, and since most of the knightly effigies made during the next hundred years were shown with crossed legs, the supporters of this theory must credit English man-power with having played a bigger part in the Crusades than history will warrant.[8] Some cross-legged effigies may indeed commemorate Crusaders. A fine Purbeck marble effigy in the nave of Salisbury cathedral is said to be that of William, Earl of Salisbury who fought under St. Louis and died at Mansourah in 1250, but we must always be on our guard against identifications of such effigies based only on this attitude, without corroborating evidence from either records or heraldry. The fine cross-legged knight in Dorchester Abbey (Oxon) (Plate 92), has been described as commemorating someone who fell in the Second Crusade of 1146–9 although the fashion of its arms and the style of the carving show that it dates from the very end of the 13th century.

It is harder to say why this fashion did develop; perhaps it strengthened the effigy at a thin place, or merely gave it a definitely recumbent look. The art of the effigy emerged slowly out of that of the memorial slab on which a standing figure was represented, and the extent to which an effigy reclines on its tomb, instead of apparently standing on a corbel, is an indication of the progress of this development. Although the cross-legged effigies have no direct connexion with the Crusades, it is possible that these inspired the still more animated pose of knightly effigies introduced *c.* 1260 and which expresses the conception that the soul's salvation, like knightly honour, could be won at the sword's point. If it was the Templars who were first represented in effigy as ready to start up drawing their swords, the position would have been as typical of their religious duties as the gesture of blessing adopted for episcopal effigies.[9]

One reminder of the Crusades which is often seen, but less often recognised as such, is the heraldic 'mantling' or decorative scrollwork attached to a helmet (Plate 84). This represents the linen covering which was actually worn to mitigate the effect of the fierce sun beating on a steel helm.

Since it was not the custom until after 1400 to inscribe a name upon a tomb, and the painted heraldry which made this seem unnecessary has now faded utterly, we can rarely identify any early tomb. An effigy at Loversall (Yorks) shows a man in civilian dress with a sword and a shield carved with a cross *formy*, who may have been a member of one of the Military Orders, but there is no doubt about the tomb at Rushton (Northants) on which the effigy wears the robes of office of a Grand Prior. He is Sir Thomas Tresham (died 1559) who was Grand Prior of the Hospitallers during the brief revival of the Order under Queen Mary, and his memorial may serve as the logical end of this chapter.

Chapter 3

THE PILGRIMS

THE PILGRIMS to the Holy Sepulchre at Jerusalem, whom the fighting Orders were originally founded to protect, were less influential, in our present context, than those who went to Santiago de Compostela and who sometimes reproduced in English churches details which they had noticed on their journeys. A particularly interesting example of such copying by an observant pilgrim concerns a group of 12th-century Herefordshire churches which are so individual in the style of their ornamental sculpture that all seem likely to have been produced by the same workshop. The earliest church in this group was built at Shobdon and a Priory was founded there by Oliver de Merlimond, steward to the Lord of Wigmore, who is known to have gone on pilgrimage to Santiago when the work was started. He travelled through France, staying with the canons of Saint-Victor in Paris, and may have taken his master carver with him.[1] De Merlimond's church was pulled down in the 18th century but its two doorways, with sculptured tympana, were re-erected in Shobdon Park as a landscape ornament. Although now almost obliterated by weathering, the sculpture of these doorways shows the same mixture of the wiry interlacings seen on some late Saxon crosses, and in Scandinavian stave churches, with sculptural motives copied from French and Spanish churches, which characterises the better preserved work at Kilpeck, and Rowlstone and on the later fonts of Eardisley and Castle Frome (Plate 33). Professor Zarnecki has pointed out the resemblance between the small human figures placed one above the other on the shafts of the chancel arch at Kilpeck and the treatment of figures on the famous *Puerta de las Platerias* of the cathedral at Compostela He also suggested that the carvings of Samson and the lion and of a mounted man riding down an opponent on the tympana at Parthenay-le-Vieux (one of the churches visited by pilgrims on the way from Paris to Santiago) had furnished models for the Samson tympanum at Stretton Sugwas, and the St. George at Brinsop. The French sculptor is thought to have modelled his horseman on a Roman statue of Marcus Aurelius, then mistakenly supposed to represent Constantine the Great, and in Herefordshire the design was further changed by its fusion in the carver's memory with the mythology of his Viking ancestors. The two birds placed fore and aft of the saint have no place in his legend but a similar design on a king's helmet of the early Viking period, found near Uppsala, shows Odin on horseback attacking a great serpent with his spear, and accompanied by his two magic ravens.[3]

We are constantly reminded of the pilgrims who sought the shrine of St. James at Compostela, by the imagery which represents this saint wearing their distinctive dress. On a desk-end at Yarcombe (Devon) (Plate 60) we see him wearing the large hat turned up in front with the scallop shell badge of a pilgrim to Compostela. He holds a pilgrim's staff and his small pouch, or scrip, hangs from a strap crossing his chest.

The legend of St. James does not explain why he was particularly associated with the scallop shell, and some English representations, such as the windows at Doddiscombleigh (Devon) and East Brent (Som) show his robe trimmed with other shells, so it has been suggested that St. James absorbed the cult of some local sea god.[4] The East Brent window, together with others at Malvern, Coombe (Oxon) and St. Peter Hungate, Norwich, show St. James with a slender rod strapped to his staff. The Cathedral of Compostella still venerates the staff of St. James and a carving on the *Puerta de las Platerias* shows the saint, without attributes, standing between two trees from which the side shoots have apparently been lopped. These may record a custom of giving pilgrims a rod cut from some special trees as a memento, for a hazel rod, together with some shells, was found in the tomb of Bishop Richard Mayo (died 1516) in Hereford cathedral.[5] On the tomb of Sir Richard Vernon at Tong (Salop) St. James has two rods strapped to his staff.

Sometimes we find in churches memorials of individual pilgrims who, perhaps, died on their way to his shrine. A much battered effigy in St. Mary's church, Haverfordwest, is identified as a pilgrim by the scallop-shells on its scrip, while the recumbent effigy in the church of Ashby-de-la-Zouch (Leics) must have represented a man of consequence, for he wears the SS collar with his pilgrim's dress, both hat and scrip being adorned with scallop-shells. To neither of these tombs has a name been attached, but a pilgrim shown in a window at Cockington (Devon) is said to represent Robert Cary who went to Compostela.[6]

Pilgrimage to the Holy Land cost an ordinary pilgrim about a hundred marks of silver in the 12th century,[7] and even a journey to Rome or Compostela was so expensive that many guilds made provision for helping their members who wished to go on a pilgrimage. The rules of both the Guild of the Resurrection and the Fullers' Guild, at Lincoln, provided that their members should accompany the pilgrim to the city gates and there contribute to his expenses, and also welcome him on his return.[7] The window set up by the Palmers' Guild at Ludlow, although much restored, provides us with many illustrations of pilgrim life. We see the pilgrims receiving from St. John, in the Holy Land, the ring which Edward the Confessor had given in alms to the saint, taking him for a beggar. They fulfil the saint's command to return the ring and are shown receiving from the king the charter of the Palmers' Guild. Other panels show them walking in a procession, followed by choristers and being welcomed by the leading citizens of Ludlow.[8] All members of the Guild felt that they had thus, to some extent, shared in the spiritual benefits of the pilgrimage.

For those who could not undertake the hazards of foreign pilgrimage there were many shrines in Britain which attracted large numbers of pilgrims. Canterbury inevitably dominates our mental picture of such pilgrimages, but Glastonbury, Walsingham, Peterborough, Holywell, St. David's, St. Andrew's, to name but a few, attracted many pilgrims, and each county boasted some churches whose holy relics were thought to have the power to alleviate sickness, whether of body or soul.

A modest example of one of these local shrines can be seen at Whitchurch Canonicorum (Dorset), where the leaden reliquary containing the body of St. Candida survives inside the stone tomb-chest, the sides of which are pierced with three holes through which the pilgrims stretched their hands to touch it. Another unusual relic of pilgrimages is the 13th-century inscription on brass by the south door of the chapel of St. Catherine, on the hill overlooking Milton Abbey, which promises to worshippers in this holy place an indulgence of 110 days. This chapel marks the spot where St. Samson of Dol appeared to King Athelstan and foretold his victory at Brunnanburgh; the earthworks which surround the chapel are sometimes said to have defended the camp of his army.

The old Norfolk term for the Milky Way, 'the Walsingham Way', recalls the phial containing some drops of the Virgin's milk, that was shown to pilgrims in the great Abbey which grew up round a small wooden chapel, reputed to have been constructed under the instruction of Our Lady, as a copy of the Casa Santa at Nazareth. Pilgrims coming to Walsingham could also have visited the strange Red Mount Chapel at King's Lynn, built by Robert Corraunce in 1483 to house a relic of the Virgin. The double staircase in the octagonal outer shell of brick allowed them to circulate freely through the cruciform, vaulted central chamber in which the relic was doubtless displayed. Still nearer to their goal they passed Houghton-in-the-Dale, where the charming little 14th-century 'Slipper Chapel' recalls that here the pilgrims (including Henry VIII) doffed their shoes and walked the last two miles to Walsingham barefoot.

Holywell (Flint) drew thousands of pilgrims to St. Winifred's shrine, and, in the valley by which they approached it, can be seen the stones marking the stations at which they prayed. An inconspicuous mark of their further journey over the wild Welsh hills to St. David's can be seen on the hill behind Nevern church. By the side of a narrow hill path the laminated face of natural rock has been carved with a cross in low relief, and below is the niche, also marked with a cross, in which the pilgrims knelt in prayer.

Offerings made by pilgrims and other travellers were an important source of revenue to medieval churches. A pilgrim was despatched to Walsingham under Katherine of Aragon's will with 200 nobles to distribute in charity on the way. Some of the churches lying on, or near, the so-called Pilgrims' Way, leading along the Downs from Winchester to Canterbury show unusual features which seem to have been connected with the display of relics to large crowds of pilgrims. At Compton (Surrey) the east walls of a small Norman church were strengthened in the late 12th or early 13th century, and an upper chapel was built over the High Altar. The low wooden screen which fences the open edge of this upper chapel is said to be contemporary with it, and may be the oldest surviving screenwork in any English church. This alteration must have been made at the time when pilgrims first began to flock towards Canterbury. On a hill overlooking the river by Guildford stands the ruined chapel of St. Catherine which is remarkable because of its five doorways, two of them built into window spaces above the north and south entrances. It has been suggested that these upper doors were reached by wooden stairs from without and gave access to an interior gallery from which relics could be viewed.[9] A similar use of a double staircase to avoid congestion was tried in the north porch at Grantham (Lincs) where holy relics were displayed in an upper chamber, and this church also has two external stairs leading to the crypt. This feature is also found in the 12th-century crypt at Berkswell (Warcs). At Wrotham (Kent), where the Archbishops of Canterbury had one of their Palaces, the stairs to the rood-loft are continued up to a passage over the chancel arch, in the thickness of the wall, from which windows look down upon both chancel and nave as if from a watching loft.

At Harbledown, about a mile from Canterbury, the parish church was originally the chapel of one of our oldest leper hospitals, where Henry II stopped, on his penitential pilgrimage, before continuing the journey, barefoot, and the yearly grant of money with which he endowed it is still paid. In the church is the alms box which used to be chained to a tree outside so that pilgrims could insert their offerings without coming dangerously near.

Until Henry VIII declared open war upon the cult of St. Thomas, as affording an unpleasantly apt parallel to his own strife with the Church, there was probably some reminder of the martyr in every church in the country, for a surprisingly large number still remains, although the King's men broke and defaced all that they could find.[10] Bosses were too high to be reached, as at Exeter and Norwich, and wall-paintings could either be preserved by a coat of whitewash, as was probably done to the fine single figures at Hauxton (Cambs) and Hadleigh (Essex), or altered to avoid offence. An interesting example of the latter method can be seen at Earl Stonham (Suffolk) where a martyrdom of St. Thomas, painted *c.* 1400, was later transformed into the execution of an unspecified female saint.[11]

Many fine retables in which the Nottingham alabaster carvers had illustrated scenes of the Archbishop's career were probably destroyed, but single panels can be seen at Elham (Kent), and St. Mary's church, Nottingham. At Elham we see Becket blandly defying both the anger of Henry II and the drawn sword of one of his retainers, at the Great Council held at Northampton, in October 1164, which marked the climax of their strife (Plate 40), and the panel at Nottingham shows him laying his case before Pope Alexander III. The scene of the Archbishop's home-coming is shown in a window at Nettlestead (Kent) where the monks of Canterbury are depicted welcoming him. A wall-painting, at Pickering (Yorks), shows him in defiant parley with the knights, before their murderous onslaught, and a carving of this subject on a boss in the Norwich cloisters makes clear its lesson by representing two hideous demons standing behind the knights. At Bramley (Hants) there is a realistic 13th-century painting which avoids the usual mistake of showing Becket vested for Mass and kneeling at an altar. Here he is shown in the cassock and fur-lined mantellum which he probably wore when the frightened monks hurried him into the cathedral.

A wall-painting at South Newington (Oxon) follows the general tradition of the scene of martyrdom. Reginald Fitzurse, stung by Becket's denunciation of his treachery, strikes a vertical blow which is averted by the faithful Grim. The second knight cleaves Becket's skull, the third stands by with sword bared and the fourth is shown in the act of drawing his weapon. This wall-painting gains in interest by its association with another, unique, so far as I know, in English churches, showing the execution of Thomas, Earl of Lancaster, at Pontefract in 1322 (Plate 3). Although history tells us little positive good of the rebel Earl's life, he was acclaimed as a saint and Froissart records that 'many fair miracles' were performed at his tomb, in the Priory church of Pontefract, which has been destroyed. Official disapproval expressed by the Archbishop of York as well as by King Edward II did not lessen popular fervour, and Parliament demanded his canonisation.[12] Reverence paid to the tombs of those whom the King had put to death was quite a usual way of expressing opposition to the Crown in the Middle Ages. In spite of the fact that Simon de Montfort died excommunicate, Henry III had to forbid his people to regard him as a saint, and miracles were freely reported by those who went on pilgrimages to his tomb in the Abbey of Evesham.[13] The decoration of the little church of South Newington may have been ordered by one who wished to express thereby his hostility to royal authority. Thomas of Lancaster is shown wearing a rich striped mantle, and shoes of lattice work; he kneels with an expression of beatific detachment, although the blood spurts from a wound in his neck, for the executioner's first blow miscarried. The man's half-obliterated figure is contorted by the effort with which he prepares to give the second stroke.[14]

The posthumous triumph of St. Thomas is not often shown. In the stained glass at Checkley (Staffs) and in a window from Rollright church, now in the Bodleian Library, Henry II is shown being scourged at the tomb. Two bosses in the cloisters at Norwich illustrate his penance: in the first he kneels, wearing only his shirt and his crown, before a figure, now headless, presumably a monk, so it may represent his arrival, barefoot, at Canterbury; the second boss shows him being scourged, the ornate sides of the saint's tomb showing in the background, and an attendant standing by with a cloak to throw over the King's shoulders when the last stripe had been inflicted (Plate 71). Yet another boss at Norwich shows the translation of the body of St. Thomas.

St. Thomas' power to heal the sick who invoked his aid was far famed. A window at Nettlestead (Kent) shows a monk standing by the Altar of Martyrdom with his hand on the shoulder of a child and beckoning to two other figures,[15] but the finest representation of his miracles are naturally those in the glass of Canterbury cathedral. These show us not only the original tomb and the magnificent shrine which replaced it, but also illustrate some of the procedures of medieval faith-healing. In several panels of the Canterbury windows pilgrims are shown laying upon the shrine coils of pale cord. It was the practice in the 12th century to measure either the whole body of the sick person, both in length and breadth, or only the afflicted limb, and then to offer a corresponding length of candles to the saint. In the background of the panel shown on Plate 21 two monks stand by a reading-desk, one holding a slim rod, with which, perhaps, he has measured the cord, and the other pointing to an open book which, if we are inclined to make dangerous guesses, may have been the ledger in which such offerings were recorded. In the St. William window of York Minster we can see a man having his injured leg measured, in one panel, while another shows us the wax model of his leg being offered at the saint's shrine.

Monastic chroniclers recorded many marvellous cures at the shrines of saints, and their accounts form an interesting comparison with the treatment of psychosomatic cases today.[16] Our picture of medieval pilgrimages will be too brightly coloured if we base it solely on Chaucer. Along the roads by which his pilgrims rode so happily, the sick and maimed dragged themselves, sometimes with incredible endurance, towards the shrines where lay their last hope of cure, and lunatics were driven forward, bound and beaten, to wake the echoes of the great churches with their eldritch screams.

Chapter 4

MERCHANTS AND MARINERS

IN THE Age of Faith the wealth of a district was reflected in its churches and we may reasonably conclude that any area in which almost every village has a fine medieval church was once an important centre of the wool trade upon which the national economy depended. The great 'wool churches' of East Anglia, the Cotswolds, Somerset, and parts of Yorkshire, remain as memorials of the power, as well as the piety, of the 15th and 16th century clothiers who built them, while we are more likely to find small Norman churches left unaltered in areas which did not share in this prosperity. The curious ground plans of some Midland churches show that, during long periods of moderate affluence, the parishioners made minor improvements to their church, but could never afford to pull it down and start afresh.

English churches show an extraordinary variety of plan due largely to the piecemeal addition of chantry chapels, either by wealthy individuals, or by guilds.[1] The curious projection at the south-west corner of Burford church (Oxon) is the 13th-century guild chapel, which was originally detached, and differently orientated, but was joined to the parish church in the 15th century. The building accounts of Bodmin church give the names of forty guilds which were concerned in the work. At Coventry, in the 16th century, the aisles of St. Michael's (later the cathedral) were doubled in order to accommodate six guild chapels, now only commemorated by tablets fixed to the scorched shell of the outer walls. Chapels belonging to the Dyers, Mercers, Butchers and Tanners, as well as to the fraternity of Corpus Christi were added to Holy Trinity Church, Coventry, obscuring its cruciform plan. The connection between the guilds and the parish church was particularly close at Cirencester where four of the town's guilds had chapels in the church and the rooms in the great three-storied south porch were used as Guild Halls. This church is rich in heraldry, carved on the capitals of the nave or painted on the remaining fragments of ancient glass. The hierarchy of these shields ranges from the arms of England, impaling France, through those of many ancient and noble families to the merchants' marks of clothiers who contributed to the building costs.[2] In the upper part of the east window we see both the merchant's mark of the Garstang family and their coat of arms: three mascles or and a chief azure. These devices recur on corbels in the south aisle and also on the tomb of Henry Garstang (1464). On the capitals of the north side of the nave we see the marks of two other merchant benefactors, Henry Tapper, grocer, and Robert Rychards who founded a chantry. Women's heads are carved on shields, recalling those who left bequests: in one case the name is added: *Alys Avening*.

Medieval donors did not let their munificence pass unrecorded, for the release of their souls from Purgatory might depend upon the grateful prayers of their successors. The donor of a 16th-century screen at Fritton (Norfolk), John Bacon, is painted on one panel together with his wife and their many children. At Tiverton (Devon) the carved decoration on the exterior of the south aisle contains so many references to the trading activities of its founder, John Greenaway, as to be almost a carved biography. More often we see only the merchants' marks of the donors on the corbels, capitals or bench-ends of the churches they helped to build, and the social rise of the Spring family of Lavenham (Suffolk) can be traced from the variants of their merchant's mark on the base of the tower to their coat of arms at its summit.

These merchants' marks (Fig. 17) were used, like the badges of noblemen, to identify their belongings. In an illiterate age it was obviously essential to use markings on woolsacks, or other packages, which could be readily recognised, particularly when goods were carried by sea, since, to spread the risk of loss, one ship might carry many small consignments belonging to different people. The basic elements of some of the marks we see in churches resemble characters of the ancient Runic alphabet and the earliest personal marks are thought to have been derived from the devices, often including runes, which were displayed on the roofs of houses, as protective symbols.[3] Many marks include a cross, which often has stylised streamers, or pennons, attached to its shaft. As we have seen (page 96), a bannered cross was always associated with the Agnus Dei, a symbol particularly appropriate for those who dealt in wool, and it may have been through careless repetition of such crosses, with their drooping pennons, that a reversed 4 became a common element in merchants' marks, particularly in the wool trade.

Sometimes the tools of a trade are shown on buildings perhaps financed from its profits. Thus a pair of shears is shown on buttresses of the Lane aisle at Cullompton (Devon), the tower of Fairford (Glos) and a wall-plate at Cirencester (Glos). A bench-end at Spaxton (Som) shows a fuller surrounded by various implements and working on a length of cloth. At Darley Dale (Derbs) a 17th-century tomb-chest is ornamented with carvings of a bobbin, spinning-wheel, loom and what looks like a pair of lazy-tongs.[4] The distaffs which figure in so many illustrations of domestic life remind us that, in the Middle Ages, every woman was a spinster in the literal sense of the word.

The names of some successful wool merchants, together with an impression of their general appearance in dress and accoutrements, if not their actual portraits, are recorded on many fine monumental brasses.[5] Northleach (Glos) has perhaps the greatest number, but others can be seen at Chipping Campden and Lechlade (Glos), Witney, Thame and Chipping Norton (Oxon), Wymington (Beds) and Linwood (Lincs) to name only a few. Their surprising rarity in Norfolk (there is one at Mattishall) is perhaps due to the diligence of 17th-century Puritans in destroying any monument on which prayers were solicited for the souls of the departed.

The importance of the wool trade must not make us overlook traces of the contributions made by less affluent professions. The Free Miners of the Forest of Dean formed a corporation with special privileges confirmed by ancient customs[6] and their arms, six picks and two shovels, are faintly carved upon the font in Abinghall church (Glos) together with the horseshoes and tongs of the Free Smiths arms. On a fragmentary brass in Newland church (Glos) (Plate 84) the figure of a Free Miner is shown as a crest. He wears a cap and his breeches are fastened below the knee with thongs. He holds a candlestick between his teeth, and a mattock in one hand while a hod is fastened to his shoulders. Another figure of a miner, with pick and bucket, appears on a stone slab at Wirksworth (Derbs). These figures are anonymous but on the desk fronts in the chancel at St. Ives (Corn) we see busts of Ralph Clies, smith, and his wife, surrounded by his tools. In the north aisle of York Minster, the window presented in 1380 by Richard Tunnoc, bell-founder, illustrates two of the processes of his trade.

The general destruction of the stained glass and statuary which occurred at the Reformation has made it impossible to estimate, by the relative popularity of various saints, the importance of the guilds which honoured them as their patrons, yet it was probably often by paying for a representation of their patron saint that the smaller trade fraternities contributed to the decoration of their parish churches. We know that individual members of guilds who made gifts to their parish churches were so influenced in their choice of subjects. In his will, dated 1481, John Walker of York made bequests to the city guilds of Corpus Christi and of 'the Holy Martyrs Christopher and George'.[7] Eleven years before, he had given a window to Holy Trinity Goodramgate, York, in which is shown the figure of God the Father holding the body of the dead Christ, in the centre, while the saints in the outer lights are SS. Christopher and George. These two guilds were of a semi-political character, and references to them are often connected with matters of civic authority. The kneeling men and women painted on the screen panels in St. Matthew's church, Ipswich, may have been members of the Guild of St. Erasmus which was connected with this church.

On many 16th-century brasses we find the arms of the Merchant Companies, either placed as single shields in the corners of the slab of stone, or in conjunction with the merchant's mark of the dead man.[8] The arms most commonly seen are those of the Merchant Adventurers which were incorporated in 1296 (Fig. 16); examples can be seen at Ipswich (Suffolk) on the brass of Thomas Pownder in St. Mary Quay, and on those of John Terri, in St. John Maddermarket, Norwich, and Robert Chapman at Stone (Kent). The inscription of this last tells us that

what tyme he lyvved was he
Esquier and Marchaunte Venturer of London Draper ffree,

and most Merchant Adventurers were also members of a Trade Company. We find the '*demi-virgin*' of the Mercers' Company on brasses at Antingham (Norfolk), Hinxworth and Digswell (Herts) and Lambourne (Essex), and in 16th-century glass at Stonesfield (Oxon). The leopards' heads and covered cups of the Goldsmiths' Company are engraved on brasses at Sandon (Essex), Thorpe (Surrey) and Datchet (Bucks). The three crowns and caps of the Skinners appear on the brass of William Shosmyth, 'pelliparius' of London, at Mereworth (Kent) and the Drapers' three clouds surmounted by triple crowns at Stone (Kent) and Walthamstow (Essex). The Grocers' arms are engraved on the brass of Raulf Grenewey (1558) at Wiveton (Norfolk). Sometimes a Company had more than one grant of arms; on a brass in St. Helen's Bishopsgate, London, the arms of the Merchant Taylors appear in the form granted to them in 1480, with the Agnus Dei in chief, while the 16th-century form with the golden lion appears on brasses at Kirkleatham (Yorks) and Dunstable (Beds). The armorial glass in the east window of Clare (Suffolk) records that 'the Honourable Company of Haberdashers were very good benefactors to this church' in the 17th century.

The decoration of churches demanded an overseas trade both in raw materials and finished articles. From Cologne came the 'Cullen Plates' of latten from which English metal-workers cut out and engraved figures to be inlaid in stone slabs. This process was peculiar to England and may have been developed in order to reduce imports, but it made our medieval brasses sadly vulnerable, and often only empty indents show where a fine brass must have been laid.[9] The examples of Continental type brasses engraved on a solid sheet of metal are mostly found in the eastern counties and the close connection between the two finest specimens, the Walsokne and Braunche brasses in St. Margaret's church at King's Lynn, and those of German merchant princes at Lübeck and elsewhere, suggest a common place of origin[10]. The Hanseatic League, founded in 1266, had established an affiliated house at King's Lynn by 1272. Engraved at the foot of the Braunche brass we see a Peacock Feast in progress, perhaps recalling that to which Robert Braunche entertained King Edward III.

Glass was imported, to be designed and stained by English glaziers, and much of the fine stone used in East Anglia came from Caen, since there were no local quarries. In return England exported the finest products of her embroiderers and large quan-

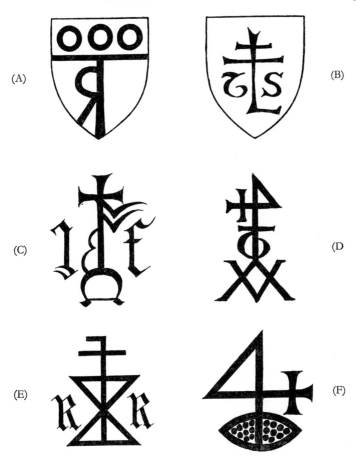

FIG. 17. Merchants' marks

(A)—ROBERT TAWKE: Westhampnett (Sussex).
(B)—THOMAS SPRING: Lavenham (Suffolk).
(C)—JOHN FORTEY: Northleach (Glos).
(D)—THOMAS POWNDER: Ipswich (Suffolk).
(E)—ROBERT RYCHARDS: Cirencester (Glos).
(F)—JOHN LANE: Cullompton (Devon).

tities of alabaster panels. We may see complete retables of English alabaster in Spain, Germany or Iceland, but in no English churches, for the material was all too easily broken, or burnt, by the iconoclasts. The five panels found buried in the churchyard at Drayton (Berks) and replaced in the church are the most complete example recovered, but single panels can be seen at Yarnton, Elham (Plate 40) and many other places. As the production of these panels became more mass-produced, in the 15th century, the quality of the work deteriorated. Heads of St. John the Baptist (Plate 86) were a 'special line' of the Nottingham alabasterers and one record refers to payment owing to a single carver for fifty-eight of them.

The foreign contacts formed by wealthy traders influenced their taste in church-building. The Flemish influence preponderates, and sometimes we can see the means by which it was largely introduced. The flamboyant character of the tracery upon the church chests at Crediton (Devon) or North Frodingham (Yorks) reveals their imitation of the chests which were imported from the Netherlands in such numbers that even chests made in England were known as 'Flanders' chests'. The markedly foreign character of the 16th-century rood-screens at Brushford, Colebrooke and Coldridge, all in Devon, was probably derived from similar imported work. Foreign influence can also be detected in the woodwork of the Oxfordshire churches of Thame and Charlton-on-Otmoor, in the screen of the Spring chapel at Lavenham and on the bench-ends of Wiggenhall St. Mary the Virgin (Norfolk), to name but a few examples.[11] On painted rood-screens foreign influence sometimes makes itself apparent in the choice of saints. Thus, at Tor Bryan (Devon) we find such unusual saints as St. Catherine of Siena, St. Armil of Ploermel and a saint with a ladder who may be St. Emmeran of Ratisbon. At Tacolneston (Norfolk) one sadly defaced panel from the 16th-century screen depicts the Temptation of St. Anthony and is clearly based on an engraving (dated 1509) by Lucas van Leyden,[12] and this brings us to the consideration of the import trade in books and engravings, whose influence upon early 16th-century carvings in English churches has received less attention than it merits.

England lagged behind other countries of Europe in the production of woodcuts and early printed books, but foreign booksellers were very ready to serve the English market and a single Customs House return for the Port of London in 1479–80 records the import of 1400 books.[13] The cities from which they mostly came were Paris, Antwerp and Rouen. Among the foreign booksellers who set up shops in St. Paul's Churchyard was Simon de Vostre, who, in conjunction with Thielmann Kerver and Philippe Pigouchet, produced in Paris many books with decorative margins including figures of half-length prophets, Biblical scenes and groups from the Dance of Death, as well as fantastically grotesque monsters. (See title page.) From the decoration of these Parisian Books of Hours the carver of the de la Warr chantry at Boxgrove (Sussex) copied the designs of his decorative sculpture; the Dance of Death on one pillar, the man climbing a tree while a maiden stands at its foot on another, the grotesque subjects of naked men and monsters in the panels immediately below the cresting (Plate 78), all these can be traced on the blocks which these French printers used in many books and in all sorts of combinations. This repetition of designs makes it impossible to say which particular book is likely to have been bought, either in Paris or London, by Thomas West, ninth Lord de la Warr, and used by the craftsmen whom he employed to build his chantry chapel. Nor shall we ever know whether it was the same book, or merely another volume from the same source, which inspired the carver of the misericords in Bristol cathedral. One misericord, which represents three naked figures fleeing from a two-headed dragon, offers us an interesting impression of an English carver copying a model in another medium. The engraver's foliage background he has discarded entirely, although the stone carver at Boxgrove had attempted it. The three fugitives and the dragon are faithfully repeated, except for one significant alteration. The engraver had shown his central figure from the back, with the face appearing in *profil perdu* over the right shoulder, as though glancing back at the fearful monster (Fig. 18). This form of perspective is unusual in English medieval carving and the Bristol craftsman evidently recoiled from the idea of attempting it. His central figure has its face turned to look at the spectator in the manner normal for such groups. Unfortunately for the realism of his perspective he did not make a corresponding change in the pose of the back and arms, with the result that the figure is anatomically impossible. One can almost hear him blaming his employer for having insisted on an honest British workman copying such an outlandish foreign design! The designs of two other Bristol misericords came from the same source; a mermaid between two grotesque monsters and an ape astride a

FIG. 18. Marginal Ornament from a Book of Hours printed in Paris about 1500, by Thielmann Kerver

strange quadruped which is being driven by a man holding its tail. Two of these same grotesque designs were followed by another carver of misericords at Throwley (Kent). A strong likeness between the faces and crowns of King Noble the Lion and his consort, as shown in the fine series of Reynard the Fox carvings at Bristol (Plate 59), and one of the two surviving woodcuts from the early version of this book printed by Wynkyn de Worde raised hopes which comparison with later imprints of the other designs did not confirm. The search for the originals of strange carvings is a pursuit full of disappointments, but the delight of success obliterates all memory of them.

It is impossible to separate the subject of foreign trade from some remembrance of the ships in which it was carried. We are apt to think of ourselves as having always been a sea-going people, but the incidence of ships in the imagery of our churches might remind us that, between the period of the Viking long-ships, which are represented on hog-back tombs and the ironwork on doors of this period, and the late 15th-century, England was primarily a land power, whose armies merely had to be ferried across the Channel. The famous 13th-century *Mappa Mundi* in Hereford cathedral offers at least a partial explanation of this. It reflects the opinion of the time that, to the west of Britain lay only a few unimportant islands and then the limitless, hostile ocean. Across the narrow division of the Channel lay the countries familiar through commerce or campaigns, and beyond them strange lands populated by monsters.[14] Yet some of the few surviving 12th-century carvings of ships are sufficiently detailed to have historical value. For instance, the curious craft on the font at Winchester (which dates from *c.* 1180) (Plate 34) may have the earliest known representation of a stern rudder and thus mark the beginning of a new phase in shipbuilding.[15] The long ships of the Norsemen were double-ended, bow and stern being approximately the same shape, and, so long as ships continued to be steered by an oar, or by rudders fixed to the sides of the hull, there was no incentive to alter this shape. When, however, the advantages of having a single rudder fixed to the stern were realised, it became highly desirable that ships should be built with a straight sternpost on to which the rudder could easily be hinged.

A bench-end, originally in St. Nicholas' church, King's Lynn, but now in the Victoria and Albert Museum, shows a carving of a single-masted vessel of about 1400 with crenellated fore- and after-castles and fighting-top; three dried fish are introduced into the panelling as a reminder of the important fisheries at King's Lynn which were protected, from very early times, by royal charters.[16] With this exception I can recall no ships carved in the 13th or 14th centuries which can claim to be more than stage properties.

If we wish to find illustrations of real ships dating from the late 14th or early 15th centuries, we must rely on scratched drawings, made by seamen rather than artists, on the walls and pillars of churches in coastal areas, such as Blakeney, Cley, Salthouse and Wiveton in Norfolk, Newbourn (Suffolk) or Welbourn (Lincs). The church of St. Margaret-at-Cliffe (Kent) is particularly rich in such *graffiti* of ships and one of the largest and most elaborate of these is cut on a pillar beside the font. This shows a vessel with a stern-hung rudder and overhanging aftercastle. She carries a bush, or a branch of a tree, on both stemhead and bowsprit and a larger bush on her aftercastle, presumably as a recognition mark, for a similar use of a bush is shown on the 13th-century seal of Melcombe Regis. Her square sail shows four bands of reef-points.[17]

The rounding of the Cape of Good Hope in 1488 and the

discovery of America revolutionised man's conception of the world as shown on the *Mappa Mundi* at Hereford. Britain was no longer situated on the outer fringes of the world but lay in a strategic position between Europe and the new worlds that the explorers had revealed. In Henry VII she had a king who, having come to the throne by means of a successful invasion, realised the importance of sea-power and who, by his own ventures in shipbuilding, set a new standard. From the 15th century onwards we see many ships in the carvings and glass of medieval churches and to those whose knowledge of either ecclesiology, or shipbuilding, is sufficiently sure to allow of accurate dating, the two subjects can be interrelated with advantage. A peculiarity in ship construction may date the part of the building on which it is represented, or the arms in a stained-glass window fix a date at which some particular form of rigging was in use, even if the artist is not altogether accurate in his portrayal of a ship. In a window representing St. Christopher at Thaxted (Essex), a boat is shown sailing down the river, steered by a single sailor with an oar.[18] Although the painter obviously meant to show a small river craft, it is clear from details of construction that he based his design on sea-going vessels. It is therefore of importance to students of rigging that the square sail should be shown with several bands of reef-points in the window of a chapel which was built about 1510. The painter has also shown the parrel (or band holding the yard to the mast) as consisting of wooden balls strung together on rope, like a bead necklace. Stylised carvings of ships occur on West Country benchends, as at East Budleigh (Devon) or Bishop's Lydeard (Som.)

The concept of a fighting Navy defending unarmed merchantmen was a 16th-century development and although the *Sovereign* and the *Regent* built by Henry VII were the most powerful ships of war then afloat, they were designed as though intended to carry cargo. The King thought that a large fleet of stoutly built merchant ships would prove the country's surest defence in case of war, so the first Navigation Act, in 1485, forbade the importation of Bordeaux wine into England unless carried in English ships.[19] This trade counted so largely in the plans of shipwrights that the capacity of British ships was, and still is, calculated in terms of 'tonnage' which originally meant the number of tuns (huge barrels) of Bordeaux wine which they could accommodate in their holds. These tuns also figure largely in ecclesiastical art. A tun was the invariable symbol for the syllable 'ton' in any rebus: the babe-in-a-tun of the Babingtons at Kingston-on-Soar (Notts) and the beacon-on-a-tun of Bishop Beckington in Wells cathedral are examples. A more direct connection between carvings and the Navigation Act can be seen at Tiverton where the carvings on the exterior of the Greenaway Chapel, built in 1517, include tuns as a recurring feature of the decorative designs, combined with anchors, ropes, bales of wool and other emblems of the trade by which John Greenaway imported wool from Ireland and sent cloth to France and Spain in exchange for oil and wine. This chapel has perhaps the finest existing muster of carved ships, including one which is actually shown unloading cargo, although exposure to weather has blurred some of their details, like those of the similar carvings at Cullompton.

Several of the ships at Tiverton are clearly armed with canon (Plate 87) but one also has men armed with cross-bows in her tops, a reminder that the cannon had not yet achieved supremacy over the older weapons. Henry VII ordered his ships to carry guns, not only in their castles but in the waist, and they are shown there on most of the carved ships. Some ships are shown which have both oar propulsion and sails, including one strange craft on the wall of the south chapel which shows the rowers sitting on an outrigger, or long platform suspended over the side of the ship by three massive chains. Henry VIII experimented with vessels which could combine the advantages of sailing ship and galley. His *Great Galley*, launched in 1515 when John Greenaway was probably planning his chapel, was a fourmasted vessel with 60 oars on each side,[20] but she was not a success and it is more probable that the sailing galleys shown at Tiverton refer to the ships of the Venetian trading fleet which came yearly to Flanders and the English ports.[21]

In North Stoneham church (Hants) we find an unexpected memorial of these Venetian traders:[22] a slab of stone in the floor which bears the inscription SEPULTURA DE LA SCHOLA DE SLAVONI ANNO DNI MCCCCLXXXXI. In the centre of the stone is a shield showing a double-headed eagle. The Riva degli Schiavoni in Venice and the famous church built on the site of their hospice commemorate these Dalmatian sailors who certainly

provided 180 oarsmen for the first 'Flanders Fleet' that sailed
from Venice in the 14th century, so it seems reasonable to suppose that these men must have come to Southampton in the same
way. Whether some outbreak of plague in 1491 caused their
deaths, or they were killed in one of the, not infrequent, quarrels
between the Venetian traders and the people of Southampton, we
shall never know, nor is it certain whether this stone marks their
actual burial place. North Stoneham seems rather far inland for
this although the Itchen was then navigable much further up,
and perhaps the memorial was brought here from St. Mary's
church, Southampton, which stood in the main medieval cemetery,
when this church was destroyed.

Only a few of the many memorials to later navigators and
traders can be mentioned. One of the ships which fought under
Drake's command is shown on the memorial to Sir James Hales
in Canterbury cathedral. He was Treasurer to the fleet which went
to Portugal in 1589 and died on the way home, so his burial at
sea is represented with an over-large corpse being lowered over
the side as the ship sails on. In the little church of Sutton-at-
Hone (Kent) there is a grand monument to Sir Thomas Smith,
died 1625 who is described in the epitaph as 'late Governour of ye
East Indian, Moscovia, French and Sommer Iland companies.
Treasurer for the Virginian Plantation, Prime Undertaker (in the
year 1612) for that noble designe the Discoverie of the North West
Passage. Principal Commissioner for the London expedition
against ye Pirates and for a voiage to ye Ryver Senega upon ye
coast of Africa. One of ye cheefe Commissioners for ye Navie
Roial and sometyme Ambassadour from ye Ma/te of Gr. Brit. to
ye Emperour and Great Duke of Russia and Moscovia'.[23] It was
indeed a rapidly expanding world!

Memorials to less important 17th-century sailors can be seen
at Waltham Abbey (Essex) where a ship in full sail, inscribed
Industria decorates the great ledger on the tomb of Captain Smith,
died 1679. At Rotherhithe a three-masted ship is carved on the
tombstone of Captain Anthony Wood, and here also was buried
Christopher Jones, the master of the *Mayflower*.

The 18th century was the age of pictorial reliefs and the monuments to distinguished sailors offer us a wealth of historical
illustration. Several of these reliefs illustrate the battle, or ship-

wreck, in which the dead man lost his life and two of them refer to the terrible storm which scattered the British fleet returning from the Mediterranean in 1703. The wreck upon the Scilly Isles of Sir Cloudesley Shovell's flagship is carved upon the monument to that admiral in Westminster Abbey, and we find a simpler version at Knowlton (Kent) on the memorial to Lady Shovell's two sons (by her first husband, Sir John Narborough), who also perished in the wreck. The decoration of the stern galleries, which were the pride of 17th-century ships, has evidently interested the carver much more than the problem of conveying the tumult of the elements. Heavy clouds and disordered rigging are shown, but the ship rides on an even keel. Another wreck is shown at Great Waltham, Essex, where the ship which carried Hugh Everard founders on the Goodwin Sands. The foundering in the Channel of Admiral Balchen's flagship, in 1744, is shown upon his monument in Westminster Abbey, where the *Buckingham*, in which Admiral Tyrrell was lost in 1767, is represented under water on his tomb. Less celebrated disasters are depicted on some of the 18th-century gravestones at Warblington (Hants). One of these shows a ship being shattered by the explosion of her powder magazine, and another has a carving of a ship sinking at the entrance to a port whose castellated walls and quayside steps are shown in the background.

Victory appears on the tombs as well as disaster; at North Stoneham, near Southampton, Hawke's monument bears a relief showing the Battle of Quiberon Bay, in 1759, when his ships destroyed the French fleet intended for the invasion of England. A relief by Rysbrack, on the monument to Admiral Wager in Westminster Abbey, gives a vivid impression of the flaming wreck of a Spanish ship destroyed by his fleet in the West Indies. Anson's victory off Finisterre, in 1747, is shown in the Abbey on the tomb of Captain Saumarez, and an engagement between two ships is carved on the tomb, at Chitterne (Wilts), of Mathew Michell who, his epitaph tells us, went to sea at the age of eight and sailed round the world with Anson in 1743. From the pitiful recollection of what this child must have endured when he went from the nursery to the Navy, let us turn with relief to consider older, and grander men, whose travels were undertaken solely for their own pleasure and enlightenment.

Chapter 5

THE COUNTRY GENTLEMAN
TURNED ARCHITECT

AS I WROTE, at the beginning of this book, there is plenty
of material which will help us to create a mental picture of
18th-century life, and the illustrations which we can find
in our churches are easily recognised. The pompously periwigged
personages who stand, sit or recline in effigy on 17th- and 18th-
century tombs, have left full records of their lives and, if we wish
to know more about them, we must read rather than ramble.
Occasionally an odd discovery evokes the characteristic flavour
of the period, as, for example, the wooden horse at Berkeswell
(War) which was built for a sporting parson who bestrode it
while preaching because he found his ideas flowed more easily
in the saddle![1] Many later tombs have epitaphs which give full
(and often fulsome) obituary notices. Sometimes it is hard to
believe that they were not composed in an ironical spirit, as when
the grandiloquent monument to the first Duke of Chandos at
Little Stanmore (Middlesex) praises that fantastic megalomaniac
for his modesty and dislike of ostentation! Canons House, near
Edgware, and its builder, are now chiefly remembered because
of Pope's jibes at 'Timon's villa' but the little church with its
grisaille paintings by Laguerre, in the *trompe l'œil* style which
delighted the fashionable world of the time, and the ducal box
which confronts the organ on which Handel played, is a charming
relic of this aristocratic extravaganza.

There is no space in this book to discuss these later monuments
of social history, but one aspect of the relation between the Lord
of the Manor and his parish church must be mentioned, for at
no other period did these gentlemen exercise so much influence
upon architectural style.

As long as buildings continued to be designed by master masons
in the traditional idiom of English Gothic, the churches built by
Kings, or great nobles, differed more in scale than in style from
those whose founders were more modestly endowed. The revival

2 Mobbed owl, Norwich Cathedral
3 Resurrection and appearance to Mary Magdalene, Lincoln Cathedral

64 The eavesdropping demon, Ely Cathedral
65 The dishonest ale-wife, Ludlow
66 Luxuria, Stratford-upon-Avon

7 Easter sepulchre, Hawton

69 Feast of Herod, Gresford

68 Massacre of the Innocents, St Peter Mancroft Norwich

71 Henry II scourged at the shrine of St Thomas,
cloister boss, Norwich

70 The angel with the Second Trumpet,
cloister boss, Norwich

72 The Knight of the Swan Exeter Cathedral
73 Mermaid suckling a lion, Edlesborough
74 The Locust of the Apocalypse, Exeter Cathedral

75 Flight of Alexander, Gloucester Cathedral
76 Tristan and Iseult, Chester Cathedral
77 Sir Yvain, Enville

78 Grotesque ornament, de la Warr chantry, Boxgrove
79 The Bruce Cenotaph, Guisborough

80 The chancel of Norbury Church

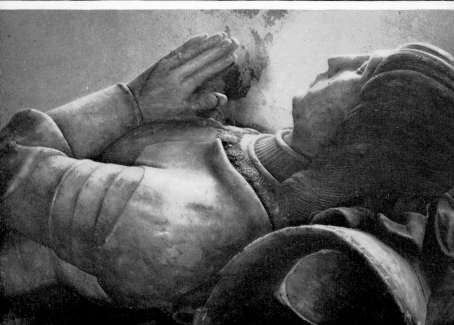

81 The effigy of Edward II, Gloucester Cathedral
82 Sir Henry Pierrepont, Holme Pierrepont

d, Lord Despenser, Tewkesbury

85 Extreme unction, Gresham

84 The Free Miner, Newland

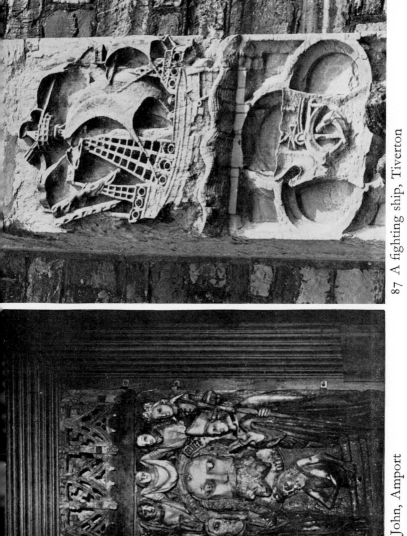

86 Head of St John, Amport

87 A fighting ship, Tiverton

88 'Gabriel leaves, Joseph advances', transept boss, Norwich Cathedral
89 Herod and the doctor, transept boss, Norwich Cathedral

90 Domestic brawl, Bristol Cathedral
91 Cutting the corn, Worcester Cathedral

92 The cross-legged knight, Dorchester Abbey
93 The sleeping Jesse, Abergavenny

of Classicism altered the whole situation. Architecture became a matter of pattern and precept rather than of instinctive sense of proportion and a living tradition. The more enterprising master masons tried to gain an understanding of the new style, but they enjoyed few opportunities of seeing fine Renaissance buildings and the number of architects who were capable of designing a church in the fashionable taste was too small to meet the demand. On the other hand, any gentleman of wealth and culture who aspired to become a patron of the arts had probably made the Grand Tour of Europe as an essential part of his education. He was thus relatively well equipped to act as the liaison officer between the distinguished architect from whom he commissioned a design and the local masons who would execute it. Many of these masons were used to working from the vague instructions which we find in some medieval contracts to make the new work like that at X—— only bigger, and, by implication, better.[2] They were therefore less dependent upon detailed drawings than successive generations were to become and so the noble patron was often able to achieve his desired end and take most of the credit for his new house, or church. The 18th century was the heyday of the amateur architect and there was apparently no prejudice against plagiarism, even among those whose designs were copied. When James Gibbs published his *Book of Architecture* in 1728, he wrote in the preface that he had been urged to do so by persons of quality to the end that it might 'be of use to such gentlemen as might be concerned in building, especially in remote parts of the country, where little or no assistance for designs can be procured'. The opinion of those who so counselled him was justified. For the next hundred years we can detect the influence of Gibbs' engraved designs not only in this country but in New England as well. The little church at Mereworth (Kent), which was built by the Earl of Westmoreland in 1744-6, was adorned with a copy of the spire of St. Martin in the Fields, which moved Horace Walpole to say that the 'poor church curtsies under it, like Mary Rich in a vast high-crown hat'.

Crossing the Atlantic for a brief digression, we can see one of Gibbs' six alternative designs for this spire as executed by Joseph Brown, in 1775, at Providence, Rhode Island. In the lovely village of Farmington, Connecticut, the white painted wooden spire of

Q

the church also strikes with familiar charm the eye of the travelling Londoner.[3] The part played by these wealthy amateurs in the transformation of their houses does not concern us here, although I may mention the tomb of Sir Joseph Danvers at Swithland (Leics) where the building of a new house is carved in low relief on the south side of the slate tomb-chest. This tomb is partly within the park of the manor house, partly in the churchyard, and the explanation of this is typical of the mentality of the period. Sir Joseph did not wish to be separated in death from his dog, and so, instead of arranging for his tomb to be in the church, he caused it to be built into the churchyard wall so that the dog, lying in unconsecrated ground, might be at his master's feet. Another Leicestershire tomb, at Scraptoft, shows James Wigley (died 1765) supervising the planting of trees, a process which at this date had such a close relation to the design of a house that landscape gardening might almost be considered as a branch of architecture. By curving banks and skilfully planted copses, the eye of the spectator was led to distant viewpoints where romantic ruins or classical buildings were disposed to focus the attention. The 'fascination frantic of a ruin that's romantic' held many a noble gentleman in its grip, and the church of Ayot St. Lawrence (Herts), designed by Nicholas Revett in 1778, was built because Sir Lionel Lyde thought that the old church would make such an ornamental ruin.[4] The new church also fulfilled a function in the scheme of landscape gardening, for it provides a beautiful termination to a vista. The Doric portico is scholarly in design (as might be expected from an architect who had collaborated with 'Athenian' Stuart on *The Antiquities of Athens*), but the open colonnades which connect the body of the church with the tombs on each side are merely scenic decorations. 'Athenian' Stuart himself gave effect to an idea originated by the Earl of Harcourt when the church at Nuneham Courtenay (Oxon) was rebuilt in 1764, as part of the improvements to the park which were then being carried out under the direction of 'Capability' Brown. They achieved their ends perfectly, and, as Horace Walpole put it, the church is 'a principal feature of one of the most beautiful landscapes in the world', but the handsome hexastyle portico with its Greek Ionic order has no structural purpose and merely shelters a blank wall.

Occasionally we find villages in which the wealth and influence of the Lord of the Manor, or his good fortune in friendship, enabled him to get the foremost architect of his day to design the new parish church, which thus offers us the rare interest of a minor work by one of the great masters of architecture. When Walter Chetwynd rebuilt the church of Ingestre (Staffs) in 1673–6 he may have relied on the good offices of Dr. Robert Plot to induce Wren to design it, for Plot was Secretary to the Royal Society when Wren was its President, and the full description of Ingestre church, which we find in Plot's *Natural History of Staffordshire*, was probably written by Wren.[5] He describes it as 'not great, but uniform and elegant . . . the windows illustrated with the Armes and matches of the Chetwynds in painted glass and the ceilings with the same in fretwork . . . an elegant skreen of Flanders oak garnish't with the King's Armes and great variety of other curious carvings'.

In 1742 James Gibbs built the church of Patshull (Staffs) for Sir Richard Astley, but the tradition that Binley (Warcs) was designed by Robert Adam lacks confirmation. It was built at the expense of the sixth Earl of Craven in 1771–3, and contemporary accounts only refer with tantalising vagueness to 'various architects employed in erecting and completing the same in an elegant manner'. The whole church has considerable dignity, and the interior has a refined charm. On faded green walls a plaster-work design of ribbons and foliage surrounds medallions in which one is almost surprised to find reliefs of such subjects as Christ and the Woman of Samaria, instead of the love scenes of classical mythology. The finely wrought iron-work of the gates to the apse might have been designed for the ramp of some grand staircase.

If Binley gives one the impression of an elegant drawing-room, the church which stands beside the ruined shell of Great Witley House (Worcs) has the appearance of a rococo *salon*.

When the house of the Duke of Chandos at Canons was demolished in 1747, the second Lord Foley bought the windows and paintings from its chapel to adorn the church near his own house, erected some dozen years earlier. Three large, and twenty smaller, paintings, all by Antonio Bellucci, were fitted on to the ceiling and this difficult adaptation from one building to another was made possible by using a very recently invented material, papier-mâché, to copy and modify the original stucco work by Bagutti.[6] The deceptive result must be reckoned successful, but the purely pictorial windows show a disastrous indifference to the true character of stained glass which would have been inconceivable to a medieval craftsman. Although the larger paintings show religious subjects, the general character of the decoration has a theatrical frivolity strangely out of keeping with an English country church. It is the stage setting for a comedy of manners on which the curtain fell, for the last time, long, long ago.

The influence of a most unexpected patron of church-building, Sir Francis Dashwood, founder of the notorious Hell Fire Club, can perhaps be detected in some of the strange features of the church at West Wycombe (Bucks). The golden ball on the top of the tower (inside which ten people can sit at table) is a picturesque landmark in the carefully ordered prospects with which he surrounded his home. The delicacy of the mouldings in the nave, where sixteen Corinthian columns support a ceiling painted to imitate coffering, reminds us that Dashwood was an enthusiastic patron of the arts. He was a leading member of the Society of Dilettanti, founded in 1736, which, by financing the careful studies of classical architecture made by Robert Adam, 'Athenian' Stuart and Nicholas Revett in Dalmatia and Greece, exercised a lasting influence on English architecture. Perhaps a memory of the darker activities of this patron can be detected in the strange painting of the Last Supper, in the chancel, which makes Judas Iscariot the principal figure.

The Grand Tourists brought back to England pictures and sculpture which made their country homes some of the richest treasure houses of Europe. A 17th-century tomb-chest (somewhat heavily restored) in the churchyard of St. Mary's Lambeth recalls three generations of Tradescants of whom two

> . . . lived till they had travell'd Art and Nature through:
> As by their choice collections may appear
> Of what is rare, in land, in sea, in air,
> Whilst they (as Homer's Iliad in a nut)
> A world of wonders in one closet shut . . .

The carvings on the sides of the tomb show exotic buildings, both classical and Oriental, whilst a welter of fallen columns, detached capitals and obelisks overthrown, convey an impression of the Roman ruins from which such antiquaries liked to enrich their private collections. Curiously enough, these carvings do not include the rare plants for the study and cultivation of which the Tradescants are also remembered.

Though some of these distinguished collectors built beautiful classical houses in which to show their treasures to the best advantage, their churches were less successful. In the second half of the 18th century some of them began to tire of classical forms and seek to revive the Gothic tradition which had been destroyed by the xenophilia of their forebears. At Shobdon (Herefs) the second Lord Bateman commissioned, in 1753, as artificial a piece of Gothick stage scenery as was ever designed at Strawberry Hill. The architect is unknown but may have been Richard Bentley, a member of Walpole's Committee of Taste.

Few people, however, could afford to rebuild whole churches and it is on the monuments that we most often see the change of taste reflected. The effigies of the dead no longer lie as if asleep, in pious, patient expectation, but stand erect, or else recline in uncomfortably wakeful attitudes. The mason sculptors of England adapted their craft to meet new demands. At Blechingley (Surrey) the only monument signed by Richard Crutcher shows us the standing figures of Sir Robert Clayton, Lord Mayor of London, and his wife, looking as though they might at any moment begin declaiming the matter of the lengthy epitaph displayed between them. Only one detail links these grandiose figures with both past traditions and common humanity: the richly dressed baby daughter sleeping at their feet had been dead for forty years when the tomb was made. At Gayhurst (Bucks) Sir Nathan Wright and his son are similarly posed beneath a marble curtain which might just have risen upon the emotional and allegorical drama that was to be introduced by the foreign sculptors whom England welcomed in the late 17th and 18th centuries. Cibber the Dane showed the broken-hearted parents kneeling beside the tomb of Thomas Sackville at Withyham (Sussex) and John Nost, the Fleming, represented Time, with her hourglass, mourning below the statue of the great lawyer, Sir Hugh Wyndham at Silton (Dorset) while Charity is shown hanging up the portrait of the Duke of Montagu on his monument by Roubiliac at Warkton

(Northants). Personal taste must decide how much each of us welcomes this change, but need not prevent us regarding the originals of such splendid statues as that of Lord King, by Rysbrack, in Ockham church (Surrey) with gratitude for the exotic beauty which they brought to our post-medieval churches

Chapter 6

THE COMMON PEOPLE

W E HAVE looked at the monuments of the great, the benefactions of the wealthy and the impressive schemes of imagery designed by learned men. What can the churches tell us of the common people who could not afford to build chapels or commission tombs and whose frequent misunderstandings of religious symbolism introduced some strangely distorted subjects into English imagery? They too have their memorials, if we have the patience and the imagination to seek them out.

The life experience of an artist is the raw material from which he creates a new world, and, if he be a man of genius, we accept the reality of this without considering its origin. With the more humdrum craftsman, we take pleasure in detecting the biographical details which his lack of imagination has left unaltered. Bad novels are sometimes of more value to the historian than the timeless masterpieces of fiction. There are few of the outstanding events in the life of a medieval villager which cannot be illustrated by carvings, paintings or stained-glass windows in medieval churches, although in many cases the artist's intentions were didactic rather than biographical. For instance, the landmarks of life which the Church hallows with her Sacraments are plentifully represented upon the 15th-century Seven Sacrament fonts, found chiefly in the eastern counties. Some thread is necessary to string together the examples I have chosen from a wealth of alternatives, and so my last chapter shall describe an illustrated biography of the common man.

Although elements of genre painting are introduced into many medieval Nativities, they are confined to such small details as the black-and-white-tiled floor, and the basket-grate beside which St. Joseph is shown sitting, in a comfortable armchair, in the glass of the east window of St. Peter Mancroft, Norwich. The mental image of the stable at Bethlehem was too vivid in the minds of the artists for them to borrow from their daily life further touches of realism.

Baptism which is represented on the Seven Sacrament fonts at such places as Gresham, Walsingham and Cley in Norfolk, usually took place on the day of birth. The old custom of placing salt in the child's mouth and saliva on its ears and nostrils has left its trace upon the font in St. Margaret's church, Ipswich, on one panel of which is carved an angel holding a scroll inscribed SAL ET SALIVA.[1]

A very early stage of life may be represented on a bench-end at Sheringham (Norfolk), where a swaddled baby for ever seems in danger of slipping off the shoulder of the standard, but, if we admit that the carver may have been careless in his reproduction of the enveloping folds, it may equally well represent early death. Children who died before their mother had been churched were termed 'Chrisom children', and were shrouded in the white linen vesture placed upon them by the priest when he anointed them with Holy Oil at their baptism; this was bound about the corpse with strips of linen crossing diagonally in front. The use of the chrisom was erased from the second Prayer Book of 1552.[2]

Infant mortality was very high in the Middle Ages and much later. Along the foot of the incised slab which marks the tomb of Sir Francis Tanfield at Gayton (Northants) are small figures of his eighteen children, including eight chrisom children. There seems to have been a mistake in the instructions given to the carver, one child being forgotten, for an extra chrisom baby has been inserted, above the general level. For an actual illustration of an early death-bed we must turn to the later tombs and see at Ashbourne (Derbs) the famous carving by Thomas Banks of Penelope Boothby, tossing in fever. The epitaph, 'the unfortunate parents ventured their all on this frail bark and the wreck was total' is in poignant contrast to the casual afterthought of yet another dead baby, at Gayton.

The carvings on the fonts at Gresham, Sloley and West Lynn in Norfolk may remind us that the Synod of Exeter, in 1287, ordered that the parents of children who were not confirmed by the time they were three years old, were to fast upon bread and water every Friday until the ceremony had taken place.[3] On these fonts the children are represented as infants held in the arms of their sponsors.

Education was a painful business in the Middle Ages and many boys had their little learning literally knocked into them by the parish priest, or one serving a chantry chapel. On misericords at Sherborne, Boston and Norwich the schoolmaster is shown hard at work! An amusing illustration of the medieval undergraduates can be found in the little figures which form the foot-rest to the effigy of William of Wykeham in Winchester cathedral. Although these are sometimes said to represent the Clerk of the Works, Master Mason and Master Carpenter concerned in the great Bishop's building enterprises at Winchester and Oxford, the analogy with the frequent appearance of bedesmen on such foot-rests seems to support the alternative theory that the figures commemorate the poor scholars for whom he made such munificent provision.

Schooling was not a subject which appealed much to the carvers; sport was far more attractive. We find lively representations of football on a misericord at Gloucester, and are made sadly aware of the truth of Sir Thomas Elyot's strictures that it was 'nothyng but beastely fury and extreme violence, whereof procedeth hurt' by the effigy of the eleven-year-old son of Sir John Stanley, at Elford (Staffs), who was killed by a ball striking his temple. The boy is dressed in a long gown and holds a ball in one hand while a finger of the other is pressed to his temple. The inscription tells us that 'where the pain is, there is the finger'. Various forms of wrestling appear; on a capital at Pocklington (Yorks), a roof boss at Lechlade (Glos) and on misericords at Norwich and Bristol, the figures are engaged in collar wrestling, while the usual holds are employed on a misericord at Halsall (Lancs). A later, and more curious, reminder of past wrestling matches is the tomb of Sir Thomas Parkyn of Bunny (Notts) who caused his effigy to be carved 'in a bruising position, even in an encounter with Master All-bones, alias Death'.[4] Bear-baiting appears frequently on misericords; there are three in Beverley Minster alone; and a beautiful example at Enville (Staffs) shows us the detail of the staff with which the bear-ward controlled his charge. Cock-fighting is not shown, to my knowledge (although there is an old cock-pit in the churchyard at Pennant-Melangell) except as the term was applied to a child's game. This is shown on a misericord in St. George's Chapel Windsor, where two boys fight, with their knees drawn up between their tied hands and fastened there with sticks. All forms of hunting are commonly represented in churches, sometimes in unexpected places, as on the tomb of the Duke of Exeter from St. Katherine's Hospital, now in the chapel of St. Peter-ad-Vincula in the Tower of London, or round an arch in the south transept of Lambourn (Berks).

The churches are full of very charming carvings and brasses showing children of all ages as they must have appeared at their devotions, for it was the common custom to represent all the children of a family kneeling on the tomb of their parents. It is impossible for me to choose from such a wealth of illustration, each reader probably has his, or her, own favourite.

The Seven Sacrament fonts show us several scenes of marriage. It is to be hoped that our imaginary hero was not so ungallant as to insist upon his bride wearing nothing but her smock, so that he could evade all future responsibility for her debts, but entries in the parish registers of Much Wenlock in 1547, and Chitterne (Wilts) in 1714, record such marriages.[5] Happy family life was rarely represented, as the carvers much preferred the slap-stick humour of violent quarrels. The universal distaff is used as a weapon on misericords at Carlisle, Stratford-on-Avon, Bristol (Plate 47) and elsewhere. Usually the husband gets the worst of it, and on a misericord in Henry VII's Chapel, Westminster, he is shown holding a ball of wool and a winding frame which suggests a reference to the humiliation of man by woman in stories akin to the legend of Hercules. An ill-treated man could have recourse to the law and get his unruly wife condemned to the Scold's Bridle, of which a specimen is still preserved in the church of Walton-on-Thames (Surrey). This instrument is dated 1632 and inscribed:

> Chester presents Walton with a bridle
> To curb women's tongues that talk too idle.

and the bridled scold is said to have been chained in the church porch for a length of time which varied according to the seriousness of her offence.[6] If the bridle was not effective the ducking-stool, such as that kept in Leominster church (Herefs), might have been brought into play!

If we would choose a profession for the hero of our imaginary biography, the artists provide us with a wide range. If, like the majority of the working population of medieval England, he is to be an agriculturist, the carvings of the 'Labours of the Months'[7] display the varied cycle of his year. Most of these were copied from the illuminations which adorned the calendars in psalters; the leaden font at Brookland (Kent) includes the signs of the Zodiac with their Norman names, and the names of the months are also given. Thus, over the figure of a man treading out grapes in a vat we read '*Vitovvre*', which is probably a corruption of Huitobre, the eighth month of the old year which began in March.[8] Wine was made in England, though not to any large extent, in the Middle Ages, and the inclusion of the vintage in many of these carved calendars probably points to the copying of imported manuscripts. On misericords at Ripple, where there is a complete set of 'Labours of the Months', we see the stubborn toil of ploughing and the reward of a back-breaking harvest and threshing. Perhaps the most beautiful harvest scene is that shown on the 12th-century font at Thorpe Salvin (Yorks). The farmer's enemies, the birds, are shown hovering round the sower who is casting seeds from two big bags on a misericord at Worcester, and the fox is often shown making off with the poultry.

When the winter came on the surplus stock had to be killed off, so the killing of the ox (Worcester), the cutting up of the carcass (Bristol) and the feasting (Malvern) show the pleasanter side of the farmer's life. At Ripple he is shown cutting up logs for the fire, and at Worcester the husbandman warms his feet by the fire, with a good side of bacon hanging up behind him. All these carvings are on misericords.

As alternative professions the misericords at Wellingborough (Northants) show us the shoemaker with his tools and the wood-carver. At Ludlow we can see the sexton with his two shovels above a tomb, and also a holy-water bucket and aspersor, for it was one of the perquisites of the office that the sexton might earn small fees by carrying holy water round the parish to asperse the faithful.[9] The parish beadle of the time of Queen Anne is repre-sented by a statuette which surmounts the poor-box at Pinhoe (Devon). The post-medieval tombs provide some further illus-trations. The forester of the time of James I, at Newland (Glos), holds a bow in one hand and an arrow in the other, and in the same churchyard there is a table-tomb, ejected from the church, with an effigy of John Wyrall (1457), hereditary forester of Dean, in his hunting costume. A 17th-century builder is depicted on the grave-slab of ANDRO PATRIK Mr OF WORK AT DRUMLANRIG 1685 at Durisdeer (Dumfries); he wears a long coat with an apron over it and holds a chisel and a mell.

My last alternative is perhaps the most interesting. At Abergavenny, on the tomb-chest of Dr. David Lewis, Judge of the High Court of Admiralty in the time of Queen Elizabeth, is carved a burly figure in a long gown with hanging sleeves, who holds a short-stemmed oar in his hand. The arch of the niche is inscribed THE SARGENT OF ADMIRALTEE. The figure represents the Sergeant-at-Mace, in his official dress, holding the silver oar which is still the particular mace of the High Court of Admiralty. The badge of the Admiralty can still be seen on the carving, but the Royal arms, with the supporters of Henry VII, which were formerly decipherable, have now been worn away completely.[10] Since these arms, clearly of much earlier workmanship than the rest of the mace, appear on the 18th-century Oar now borne by a Marshal in the High Court of Admiralty, this carving may show us the original form of the mace as well as a portrait of one of its Elizabethan bearers.

We have already considered the various sins which might have brought about the downfall of our imaginary hero, but it is surprising to find an individual act of intemperance recorded in a church; the font at Upper Tollesbury (Essex) is inscribed:

> Good people all I pray take care
> That in ye church you doe not sware
> As this man did.

The parish register for 1718 records that a man who came drunk to church and talked and swore aloud during the service paid £5 to avoid being prosecuted for this offence, the money being spent on a new font. A curious niche in one of the piers supporting the central tower at Claverley (Salop) is said to have been either a confessional or a seat of penance.

Punishment was not always to be avoided by payment, and in the windows of All Saints church, York, we see a pious man fulfilling one of the Seven Works of Mercy by visiting those who sit in the stocks with chains on their wrists and necks. A poppyhead at Blythburgh shows a chained man in the stocks and another, at Feltwell (Norfolk), shows the merciful person stooping outside a prison which is very like a sentry-box. That the Devil was responsible for all sins was made clear in the scenes of Penance, where evil imps are shown fleeing from the penitent who kneels in confession, or receives the lash, as on the font at Walsingham or a misericord in New College, Oxford.

Sickness or toothache were ills which the carvers seem to have thought more tolerable than their cure by the methods of medieval medicine. Doctors are almost always represented as apes holding up urine flasks (Plate 58), and one can more readily imagine such creatures prescribing an ointment made of crickets' wings and pounded dung beetles than the actual inventor of this medicament, John of Gaddesdon, physician to Edward II. The hideous ape which holds out a draught to a bedridden patient on a misericord in Malvern is a creature born of delirium! From such vile caricatures of a noble profession, let us turn with relief to the worthier portrayal of a doctor on the brass of Dr. Duncan Liddle (died 1613) in St. Nicholas' church, Aberdeen. This brass was engraved at Antwerp, by Gaspar Bruydegone of the Antwerp Mint, and shows the doctor writing at a table surrounded by his books and implements.[11]

And so we come at last to the deathbed of our hero, and see him, upon the font at Gresham (Plate 85), propped high against his pillows to receive the Extreme Unction. On each side of the priest stands an acolyte; one holds the book and the other the chrismatory. On the bed lies a dish containing something which may represent the five wisps of wool with which the priest wiped the places he had anointed; mouth, nostrils, ears, eyes and hands, and which were afterwards carefully burned or buried in the churchyard. A later deathbed scene is portrayed with more poignant expression of sadness on the Dormer tomb at Quainton (Bucks) where Roubiliac has shown the father and mother kneeling beside their dying son. The contrast between this highly dramatic representation of human sorrow and the impersonal calm of a great medieval tomb, whose host of 'weepers' neither shed, nor draw, a tear, is one indication of the long road which our minds have traversed in this book, and which now draws near to its end.

One last scene ends our imaginary biography. Burying the dead who had no friends to perform this last duty for them was included in the Works of Mercy, and a bench-end at Feltwell (Norfolk) shows us three pious persons so employed. One of the Blythburgh poppy-heads, also, probably represents a man lowering a shrouded corpse into a grave, the edge of which is clearly shown, but the fact that the head of the corpse has been broken off square has led to this carving being described as a man binding a sheaf, although an old engraving shows the original form. In both these carvings the body has not been placed in a coffin but merely wrapped in a shroud, probably made of woollen cloth. The parish registers of the 16th and 17th centuries make it clear that burial in a coffin was confined to the wealthy; references to uncoffined burials are frequently found in parish registers, with a lower scale of fees than for coffined ones. Up to the 19th century uncoffined burials took place, the corpses being carried to church in the parish coffin, examples of which were to be found in two Yorkshire churches, Easingwold and Howden. Even burial did not finally end a poor man's wanderings, unless he was wealthy enough to have a gravestone, or lucky enough to lie in a churchyard with ample room. When the marks of burial had disappeared, fresh corpses were often interred in the same plot of ground, any remaining bones being carefully preserved in a Bone-hole under the church. At Micheldean (Glos) the rood-loft stair continues down into a barrel-vaulted chamber, with a bone-shoot at the east end, which still contains bones.

The results of these superimposed burials can be seen in many churchyards where the level of the earth outside is above that of the church floor, sometimes reaching up to the sills of the windows. Above the grass and flowers that feed on human dust falls the shadow of the same churchyard yew from which their friends once cut sprigs to deck the shroud or scatter in the open grave. The tolling bell which mourned the end of their earthly journey is perhaps the same which sets the heavy summer air vibrating today, reminding us of the many strange beliefs which can be traced on the inscriptions of these bells. At Weedon Lois (Northants) an early 18th-century bell is inscribed DEFUNCTOS PLORO CAELUM REDDOQUE SERENUM, because bells were supposed to avert thunder, while the inscription PESTEM FUGO at Guilsborough (Northants) recalls the belief that they could also avert pestilence.[11] The Church did not accept the popular belief that the sound of bells could drive away evil spirits at all times, but the belief that the passing soul could be protected from the attacks of demons by the ringing of bells (which is to be found in all ages and in many countries) led to the custom of the Passing Bell. In English campanology nine 'tellers' announce the death of a man and six are tolled for a woman, followed, in each case, by one stroke for every year of the deceased person's life. At Ayot St. Peter (Herts) the nine tellers are rung on Good Friday, followed by thirty-three strokes for the years of Our Lord's life, and to those who listen with minds enriched by imagination and memory, the faiths and fears of thousands of generations, in all continents of the world, are implicit in that tolling bell.

*Appendices, Bibliography and Notes,
County Index and General Index*

R

ARRANGEMENT OF SUBJECTS IN THE
BIBLIA PAUPERUM

(From Block-book printed in Netherlands)

Eve tempted

The Burning Bush

Abner visits David at Hebron

Presentation of first-born in the Temple

Rebecca sending Jacob to Laban

Adoration of the Golden Calf

Saul causing Ahimelech and the priests to be slain

David consulting God about his return after death of Saul

Passage of the Red Sea

Esau sells his birthright

Elijah and the widow's son

Abraham and the angels (Plate 29)

Nathan reproving David

David with head of Goliath

Esdras asked by Darius to purify the Temple

Jacob told of death of Joseph

Joseph sold to the Ishmaelites

Melchizedek meets Abraham

Micaiah prophesies the death of Ahab

Foolish virgins

Annunciation

Nativity

Adoration of Magi

Purification

Flight into Egypt

Destruction of the idols in Egypt

Massacre of Innocents

Return out of Egypt

Baptism of Christ

Temptation of Christ

Raising of Lazarus

Transfiguration

Mary Magdalene at the feet of Christ

Entry into Jerusalem

Christ driving out the money-changers

Judas betrays Christ

Judas paid 30 pieces of silver

Last Supper

Christ leaves the disciples at Gethsemane

Christ in the Garden of Olives

Gideon and the fleece

Aaron's rod burgeons

Queen of Sheba visits Solomon

Presentation of Samuel in the Temple

Mychal assisting David's escape

Dagon falling

Athalia's massacre of the sons of Ahaziah

Return of Jacob to his country

Spies bearing grapes

Fall of Man

Widow's son restored to life by Elisha

Children of Israel in the fiery furnace

Miriam punished with leprosy

Children of the prophets meet Elisha

Judas Maccabeus orders the purification of the Temple

Absolom incites the people to rebellion

Joseph sold to Potiphar

Manna from Heaven

Elisha prophesies plenty in Samaria

Fall of the Angels

Abner treacherously killed by Joab

Kiss of Judas

Tryphon treacherously takes Jonathan captive

Jezebel seeks to kill Elijah

Pilate washes his hands

Daniel accused by the Babylonians

Shem covers nakedness of Noah

Crowning with thorns

Children mock Elisha and are eaten by bears

Isaac carrying faggots

Christ bearing the Cross

Widow of Zarephath holding two pieces of wood crosswise

Sacrifice of Isaac

Christ on the Cross

Moses and the brazen serpent

Creation of Eve

The soldier pierces the side of Christ

Moses striking the rock

Joseph put into the well

The Entombment

Jonah swallowed by the whale

David cuts off the head of Goliath

Descent into Limbo

Samson and the lion

Samson and the gates of Gaza

The Resurrection

Jonah cast up

Reuben seeking Joseph at the well

Three Maries at the Sepulchre

Daughter of Sion seeking her spouse

Daniel released from the lions' den

Christ appears to the Magdalene

Daughter of Sion finds her spouse

Joseph discovers himself to his brothers

Christ appears to the disciples

Return of the prodigal son

Angel appears to Gideon

Incredulity of St. Thomas

Jacob wrestles with the angel

Enoch taken up to Heaven

Ascension

Elijah in the chariot of fire

Moses receives the Tables of stone

Pentecost

Sacrifice of Elijah consumed by fire from Heaven

Solomon seats his mother by his side

Coronation of Blessed Virgin

Esther and Ahasuerus

Judgment of Solomon

Last Judgment

The Amalekite who slew Saul is slain

Destruction of Korah, Dathan and Abiram

Hell

Sodom and Gomorrah (Plate 29)

Feast of the children of Job

Christ holding His saints in His mantle

Jacob's ladder

Daughter of Sion crowned by her spouse

Reward of the righteous

St. John and the Angel

THE LABOURS OF THE MONTHS

Month and Sign of Zodiac	Brookland Font	Ripple Misericords	Worcester Cathedral Misericords
January (*Aquarius*)	Two-faced Janus drinking at table	Man emptying two jugs (Aquarius)	Woman with distaff. Man with spade
February (*Pisces*)	Man sitting by the fire	Man and woman sitting by the fire	Man by the fire
March (*Aries*)	Man pruning a vine	Man sowing and leading horse and cart	Sowing seed
April (*Taurus*)	Figure in long robe holding foliate branch	Bird-scaring	Man holding branches (Plate 11)
May (*Gemini*)	A mounted knight hawking	Woman holding nosegay between sheaves of flowers	Man with hawk, horse and page
June (*Cancer*)	A man mowing hay	Full Sun	Mowing with scythe
July (*Leo*)	Man raking hay	Building?	Weeding with crotch and hook
August (*Virgo*)	Man reaping with sickle	Man and woman cutting corn	Reaping with sickles (Plate 91)
September (*Libra*)	Man threshing with flail	Hunting with hawk (broken) and hound	Huntsman with horn
October (*Scorpio*)	Man treading out grapes	Pruning	Swineherd knocking down acorns for his pigs
November (*Sagittarius*)	Swineherd getting acorns for his pigs	Pig killing	. . . .
December (*Capricornus*)	Pig-killing	Splitting logs	Killing an ox

Note.—On the Brookland font the names of the months are given in Norman French, also those of the signs of the Zodiac, although the latter are sometimes incorrectly allocated and spelt. In most other cases there is some measure of uncertainty as to which Labour is supposed to represent which month. The agricultural programme varies according to local climatic conditions and the general weather conditions and the craftsmen's work reflected their own experience or that of the scribes whose illuminated psalters they copied. That the latter influence was the stronger is shown clearly by the fact that sheep-shearing, the most important event to an English medieval farmer, is not included, while the tending of vines often appears. Many of the illuminated calendars were probably of Continental origin, or based their conception of the agricultural year upon foreign prototypes.

THE APOSTLES AND PROPHETS OF THE CREED SEQUENCE

St. Peter (keys): 'I believe in God the Father Almighty, Maker of Heaven and earth':

St. Andrew (saltire cross): 'and in Jesus Christ, His only Son, Our Lord',

St. James Major (pilgrim's habit): 'who was conceived by the Holy Ghost, born of the Virgin Mary',

St. John (dragon emerging from chalice): 'Suffered under Pontius Pilate, was crucified, dead and buried',

St. Thomas (spear): 'He descended into Hell; the third day He rose again from the dead',

St. James Minor (a club): 'He ascended into Heaven and sitteth on the right hand of God the Father Almighty';

St. Philip (loaves or tall cross): 'From thence He shall come to judge the quick and the dead'.

St. Bartholomew (flaying knife): 'I believe in the Holy Ghost';

St. Matthew (money-box, bag, or sometimes a sword): 'The Holy Catholic Church; the Communion of Saints';

St. Simon (fish, oar or sword): 'The forgiveness of sins';

St. Jude (a boat): 'The resurrection of the body',

St. Mathias (halberd): 'and the life everlasting'.

Jeremiah: 'Thou shalt call me, My father' (iii. 19). 'Ah, Lord God behold, thou hast made the heaven and the earth by thy great power.' (xxxii. 17).

David: 'The Lord hath said unto me, "Thou art my son; this day have I begotten thee" ' (Psalm ii. 7).

Isaiah: 'Behold, a virgin shall conceive, and bear a son' (vii. 14).

Zechariah: 'They shall look upon me whom they have pierced' (xii. 10).

Hosea: 'O death, I will be thy plagues; O grave, I will be thy destruction' (xiii. 14).

Amos: 'It is he that buildeth his stories in the heaven' (ix. 6).

Zephaniah: 'And I will come near to you to judgment; and I will be a swift witness'. (This mistaken attribution of Malachi iii. 5 is often seen.)

Joel: 'I will pour out my spirit upon all flesh' (ii. 28).

Micah: 'They may all call upon the name of the Lord, to serve him'. (Mistaken attribution of Zephaniah iii. 9.)

Malachi: 'The God of Israel saith that he hateth putting away' (ii. 16).

Daniel: 'Many of them that sleep in the dust of the earth shall awake' (xii. 2). By confusion the text given to Daniel is often 'I will open your graves' (Ezekiel xxxvii. 12).

Obadiah: 'The Kingdom shall be the Lord's' (21).

Note.—The order of the Apostles is generally the same but that of the Prophets may vary, or different texts be allotted to them.

ANIMALS IDENTIFIABLE IN CHURCH IMAGERY
Real Animals

ANTELOPE According to Bestiary has long serrated horns which become entangled in bushes as man is trapped by his sins. Bench-end Walpole St. Peter, misericord Manchester cathedral. Used heraldically the antelope has tushes like a wild boar and often a chain round its neck. Bench-end Wiggenhall St. German (Norfolk).

APE Typified fraud and indecorum. Largely used in animal satires and fables.

BAT General appearance naturalistic but wing structure never correct. Misericords at Chichester, Christchurch, Lincoln, Wells, Edlesborough.

BEAR Mostly shown in scenes of bear-baiting, or dancing, as on misericords in Beverley Minster. Heraldically the bear and ragged staff of earls of Warwick often seen. Also figures in Reynard the Fox epic at Bristol and elsewhere.

BOAR Associated with pre-Christian protective magic, on helmets. Shown on tympanum of St. Nicholas' church, Ipswich. Bench-end Stowlangtoft (Suffolk). Otherwise appears only in boar-hunting scenes.

CAMEL Mostly found on bench-ends in eastern counties: Eynesbury (Hunts), Isleham (Cambs), Stowlangtoft, Ufford and Tostock in Suffolk. Only recognisable by its hump.

CAT Usually shown holding a mouse. Figures in Reynard the Fox subjects on Bristol cathedral misericords.

COCK Fine misericord Wells cathedral. With hens, Tewkesbury.

CRANE According to the Bestiary, one crane stands sentinel while the others sleep, holding a stone in one uplifted claw, so that, should it sleep, the falling stone would wake it. Misericords at Denston (Suffolk) and Lincoln cathedral show it holding the stone.

CROCODILE The real appearance of the beast was unknown. In some Bestiaries it looks like a wolf, so it can only be identified when it swallows the hydrus (q.v.) as on the corbels at Kilpeck.

DEER Shown naturalistically in hunting scenes or legends of SS. Hubert or Giles. Said in Bestiary to 'pant for cooling streams' because of thirst engendered by fighting fiery serpents. Combat shown on cross shaft at Melbury Bubb (Dorset) and door at Dalmeny, West Lothian.

DOG   Bestiary tells that dogs lick their wounds to heal them. Bench-end Lakenheath (Suffolk).

DOLPHIN   Shown leaping, or in attendance on mermaids.

DOVES   Symbol of the Eucharist when shown drinking from chalice or pecking at grapes. Grave slab Bishopstone (Sussex).

DUCK   Naturalistic where shown as on misericord Stratford-upon-Avon.

EAGLE   Bestiary says it renews its youth by flying up towards the sun until its old plumage and the film over its eyes are burned away and then diving into a fountain. Bench-end built into altar at Forrabury (Corn) shows bird diving into water and misericord at Higham Ferrers an eagle rising from water with a halo behind its head. See page 96.

ELEPHANT (see page 152)   Said to have no joints in its legs and rests leaning against a tree. The hunter cuts through the tree, the elephant falls. Other elephants (the prophets) try to raise it but cannot until a young elephant (Christ) puts his trunk under the fallen one. Mortal feud with the dragon (font Dunkeswell (Devon)).

FOX   Shown shamming dead to trap birds (misericord Whalley, Lancs). Often shown stealing poultry. Symbolises Devil capturing souls. Hero of Beast Epic. Windsor, St. George's, stalls and Bristol cathedral misericords. Preaching fox common subject). See page 150.

FROG   Symbol of heretics. Shown issuing from dragon's mouth on boss Norwich cloisters. Used in necromantic medicine. Misericord at Windsor shows man being made to swallow a whole frog.

GOAT   Usually shown browsing on bushes (Winchester College misericord) because the Bestiary derives its name from *carpendo* and says goats called *caper* from this way of feeding.

HAWK   Shown with rabbit, or other animal, in claws.

HEDGEHOG   Said to roll on fallen grapes to carry them back to its young impaled on its prickles. Misericord New College, Oxford.

HIPPOPOTAMUS   Misericord St. George's Chapel, Windsor.

HOOPOE   Young birds tend their parents by plucking out the old feathers. Shown on misericord in St. George's Chapel, Windsor, and perhaps at Carlisle.

HORSE   Only shown incidentally.

HYENA   Shown devouring corpses in Bestiaries and on boss Queen Camel (Som) and misericord Carlisle cathedral.

IBEX   Said to throw itself over precipices and land on its horns. Possible example, bench-end St. Nicholas', King's Lynn.

IBIS   Said to feed on carrion and snakes in shallow water because it cannot swim out to clean food = man who will not leave his sins. Misericords Lavenham, pecking at a human head and Windsor, eating a snake.

LION   Breathing on dead cubs to bring them to life = Resurrection, shown on boss in Canterbury cloister. Symbol of Goodness when it fights a dragon, corbel Beverley Minster, misericords Lincoln, Carlisle, etc. When sick eats a monkey, misericord at Windsor.

LIZARD   Corbel in Wells cathedral among foliage. Difficult to distinguish from dragon.

OSTRICH   Misericords Stratford-upon-Avon and Windsor show it with a horse-shoe in its beak, to indicate power of digesting iron. Mostly shown with hooves to indicate speed in running (Plate 11). Misericord in Henry VII's Chapel, Westminster, more naturalistic.

OWL   Different species sometimes indicated. Short-eared on misericord Hemington (Northants), Long-eared Edlesborough (Bucks). Sometimes shown mobbed by small birds.

PANTHER   Said to hide for three days after which it roars and draws all animals to it by a sweet smell = Christ in the tomb and after Resurrection. Shown attracting animals on roof boss at Tewkesbury. Only the dragon resists it and retreats to its lair (Alne doorway).

PARD   Hybrid of panther and lioness. Very bloodthirsty. Distinguished by branching tail and usually shown full face with tongue extended.

PARROT   Pair of them on misericord in Wells cathedral. Rare.

PEACOCK   Flesh supposed not to decay, so became symbol of immortality. Eyes in tail = foresight which a man loses, as the bird moults. On font at Hodnet, misericord at Lincoln and elsewhere.

PELICAN   Always shown with young birds at its breast. See page 152.

PIG   Sow and farrow a symbol of a divinely selected site. Common in west country.

RABBIT   Scenes of hunting, hawking, etc.

RAVEN   Only identifiable in connection with Noah.

SERPENT   Biblical serpent always shown as dragon, so naturalistic snake is rare. Said to scrape off its old skin by wriggling through a tight crack in rocks = man putting off sin. Snake represented as though crawling through the font bowl Ashover (Derbs) with this meaning.

SHEEP   Only incidentally shown, except for Agnus Dei.

SQUIRREL   Naturalistic.

SWAN   Often shown with coronet round its neck, heraldic or referring to romance of the Swan Knight.

TIGRESS   See page 152.

WHALE   Sleeps floating on surface and sailors mistake it for an island and land on it (boss Queen Camel (Som)). Swallows small fish while larger, and wiser, ones keep away. Carvers often show fish swallowing others, but make mistake of showing them of equal size.

WOLF   Said to bite its own paws to make them tread more quietly, misericord Faversham (Kent). Usually shown with rough mane down its spine. Guarding a crowned head, it refers to St. Edmund. See page 45.

Mythical Creatures

AMPHISBAENA   Winged serpent with a second head at the end of its tail which the Greeks knew as a symbol of deceit. Medieval artists tended to apply this second head to any monster they wished to make more horrific.

ASP   Supposed to lay one ear to the ground and block the other with its tail. Misericord Exeter cathedral possible example.

BASILISK   Hatched from egg of a cock incubated by a toad. Has head, feet and wings of a cock and serpent's tail. Its glance kills, and can be reflected back on to itself from a mirror or polished shield. Bench-ends Stowlangtoft and Tostock (Suffolk), and Sheringham (Norfolk). See page 151.

BLEMYA   Human abnormality with face in stomach. Misericords Norwich cathedral and Victoria and Albert Museum.

CALADRIUS   White bird which can foretell whether a sick person will recover or die. In the latter case it turns away from them. Only identifiable on doorway at Alne (Yorks).

CENTAUR, or SAGITTARIUS   Human half typifies Christ upon earth, the horse his vengeance on those who betrayed him. Centaur aiming arrow at dragon (tympanum, Kencott (Oxon)) may symbolise Harrowing of Hell.

CYCLOPS   Possible example on cornice at Adderbury (Oxon).

CYNOCEPHALI   Dog-headed people shown on Mappa Mundi but elsewhere indistinguishable from grotesques.

DRAGON   Common symbol of evil. Distinguished from Wyvern by having four legs.

GRIFFIN   Forepart of an eagle and hindpart of a lion, supposed to guard treasure in India and destroy covetous persons who tried to seize it.

HYDRUS   Small snake said to coat itself in mud and slide down throat of crocodile, afterwards bursting through its side. Kilpeck corbels symbolised Christ descending into Hell in human form.

MANTICHORA   Monster with head of a man with three rows of teeth, the body of a lion and the tail of a scorpion. Perhaps incised on exterior of North Cerney church (Glos).

PHOENIX   Traditional design of bird rising renewed from flames only occurs on misericord in Henry VII's Chapel, Westminster. Birds with curiously branching tails may have been meant to represent phoenix. Boss Queen Camel.

SALAMANDER   Two-legged dragon with knotted tail, said to live in fire = man who can pass through temptation unscathed. Font Salehurst (Sussex).

SCIAPOD or SHADOW FOOT   Human abnormality with one large foot which it uses as a parasol when resting. Bench-end Dennington (Suffolk).

SIREN   Two types: the classical bird-siren (misericords Lincoln, Exeter, New College, Oxford) is rarer than the fish-siren or mermaid. On misericords Carlisle and Hereford, All Saints, bird-sirens also have fish-tails. Lures sailors with her song (Boston misericord) and when holding fish in hand (door at Barfreston (Kent), or misericord Exeter) = Evil One holding a soul. Merman is rare alone, but on fonts at Anstey (Herts) and Cambridge St. Peter's. With mermaid at Stratford-upon-Avon.

TERROBULI   Male and female stones which burst into fire when brought together. Doorway Alne (Yorks).

UNICORN   Shown as a deer with one spiral horn. Captured by pure maiden (see page 153) misericords Cartmel (Lancs), Chester, Lincoln, etc. Fighting the dragon, misericord Durham Castle. Single unicorns on fonts at Norton (Suffolk) and Southfleet (Kent) and on many bench-ends.

WODEWOSE or WILD MAN   Shown as bearded and his body covered with shaggy hair. Very popular with carvers. Complex symbolism makes his battle with lion = spiritual man mastering the flesh. Misericords Coventry, Holy Trinity and Lincoln.

WYVERN   Two-legged dragon. Heraldic.

NOTES AND BIBLIOGRAPHY

To have given this book a complete bibliography might have doubled its length. I have therefore only quoted books of primarily historical purpose where these were my authority for some particular statement. I have given preference to articles in specialised periodicals since these, while often available in public libraries, are not easily traced by the ordinary reader, and to books whose general content will help them to fuller appreciation of the interest offered by our medieval churches. Where lists of examples would have overloaded the text, I have relegated these to the notes, hoping thus to increase the chances that readers will find matters of interest in their own locality.

INTRODUCTION *pp.* 1–5

1 The Bodmin accounts were published in the *Camden Miscellany* 1875.

Part I: The Growth of the Churches

I THE DARK ROOTS *pp.* 9–22

1 E. G. Bowen, 'The travels of St. Samson of Dol', *Aberystwyth Studies*, XIII, 1934.
2 T. D. Kendrick, *Anglo-Saxon Art* (1938), 126.
3 Louis Marsille, 'Le menhir et le culte des pierres', *Bulletin de la Soc. Polymathique du Morbihan* (1936), p. 1. At St. Thuriau en St. Jean-Brévelay a menhir has been carved into a rudimentary cross.
4 S. R. Meyrick, *The History and Antiquities of Cardiganshire* (1907), 298–9. Further examples of monoliths in, or near, churchyards can be seen at Llanbedr (Merioneths) where two pillar stones stand within 100 yards of the church; Corwen (Merioneths) a large monolith built into the wall of the north porch; Bolsterstone (Yorks, W.R.) megalithic remains in the churchyard. A monolith standing in the churchyard of Nether Swell (Glos) was pulled down in 1850.
5 St. Non has two other holy wells, in Cornwall. At Altarnon the church also is dedicated to her, but at Pelynt the dedication has been changed. See G. H. Doble, *St. Nonna*, Cornish Saints, Series No. 16.
6 F. and H. W. Elgee, *The Archaeology of Yorkshire* (1933), 189.
7 T. W. Shore, *The History of Hampshire* (1892), 32.
8 *The South English Legendary*, ed. C. Horstmann. E.E.T.S., O. ser. 87.
9 For instances of churches to which the legends of supernatural interference is applied, see G. L. Gomme, 'Traditions and Superstitions connected with Buildings', *The Antiquary*, III. These stories may have a connection with the sacrifices thought necessary to ensure the stability of a building. S. Baring Gould in *Strange Survivals* (1905), 1–35, discusses the possibility that the bones, human and animal, found in some church walls may be those of the actual victims so sacrificed.

10 Sir John Rhys, *The Origin and Growth of Religion* (1886), 203 ff.
11 W. G. Clark Maxwell, 'Church dedications and their bearing on Local History', *Shropshire Arch. Soc. Trans.*, 4th ser., I, 363.
12 F. N. Stenton, Presidential Address, *Royal Historical Soc.*, 1941.
13 James Frazer, *The Golden Bough*, x, 116 ff. See also H. R. Ellis Davidson, 'The Chariot of the Sun', *Folk Lore*, LXXX (1969), 174.
14 H. F. Humphreys, 'The Birth of a saint', *Queens Medical Magazine*, November 1948.
15 R. C. Hope, *Holy Wells* (1893), xxix.
16 F. R. Pearson, *Roman Yorkshire* (1936), 117.
17 Further examples of wells whose origin is associated with the legend of the titular saint occur at: Morwenstow (Corn), St. Morwenna; Exeter, St. Sidwell; Winchcombe (Glos) and Romsley (Worcs), St. Kenelm; Marden (Herefs), St. Ethelbert; St. Albans, St. Alban; East Dereham, St. Withburgha; Stoke, St. Milborough (Salop), St. Milburgha; St. Osyth (Essex), St. Osyth.
18 Further examples of Cornish well chapels occur at St. Clether Dupath near Callington, St. Ruan Minor, Menacuddle and Madron.
19 T. Cater Mitchell, 'St. Alkelda of Middleham', *Yorks. Arch. Soc.*, XII, 83. The writer also suggests that St. Winifred of Holywell, Flint, may be derived from the Welsh words gwynn (white), fryddan (stream).
20 I have never kept notes of the distribution of graves, but W. Johnson, *Byways in British archaeology* (1912), mentions the following examples: Morwenstowe (Corn), Burnham (Essex), North Cockerington, Saltfleetby All Saints and Springthorpe (Lincs), Norham (Northumb), Caterham and Weybridge (Surrey), Bishopstone, Upper Beeding and West Dean (Sussex), Amesbury, Bradford-on-Avon and Manningford Bruce (Wilts).
21 A red sandstone cross to the north of the churchyard at Tong (Salop) is said to mark the spot where unbaptised babies were buried.
22 W. Bonser, 'Survivals of Paganism in Anglo-Saxon England', *Birmingham and Midland Arch. Soc. Trans.*, LVI (1932).
23 *Penitentiale*, XXVII, 19.
24 Further examples of possible fertility figures carved on churches are discussed and illustrated in *Man*, xxx and xxxi, and in an article by Diana Portway Dobson in *Bristol and Glos. Arch. Soc. Trans.*, LV. For examples of Sheila-na-gig on roof bosses, see C. J. P. Cave, *Roof bosses in medieval churches*.
25 Émile Mâle, *La Fin du paganisme en Gaule* (1950), 57–8, gives instances of the Church's struggle against tree-worship, and adaptations of its practices to Christianity.
26 C. J. P. Cave, *Roof bosses in medieval churches* (1948), 65–8.
27 A. C. Seward, 'The foliage, flowers and fruit of Southwell Chapter House', *Cambridge Antiquarian Soc. Comm.*, XXXV (1933–4).
28 Lady Raglan, 'The Green Man in Church Architecture', *Folklore*, L (1939), 45, and R. O. M. and H. M. Carter, 'The foliate head in England', *Folklore*, LXXVIII (1967), 269.
29 Christina Hole, *English Folklore* (1940), 88.
30 Sir James Frazer, *The Golden Bough*, XI, 32–44. Until the beginning of the 18th century the famous giants of Guildhall, Gog and Magog, were made of wicker so that they could be used in pageants, when the actor concealed within them expressed the welcome of the City of London to its distinguished guests.
31 Julius Caesar, *De bello Gallico*, VI, 15.
32 C. E. Price, 'The roodscreen of the parish church of Charlton-on-Otmoor', *Oxon. Arch. Soc. Rep.* 41 (1901), 18.

33 R. G. Collingwood in *Roman Britain* (1923), 126, gives a list of other Celtic gods which figure with Mars in composite dedications.

34 F. Haverfield, 'Three notable inscriptions', *Arch. Journ.*, L, 308 ff.

35 N. Joliffe, 'Dea Brigantia', *Arch. Journ.*, XCVIII (1941), 36 ff.

36 James Frazer, *The Golden Bough*, II, 242.

37 J. P. Droop, 'An altar to the Mothers in Lund church', *The Antiquaries Journ.*, XIII (1933), 30.

38 Further references to Roman divinities to be seen in churches at:

> *Compton Dando (Som)*. Figure perhaps representing Jupiter set in buttress at N.E. angle.
>
> *Daglingworth (Glos)*. Possible dedication to the Mothers reused as window frame.
>
> *Haile (Cumb)*. Stone dedicated to Hercules and Silvanus built into vestry wall.
>
> *Halton (Lancs)*. Altar perhaps dedicated to Mithras.
>
> *Marlborough (Wilts)*. St. Mary's. Female figure with cornucopia and steering paddle, on a globe. Fortuna?
>
> *Scaleby (Cumb)*. Dedication to Jupiter.
>
> *Tockenham (Wilts)*. Figure of Aesculapius (?) with serpent twined round staff, in niche on outside wall.
>
> *Tunstall (Lancs)*. Stone dedicated to Hygiea and Aesculapius.

39 I. A. Richmond, 'Roman Lincoln', *Arch. Journ.*, CIII, 26–56.

40 *Mirk's Festial*, ed. Theodor Erbe. E.E.T.S., extra ser. XCVI (1905), 59.

2 MILESTONES IN THE DARK *pp. 23–31*

1 V. and A. H. Nash Williams, *Catalogue of the Roman inscribed and sculptured stones found at Caerleon*, 1935.

2 W. G. A. Ormesby-Gore, Lord Harlech, *Illus. Regional Guide to the Ancient Monuments of North Wales* (1948), 14.

3 Cyril Fox, *The personality of Britain* (1938), fig. 18, gives a map of the distribution of Ogham inscriptions. Ogham inscriptions can be seen in the following Pembrokeshire churches: Brawdy, Carnhedryn, Cheriton, Cilgerran, Clydai, Jordanston, Llandyssilio West, Llanfyrnach, in Glandwr chapel, St. Dogmaels Rural, St. Dogwells, Steynton, and also at Llandawke (Carmarthen) and Trallong (Brecon).

4 Royal Commission on Historical Monuments: Merioneth.

5 W. Johnson, *Byways in British Archaeology* (1912), 6–8.

6 G. W. Meates, F.S.A., *Lullingstone Roman Villa, Kent*, 1958.

7 Bede, *Historia Ecclesiastica Gentis Anglorum*, III, 4. See also W. Douglas Simpson, 'New light on St. Ninian', *Archaeologia Aeliana*, XXII (1922), 78.

8 G. Baldwin Brown, *The Arts in Early England*, V, 28–57.

9 J. S. Coltart, *Scottish Church architecture* (1936), 210.

10 G. Baldwin Brown, *op. cit.*, V, 93.

11 *Victoria County History of Cornwall*, I, 407 ff., gives list of Chi-Rho inscribed stones at St. Endellion, St. Just (2), Lanteglos by Fowey, Southill and Phillack. See also A. G. Langdon, *Old Cornish Crosses* (1896), and his article on 'The Chi-Rho monogram upon Early Christian Monuments in Cornwall', *Archaeologia Cambrensis*, 5th ser. X, 1893.

12 Cyril Fox, *Illus. Regional Guide to the Ancient Monuments of South Wales*.

13 E. G. Bowen, 'Travels of the Celtic Saints', *Antiquity*, March 1944, and 'Settlements of the Celtic Saints', *Antiquity*, Dec. 1945.

14 G. H. Doble, *Saint Dubritius*, Welsh Saints, Series No. 3, 1943.

15 G. H. Doble, *Saint Iltut* (Cardiff, 1944), 15–27.

16 J. Romilly Allen, 'The inscribed and sculptured stones at Llantwit Major', *Archaeologia Cambrensis*, 5th ser., 118 ff.

17 G. H. Doble, *St. Teilo*, Welsh Saints, Series No. 3, gives the centres of his cult in Brittany as Plogonnec, Leuhan, Landeleau, St. Thelo and elsewhere.

18 T. Taylor, *Life of St. Samson of Dol* (1925); Dol by St. Samson; St. Pol de Leon by St. Paul Aurelian; Treguier by St. Tutwall from British Dumnonia; St. Brieuc by St. Brieuc of Cardiganshire; St. Malo by St. Malo of Gwent.

19 E. G. Bowen, 'The Travels of St. Samson of Dol', *Aberystwyth Studies*, XIII, 1934.

3 THE FIRST CHURCH BUILDERS *pp.* 32–9

1 T. Pape, 'The round-shafted pre-Norman Crosses of the North Staffordshire area', *North Staffs. Field Club Trans.*, 1945–6.

2 A. W. Clapham, *English Romanesque Architecture before the Conquest* (1930), 62. The 'Life of St. Kentigern', by Joceline of Furness, is published in *Historians of Scotland* (1874), v.

3 T. D. Kendrick, *Anglo-Saxon Art* (1938), 179–80.

4 A. Saxl and R. Wittkower, *British Art and the Mediterranean* (1948), 15–18.

5 E. L. Cutts, *Parish Priests and their People* (1898), 27. In the 6th century Gallo-Roman bishops protested against the British practice of carrying portable altars from place to place. This was customary in Iona and from there was introduced into Northumbria. The earliest known example of such an altar is that of *c.* 687 in Durham cathedral. See S. Baring Gould, *The Lives of the Saints* (1907), I, 8.

6 J. Strzygowski, *Early Church Art in Northern Europe* (1928), 98–9.

7 A. W. Clapham, *English Romanesque Architecture before the Conquest* (1930), 26–7.

8 W. Levison, *England and the Continent in the 8th Century* (1946), has an appendix giving some of the dedications recorded in that period.

9 W. Page, 'Some remarks on the churches of the Domesday Survey', *Archaeologia*, LXVI (1915), 61 ff.

10 J. C. Cox, *Derbyshire Little Guide*, 1915.

11 G. Baldwin Brown, *The Arts in Early England*, I, 360.

12 This information is recorded on an inscribed stone in the Ashmolean Museum, Oxford.

4 THE MARTYRDOM OF KINGS *pp.* 40–9

1 E. W. Kemp, *Canonisation and Authority in the Western Church* (1948), p. 7, and *passim*.

2 Bede, *Historia Ecclesiastica Gentis Anglorum*, III, xxi.

3 *Ibid.*, I, xxix.

4 For list of churches dedicated to St. Oswald see Arnold Foster, *Studies in Church Dedications* (1899).

5 Wilfrid Bonser, 'The magic of St. Oswald', *Antiquity*, IX, 418.

6 E. W. Kemp, *op. cit.*, 29.

7 For full description of the spread of the cult of St. Oswald on the Continent, see E. P. Baker, 'St. Oswald and his church at Zug', *Archaeologia*, XCIII (1949).

8 For list of dedications, see Arnold Foster, *op. cit.*

9 William of Malmesbury, *Gesta Regum Anglorum*, Bk. II.

10 F. Sydney Hartland, 'The life of St. Kenelm', *Bristol and Glos. Arch. Soc. Trans.*, XXXIX.
11 H. H. Willmore, 'Stone coffins of Gloucestershire', *Bristol and Glos. Arch. Soc. Trans.*, LXI (1939), 135 ff.
12 Wall-paintings of the martyrdom of St. Edmund in Ely cathedral and of four scenes of his legend at Cliffe-at-Hoo (Kent) are reproduced in E. W. Tristram, *English Medieval Wall-paintings, 13th century* (1950).
13 I know of few allusions to Edward II in churches and some of these, such as a wall-painting at Babraham (Cambs), are uncertain. The crowned figure in the head of the east window at Stanford-on-Avon (Northants) probably represents this king, for Queen Isabella's royal arms of France are shown below and also those of Edward III as Prince of Wales. See article by P. B. Chatwin in *Birmingham Arch. Soc. Trans.*, XLI. The arms of Piers Gaveston (*vert six eagles displayed or*) appear in the east window at Harwell (Berks).
14 E. W. Kemp, *op. cit.*, 134.
15 C. V. Wedgwood, *The Trial of Charles I* (1964), 206–8.
16 A less elevated sentiment is expressed on a tablet on the tower of Barholm (Lincs):

> Was e'er such a thing
> Since the Creation
> A newe steeple built
> In the time of vexation. L.N. 1648

5 SCANDINAVIAN BRITAIN *pp.* 50–61

1 A. W. Clapham and W. H. Godfrey, 'The Saxon Cathedral of Elmham', *The Antiquaries' Journal* (1916), 402 ff.
2 H. St. George Gray, 'Danes' Skins', *Saga Book of the Viking Club*, 1906, 7.
3 G. W. Messent, *Parish churches of Norwich and Norfolk* (1936), gives a list of 135 round towers, including 6 only known from foundations or documentary records.
4 H. Munro Cautley, *Suffolk churches and their treasures* (1938), 33.
5 W. G. Collingwood, *Northumbrian Crosses* (1927), 137–8.
6 *Ibid.*, 88.
7 T. C. Lethbridge, *Merlin's Island* (1948), 59–60.
8 C. A. Parker and W. G. Collingwood, 'A reconsideration of the Gosforth Cross', *Cumberland and Westmorland Antiq. Soc. Trans.*, New ser., XVII, 99 ff. This article includes a comparative table of the carvings on the Cross and the subject matter of the Völuspá.
9 W. G. Collingwood, 'The Archaeology of the Viking Age in England', *Saga Book of the Viking Club*, 1906–7.
10 Cotton MS. Tiberius C. vi. fol. 14.
11 Hilda R. Ellis, 'Sigurd and the art of the Viking Age', *Antiquity*, Sept. 1942.
12 R. C. Kermode, *Manx Crosses* (1907), Nos. 93, 94 and 95.
13 St. Eloy is represented as a bishop holding a claw hammer on screens at Great Yeldham (Essex) and Hempstead (Norfolk) and at Tunstead (Norfolk), he also holds the amputated leg of a horse.
14 P. A. Munch, *Norse Mythology* (1926), 37–8.
15 Royal Commission on Historical Monuments: Essex.
16 *Introduction to the Survey of Place Names* (1924), edited by W. A. Mawer and F. M. Stenton.

S

6 THE AGE OF ABBEYS *pp.* 62–70

1 P. M. Johnston, 'Claverley Church and its paintings', *Archaeological Journal* (1903), LX, 51.
2 E. W. Tristram and W. G. Constable, *English Medieval Wall-paintings; 12th century* (1944), support this interpretation and also apply it to the two men fighting on foot shown in a 13th-century painting at Kingston (Cambs). This latter is reproduced in Professor Tristram's book on 13th-century wall-paintings (1950), plate 214.
3 John Bilston, 'Weaverthorpe and its builder', *Archaeologia*, LXXII.
4 William of Malmesbury, *Gesta Pontificum Anglorum*, Rolls Series No. 52, 135.
5 The historical background to this window is fully discussed in G. McN. Rushforth, *Medieval Christian Imagery* (1936), 120–36.
6 E. W. Tristram and W. G. Constable, *English Medieval Wall-paintings: 12th century* (1927), 35. See also Clive Bell's introductory essay in *Twelfth century Painting at Hardham and Clayton* (1947), and Audrey Baker, 'Lewes Priory and the early group of Wall-paintings in Sussex', *Walpole Society* (1946), XXXI.
7 N. J. H. Westlake, *Outlines of the History of design in Mural Painting* (1902–5), 154–5.
8 M. R. James, *Abbeys* (1925), 76.
9 A. H. Hamilton Thompson, *English Monasteries* (1923), 57–9.
10 R. Liddesdale Palmer, *English Monasteries in the Middle Ages* (1930), 76.
11 Compare with the refectory pulpit which is almost the only relic of the domestic buildings of the Abbey of Shrewsbury.
12 R. Liddesdale Palmer, *op. cit.*, 170.
13 A. Hamilton Thompson, *The English Clergy* (1947), 115.
14 G. C. Druce, 'Queen Camel, bosses on the chancel roof', *Somerset Arch. and Nat. Hist. Soc.* (1937), LXXXIII, 89–106.
15 C. J. P. Cave, *Roof bosses in medieval Churches* (1948), 15.
16 M. D. Anderson (M. D. Cox), 'The Twelfth century design sources of the Worcester Cathedral misericords', *Archaeologia*, XCVII (1959), 165 ff.
17 F. H. Crossley, 'Monastic influence on the construction of parish churches', *Chester and N. Wales Arch. Soc. Journal* (1939), XXX, 138–49, includes list of Cheshire churches belonging to monasteries.
18 Mr. Howard Colvin pointed out to me that the last part of the inscription has been rearranged by modern restoration and should read: . . . *negligens, discipulus inobediens, juvenis otiosus, senex obstinatus, monachus curialis.* The word agreeing with *negligens* has been lost and *religiosus* has been added at the other end to agree with *curialis* which properly belongs to *monachus.*
19 Edward Conybeare, *Highways and Byways in Cambridge and Ely* (1923), 198.

7 GATHERINGS IN A PORCH *pp.* 71–8

1 A. W. Clapham, *English Romanesque Architecture before the Conquest* (1930), 121.
2 Ulric Daubeny, *Ancient Cotswold Churches* (1921), gives the following list of Gloucestershire churches which have niches within their porches: Aldsworth, Ampney Crucis, Ampney St. Mary, Ampney St. Peter, Barnsley, Little Barrington, Baunton, Bibury, Eastleach, Martin and Turville, Hazleton, Notgrove, Salperton and Winson. The battered remains of the images which may have stood in these niches can be seen at Coberley and Gt. Rissington.
3 L. F. Salzman, *English Life in the Middle Ages* (1926), 136 ff.
4 G. H. Cook, *Medieval Chantries and chantry chapels* (1947), 24.
5 *Ibid.*, 60.

6 A. R. Dufty, 'The Stathum Book of Hours', *Arch. Journ.*, CVI. Memorial volume to Sir Alfred Clapham (1952), 83–90.

7 F. J. Drake-Carnell, *Old English Customs and Ceremonies* (1938), 53–7, quotes several examples of doles.

8 G. Baldwin Brown, *The Arts in Early England* (1903), I, 371 and II, 207.

9 Quoted by G. G. Coulton, *Life in the Middle Ages*, III (1928), from the translation by F. M. Nichols (1865), I, 104 ff. The painting at Stowell is reproduced on plate 67 of E. W. Tristram and W. G. Constable, *English Medieval Wall-paintings: 12th century* (1944), where it is suggested (p. 45) that it may record some notable application of the Ordeal in the neighbourhood and thus stress the connection between earthly and heavenly justice.

10 Bernard Rackham, *The Ancient glass of Canterbury Cathedral* (1949), 84.

11 A full account of this case, as given in the Year Books of Edward III (Anno xxix, Hilary Term, Case No. 34), is quoted by G. G. Coulton, *op. cit.*, 89.

12 Rackham, *op. cit.*, 94–5.

13 J. C. Cox, *Sanctuaries and Sanctuary Seekers* (1911), 9.

14 J. J. Jusserand, *English Wayfaring Life in the Middle Ages* (1891), 153.

15 W. J. Pressey, 'Sanctuary in Essex', *Essex Review*, XLIV, 137 ff., quotes the description of the procedure in smaller churches as given in the Colchester Red Book.

16 M. A. Bagnall Oakley, 'Sanctuary Knockers', *Bristol and Glos. Arch. Soc. Trans.*, XIV, 131–40. See also J. C. Cox, *op. cit.*, for the contrary opinion. There is a fine example of this type of closing ring at Dormington (Herefs).

17 L. Salzman, *More Medieval By-ways* (1913), 119.

Part II: The Picture Book of the Churches

I   THE ARRANGEMENT OF IMAGERY   *pp.* 81–90

1 C. J. Cox and C. Bradley Ford, *The Parish Churches of England* (1935), 23–44, gives a very clear account of this development of parish churches at various periods, illustrated by plans and photographs.

2 J. C. P. Cave, 'Orientation of Churches', *Antiquaries' Journal* (1949), 47–51.

3 Hugh Benson, 'Church Orientations and Patronal festivals', *Antiquaries' Journal* (1955), CXII, 205 ff.

4 M. R. James, 'The verses formerly inscribed in the twelve windows of the choir of Canterbury Cathedral', *Cambridge Antiq. Soc. Publ.*, No. 38, 1901.

5 B. Rackham, *The ancient glass in Canterbury Cathedral* (1949).

6 A. N. Didron, *Christian Iconography* (1907). English translation completed and added to by Margaret Stokes. A translation of the Byzantine Manual is printed as an appendix.

7 G. H. Cook, *Medieval chantries and chantry chapels* (1947).

8 William Durandus, *Rationale Divinorum Officiorum*, translated by J. M. Neale and B. Webb (1893), 21–34, shows to what lengths medieval scholars could go in attributing symbolical meanings to the purely structural aspects of churches.

9 C. E. Keyser, *Norman Tympana and Lintels* (1904), p. xxviii.

10 W. G. St. John Hope and W. R. Lethaby, 'The imagery and sculptures on the west front of Wells Cathedral', *Archaeologia* (1904), LIX.

11 E. W. Tristram and W. G. Constable, *English medieval wall-paintings: 12th century* (1944), 113–5.

12 J. C. Webster, *Labours of the Months* (1938).

13 Émile Mâle, *L'Art religieux du xiiie siècle en France* (1910), 18.

14 Clive Bell, *Twelfth century paintings at Hardham and Clayton* (1947), 15.

15 G. McN. Rushforth, *Medieval Christian Imagery as illustrated by the painted windows of Malvern Priory church* (1936).

16 F. T. S. Houghton, 'Astley church and its stall paintings', *Birmingham and Midland Arch. Soc. Trans.*, LI, 19 ff.

17 O. G. Farmer, *Fairford Church and its stained glass windows* (1931).

2 THE CONVENTIONS OF PICTURE-WRITING *pp.* 91–100

1 V. A. Kolve, *The Play called Corpus Christi* (1966), 4.

2 Meyer Schapiro, 'Cain's jaw-bone that did the First Murder', *Art Bulletin*, Sept. 1942.

3 *Origo Mundi*, a 15th-century manuscript in the Bodleian Library, MS. 791.

4 G. R. Owst, *Literature and Pulpit in medieval England* (1966), 492.

5 G. McN. Rushforth, 'The windows of the church of Saint Neot, Cornwall', *Exeter Diocesan Archit. and Arch. Soc. Trans.* (1937), xv.

6 Francis Bond, *Wood carvings in English churches; Misericords* (1910), 81–2.

7 D. M. Robb, 'Iconography of the Annunciation in the 14th and 15th centuries', *Art Bulletin*, XVIII, 480 ff.

8 A. N. Didron, *Christian Iconography* (1907), translated M. Stokes, 201–34, describes the forms adopted for the portrayal of God the Father.

9 *Ibid.*, 234–417, describes how Christ is either portrayed or symbolised.

10 R. Pettazoni, 'Pagan origins of the Three-headed representations of the Christian Trinity', *Warburg Journal*, IX, 135 ff.

11 K. Künstle, *Ikonographie der christlichen Kunst* (1928), ii, 25 ff.

12 Otto Brendel, 'Origin and meaning of the Mandorla in eastern art', *Gazette des Beaux-Arts*, 6e sér., XXV (1944), 5–24.

13 S. J. P. Cave, *Roof bosses in medieval churches* (1948), fig. 114.

14 These verses, from a manuscript in the British Museum, Royal MS. 17A xxvii, are printed in *Legends of Holy Rood, Emblems of the Passion and Cross poems*, ed. R. Morris. E.E.T.S. O ser. XLVI.

15 J. C. P. Cave, 'The bosses on the vault of the quire of Winchester Cathedral', *Archaeologia*, LXXVI, 161, gives a full description of these bosses with many illustrations.

16 Dom Louis Gougaud, *Devotional and Ascetic practices in the Middle Ages* (1927), 79.

17 British Museum Add. 37049. The poem about the Falconer was published in *Speculum*, XXXII, 278.

3 THE OLD TESTAMENT *pp.* 101–108

1 G. Wilpert, *La fede della Chiesa nascente secondo i monumenti dell'arte funeraria antica* (1938), *passim*.

2 Françoise Henry, *Irish art in the Early Christian Period* (1940), 169–70.

3 St. Gregory, *Homilies*, see Migne, *Patrologia Latina*, LXXVI, col. 983 and col. 1287.

4 Bede, *Historia Abbatum*, ed. C. Plummer (1896), i, 373.

5 M. R. James, 'On the paintings formerly in the Choir of Peterborough cathedral', *Cambridge Antiquarian Soc. Trans.*, IX, 178–94.

6 B. Rackham, *Ancient Glass in Canterbury Cathedral* (1949), 51–65, and M. R. James, 'The verses formerly inscribed in the twelve windows in the choir of Canterbury Cathedral', *Cambridge Antiquarian Soc. Publ.* No. 38, 1901.

7 K. Künstle, *Ikonographie der christlichen Kunst* (1928), I, 277.

8 J. H. Cornell, *Biblia Pauperum* (1926), J. Ph. Bergereau, *Biblia Pauperum* (1859), is a facsimile of a 15th-century Netherlandish block-book.

9 J. Lutz and P. Perdrizet, *Speculum Humanae Salvationis* (1907). A facsimile of a 14th-century Italian manuscript of the *Speculum* was published for the Roxburghe Club in 1926 with a preface by M. R. James.

10 A. Watson, *The early iconography of the Tree of Jesse* (1934), and A. K. Coomaraswamy, 'The Tree of Jesse and Indian parallels or sources', *Art Bulletin*, xviii, 217–20.

11 G. McN. Rushforth, *Medieval Christian Imagery* (1936), 185 n.

12 M. R. James, 'Pictor in Carmine', *Archaeologia*, xciv, 141–66.

4 NEW TESTAMENT: *Infancy and Ministry of Christ* pp. 109–16

1 Émile Mâle, *L'Art religieux du xiiie siècle en France* (1910), 288–90.

2 *Dialogue of Salomon and Saturnus*, ed. J. M. Kemble, Aelfric Society (1840).

3 *The Mirroure of Man's Salvacionne*, ed. A. H. Huth, Roxburghe Club, 1888.

4 *The Mirrour of the Blessed Lyf of Jesu Christ, by Nicholas Love*. Facsimile of William Caxton's edition. Roxburghe Club, 1908.

5 *Apocryphal New Testament*. Trans. M. R. James (1926), 74.

6 G. Wilpert, *La fede della Chiesa nascente* (1938), 24–7 repr. fig. 21.

7 *Mirk's Festial*, ed. Th. Erbe. E.E.T.S. extra ser. xcvi (1905), 22.

8 Translation quoted from J. H. Cornell, 'The Iconography of the Nativity of Christ', *Uppsala Universitets Årsskrift* (1942). This passage does not figure in the 15th-century English translation of 'The revelations of St. Birgitta', edited W. P. Cummings. E.E.T.S., O. ser. xlxxviii.

9 Mâle, *op. cit.*, 254, says that it is in a Greek chronicle, early 6th century, translated into Latin by a Merovingian monk, that the names of the Magi first appear in the forms Bithisarea, Melichior and Gathaspa.

10 This association appears in Bede's *Commentary on St. Matthew* lib. i, cap. ii.

11 *Mirrour of the Blessed Lyf of Jesu Christ* (see note 4), 51–3.

12 J. Strzygowsky, *Ikonographie der Taufe Christi* (1885). Émile Mâle, *L'Art religieux du xiie siècle en France* (1928), 110, quotes the instruction of the Byzantine Manual for Painters that angels should cover their hands beneath their robes in reverence. The first appearance in France of the angel holding out the tunic is in the windows of Chartres cathedral, *c.* 1150. See Mâle, *op. cit.*, fig. 98.

13 G. McN. Rushforth, 'The baptism of St. Christopher', *Antiquaries Journal* (1926), discusses the pouring of water from a vessel in Baptism, giving examples in glass at Birtsmorton (Worcs) and on a font at Gresham (Norfolk).

14 B. Rackham, *The ancient glass of Canterbury Cathedral* (1949), 63.

15 In *Queen Mary's Psalter*, facsimile edition (1912), ed. G. Warner, plate 198, the *architriclinus* is shown with a nimbus and the editor refers to this as being 'under his guise as St. Architriclin'. C. Woodforde, 'The medieval glass of the East Harling and North Tuddenham churches, Norfolk', *Brit. Arch. Ass. Journ.* (1940), 3rd ser. V, 5, quotes M. R. James as saying that he only knew of further references to the Architriclinus as a person, not as a saint.

16 The parable is represented in the Roman Catacombs on two 4th-century tombs of women, where it apparently expresses the prayer that the dead women shall

be numbered among the Wise Virgins. (See G. Wilpert, *Le pitture delle catacombe romane*, 833 ff.)

5 NEW TESTAMENT: *The Passion to the Last Judgment* pp. 117–28

1 O. G. Farmer, *Fairford Church and its stained glass windows* (1939). For description of the Palm Sunday processional procedure see Adrian Fortescue, *The Ceremonies of the Roman Rite described* (1943), 262.

2 Clark D. Lamberton, *Themes from St. John's Gospel in the early Catacomb Paintings* (1905).

3 E. Dobbert, 'Das Abendmahl Christi in der bildenden Kunst bis den Schluss des 14. Jahrhunderts', *Repertorium für Kunstwissenschaft* (1891), XIV, 175–203.

4 Quoted from G. G. Coulton, *Medieval Panorama* (1938), 420.

5 S. A. Callison, 'The Iconography of the Cock on the Column', *Art Bulletin*, XXI, 160 ff.

6 Dom Ethelbert Horne, 'The Crown of Thorns in Art', *Downside Review*, Jan. 1935, 48 ff. Herbert Thurston (*Catholic Encyclopaedia*, 'Crown of Thorns') suggests that the band of rushes preserved in Nôtre-Dame de Paris was used to hold a helmet of thorns on the head of Christ, these thorns being twigs of the jujube tree (*Zizyphus spina Christi*). The Crown of Thorns is not mentioned as extant by Christian writers before the late 6th century, but it was venerated at Jerusalem for several centuries before being taken to France.

7 C. R. Morey, 'Christus Crucifer', *Art Bulletin*, IV, 117 ff. The earliest examples of Christ shown bearing His Cross are on 4th-century sarcophagi of a type always associated with figure subjects suggestive of Eastern origin. The subject is treated symbolically rather than realistically. In the art of the Egyptian Church Christ often carries a small cross, like a sceptre, in scenes of his miracles, and in the Entry into Jerusalem.

8 L. H. Gondijs, *L'Iconographie byzantine du Crucifié mort sur la Croix* (1947).

9 Quoted from G. G. Coulton, *Medieval Panorama* (1938), 567. Aron Andersson, *English influences on Norwegian and Swedish figure sculpture 1220–70*, 285 ff., gives an interesting discussion on the position of the feet on a 13th-century crucifix.

10 R. J. Peebles, 'The legend of Longinus in ecclesiastical art and in English literature', *Bryn Mawr Monographs*, No. 9 (1911), discusses the relation between the legend of the blind Longinus and that of the slaying of Baldur the Beautiful by the blind Hödr, deceived by the false god Loki.

11 W. L. Hildburgh, 'Iconographical peculiarities in English medieval alabasters', *Folklore*, March and June 1933.

12 Apocryphal New Testament (see note 5), 117–44.

13 *The Book of Margery Kempe*. E.E.T.S., CCXII.

14 E. T. Dewald, 'The Iconography of the Ascension', *American Journal of Archaeology*, 2nd ser. XIX, 277 ff.

15 K. Young, *The drama of the medieval Church* (1933), quotes a description of an Ascension Image being hoisted into a ring of silk curtains under the roof, from a 14th-century *Ordinarium* from Moosberg. Such an image is preserved in the Museum für Völkerkunde in Basle. Meyer Schapiro, 'The Image of the disappearing Christ; the Ascension in English art around the year 1000', *Gazette des Beaux-Arts*, 6ᵉ sér. XXIII (1943), 135–58, ascribes this convention rather to Anglo-Saxon literary sources.

16 Abel Fabre, 'L'Iconographie de la Pentecôte', *Gazette des Beaux-Arts* (1923), 33.

17 J. C. Waller, 'On a painting recently discovered in Chaldon Church, Surrey', *Surrey Arch. Coll.*, v, 275 ff. The author's bound and annotated copy of this article is in the library of the Society of Antiquaries of London and includes a much wider range of literary parallels and comparisons than the printed version.

18 A model ladder was found in a tomb of the Ptolemaic period at Ekhmeem. See *The Times*, Aug. 22, 1887.

19 *Gesta Romanorum*. E.E.T.S. extra ser., xxxiii, ed. S. H. Heritage, 384–5. The sinners cast into the cauldron were a pair of adulterous lovers.

20 Herolt, *Sermones discipuli. De Tempore*, cxxv, *De penis inferni*, gives an elaborate description of the torments undergone by a sinful woman. Dogs devoured her hands because, as she tells, 'I stretched out my hands, in giving to dogs those things I ought to have given to the poor, that is to say meat, cakes and other things; I even adorned them luxuriously with rings and gems.'

21 M. P. Perry, 'The Psychostasis in Christian art', *Burl. Mag.*, xxii, 94 ff. The weighing of the souls before Osiris is illustrated in E. A. Wallis Budge, *The Book of the Dead* (1898).

22 Françoise Henry, *Irish Art in the Early Christian Period* (1940), 159.

23 W. L. Hildburgh, 'An English carving of St. Michael weighing a soul', *Burl. Mag.*, May 1947. Herbert Thurston (*Catholic Encyclopaedia*, 'The Rosary') dismisses the tradition that the Rosary was originally instituted by St. Dominic. The use of beads, or counters, in connection with repetitive devotions goes back to ancient Nineveh, and in 1075 Lady Godiva of Coventry bequeathed to an image of the Virgin the circlet of beads threaded on cords by which she used to reckon her prayers.

6 THE VIRGIN MARY AND THE SAINTS *pp.* 129–41

1 This carving was found built into the wall near the tomb and fitted back into the space between the hands of the effigy from which it had obviously been taken.

2 E. W. Tristram and M. R. James, *Wall paintings in Eton College Chapel and the Lady Chapel of Winchester Cathedral*, Walpole Soc., xvii (1929).

3 M. R. James, *The sculptured bosses in the roof of the Bauchun Chapel, Norwich Cathedral* (1908).

4 M. R. James and E. W. Tristram, 'Wall paintings in Croughton Church', *Archaeologia*, lxxvi.

5 Betty Kurth, 'The iconography of the Wirksworth slab', *Burl. Mag.*, lxxxvi (April 1945), 114 ff. For narratives of the Assumption of the Virgin see *Apocryphal New Testament*, ed. M. R. James, 194–227.

6 The incident of the girdle occurs only in the narrative of the Assumption attributed to Joseph of Arimathea (*Apocryphal New Testament*, 217–8) and Dr. James considered that the prominence there given to the story of the relic honoured at Prato indicated that this text, which is certainly late, was written in Italy in the 13th century.

7 Migne, *Patrologia latina*, xxxix, col. 2189. See also Herbert Thurston in *Catholic Encyclopaedia*, i, 629.

8 T. S. Houghton, 'Astley Church and its stall paintings', *Birmingham Arch. Soc. Trans.*, li, 19 ff., quotes the following examples of Creed figures:
Painted screens. Kenton and Chudleigh, Devon. The apostles only at Gooderstone, Mattishall and Weston Longueville in Norfolk. The damaged paintings at Thornham (Norfolk) may have represented the prophets.

Painted roof at Abingdon (Berks) has both prophets and kings.

Windows. Norbury (Staffs), Landwade (Cambs), Drayton Beauchamp (Bucks), Hayles (Glos). In the cherestory of the Lady Chapel of York Minster there are 7 prophets and 6 apostles.

This list could easily be prolonged, for many churches have small figures of the apostles in their tracery lights.

9 Christopher Woodforde, *The stained glass of New College, Oxford* (1951), 69.

10 Émile Mâle, *L'Art religieux de la fin du moyen-âge en France* (1931), 253–79. For a complete list of the Sybils' prophecies and attributes, see E. C. Husenbeth, *Emblems of the saints* (1882).

11 *Dives and Pauper,* edition printed by Wynkyn de Worde, in the British Museum.

12 W. L. Hildburgh, 'Folk Lore recorded in English medieval Alabaster carvings', *Folklore,* LX (1949). The feasts are: St. Peter, June 29th; Decollation of St. John the Baptist, Aug. 29th; St. Thomas, Dec. 29th; traditional date of the Crucifixion, March 25th.

13 W. H. St. John Hope, 'On sculptured alabaster Tables called St. John's Heads', *Archaeologia,* LII, pt. ii, 669 ff.

14 *Acta Sanctorum,* XXV.

15 Louis du Broc de Segange, *Les Saints Protecteurs des corporations et protecteurs spéciaux* (1887).

16 *Ibid.,* ii, 49–50, quotes several of these hymns and invocations.

17 C. E. Keyser, *List of buildings having mural decorations* (1883).

18 F. Kendon, *Mural paintings in English churches during the Middle Ages* (1923), discusses the probable influence of such woodcuts.

19 John Salmon, 'St. Christopher in medieval life and art', *Brit. Arch. Ass. Journ.,* LXI (1936), 76 ff. Also H. H. Brindley, 'St. Christopher', in Supplement to Blomefield's *Norfolk* (1929).

20 The inscriptions on the Castle Acre pulpit are as follows:

    St. Gregory. *Gloria predicantium est profectus audientium.*

    St. Jerome. *Ne te decipiat sermonis pulcritudo.*

    St. Ambrose. *Evangelium mentes omnium rigat.*

    St. Augustine. *Impletus spiritu sancto predicavit.*

21 Christopher Woodforde, *Stained glass in Somerset, 1250–1830* (1946), 260–6. For Shrewsbury windows, see H. E. Forrest, *The old churches of Shrewsbury* (1920), 75–9.

22 E. W. Tristram, 'Franciscan influence in English medieval wall-painting', in *Franciscan History and Legend in English medieval art,* ed. A. G. Little (1937).

23 Hobart Bird, *Old Warwickshire churches* (1935), 125, quotes the tradition that Wroxall Priory church was built by Hugh de Hatton as a thank-offering for his deliverance after seven years of chained captivity in Palestine.

24 G. McN. Rushforth, 'The Kirkham Monument in Paignton Church', *Exeter Diocesan Archit. and Arch. Soc. Trans.,* XV (1927).

7 THE PREACHERS *pp.* 142–55

1 G. R. Owst, *Preaching in Medieval England* (1926), *passim,* for the historical evolution of preaching.

2 G. R. Owst, *Literature and pulpit in medieval England* (1966), quotes large numbers of sermon stories and similes which have their counterparts in medieval carvings. For the latter see G. L. Remnant, *A catalogue of misericords in Great Britain* (1969).

3 Quoted from Owst, *Literature,* 420–1. St. Albans MS. fol. 17. A similar phrase occurs in Harl MS. 2398, fol. 87b.

4 E. C. Rouse, 'Wall paintings in the church of St. John the Evangelist, Corby, Lincolnshire', *Archaeological Journ.*, C 151-2.

5 John Rylands Library, Manchester, MS. lat. 367, fol. 25b.

6 R. Hamann, 'The girl and the Ram', *Burlington Magazine*, LX (1932), 91 ff.

7 Owst, *Literature*, 390-404.

8 A. Katzenellenbogen, *Allegories of the Virtues and Vices in medieval art* (1939), deals with the early development of this theme.

9 E. W. Tristram, *English Wall paintings of the 14th century* (1955), 99-107.

10 *Mirk's Festial*, ed. Theodor Erbe. E.E.T.S. extra ser. XCVI (1905), 282-7.

11 *Middle English Sermons*, ed. Woodburn Ross. E.E.T.S. ord. ser. CCIX (1940), 49-57. For fuller discussion of the possible relation of these sermons and paintings to the lost Pater Noster Plays, see M. D. Anderson, *Drama and Imagery in English Churches*, 1965.

12 G. McN. Rushforth, 'Seven Sacrament compositions in English medieval art', *Antiquaries' Journ.*, IX, 83 ff. Incomplete examples of Seven Sacrament windows are recorded at: Tattershall (Lincs), Cartmel Fell (Lancs), St. Anthony's Chapel, Burrington and Bishop's Lydeard in Somerset; Frampton (Glos), Malvern Priory, Nostell Priory (Yorks), Llandyrnog (Denbighs). A wall-painting of the subject was found at Kirton (Lincs) in 1860 but perished.

13 E. W. Ganderton and Jean Lafond, *Ludlow stained and painted glass* (1961), 32-7.

14 Owst, *Literature*, 532, quoting Caius College MS. 334, fol. 174b.

15 E. Carleton Williams, 'The Dance of Death in sculpture and paintings in the Middle Ages', *Brit. Arch. Ass. Journ.*, 3rd ser. I, 229-57.

16 E. Carleton Williams, 'Mural paintings of the Three Living and the Three Dead', *Brit. Arch. Ass. Journ.*, 3rd ser. VII (1942), 31 ff.

17 S. Glixelli, *Les Cinq Poèmes des trois morts et des trois vifs* (Paris, 1914).

18 See also F. Storck, 'Aspects of Death in English Art and Poetry', *Burl. Mag.*, XXI, 249 and 314. This article includes a list of paintings of the Three Living and the Three Dead still extant or recorded.

19 J. G. Waller, 'Wall paintings at Raunds and Slapton, Northants', *Arch. Journ.*, XXXIV, 219 ff.

20 Owst, *Literature*, 299-303, quoting from the *Summa Predicantium Judicium Divinum* of John of Bromyard.

21 E. W. Tristram, *op. cit.*, 121-5.

22 *Medieval Lore from Bartholomaeus Anglicus*, ed. Robert Steele (1924), 168.

23 Owst, *Literature*, 204.

24 Kenneth Varty, *Reynard the Fox* (1967), a study of fox-subjects in medieval art, and their relation to the literary sources.

25 The paintings are reproduced in R. S. Loomis, *A mirror of Chaucer's World* (1965), 162.

26 E. P. Hammond, *English Verse from Chaucer to Surrey* (Durham N.C., 1927) 113-8, gives the full text of the poem by John Shirley describing Lydgate's devisings for the hangings, and references to other literary allusions to Bicorne and Chinchface, the alternative spellings of the monsters' names.

8 THE PLAYERS *pp.* 156-63

1 M. D. Anderson, *Drama and Imagery in English Churches* (1963), deals entirely with the relation between medieval plays and the imagery of contemporary churches.

2 *The Northern Passion*. Ed. F. D. Foster. E.E.T.S. ord. ser. CXLV.

3 J. A. Knowles, 'Medieval methods of employing cartoons for stained glass', *Master Glass Painters' Journal*, I, no. 3, 35 ff.

4 W. L. Hildburgh, 'English alabaster carvings as records of Medieval religious drama', *Archaeologia*, XCIII.

5 A. Heales, 'Easter Sepulchres', *Archaeologia*, XLII, 263–308.

6 K. Young, *The drama of the Medieval Church* (1933), treats fully the history of this evolution of drama. Glynne Wickham, *Early English Stages*, vol. I, 1300–1576, contains much interesting material about the production methods of plays and also secular pageants.

7 J. K. Bonnell, 'The Serpent with the Human head in art and Mystery Play', *American Journal of Archaeology* (new series), XXI (1917), 255 ff.

8 In the early morality play *The Pride of Life* the King orders his soldier, Strength, to draw the curtains round him because he wishes to rest. The next scene does not require his presence.

9 M. D. Anderson, *op. cit.*, 87–104, discusses the evidence of these bosses.

10 Émile Mâle, *L'Art religieux de la fin du moyen-âge en France* (1931), 58.

9   HOW THE CRAFTSMEN GOT THEIR DESIGNS   *pp.* 164–73

1 G. L. Remnant, *A Catalogue of Misericords in Great Britain* (1969).

2 M. D. Anderson, 'The Designers of Misericords', *Connoisseur Year Book 1960*, 115–18.

3 T. S. R. Boase, *English Art 1100–1116* (1953), 24.

4 A. Saxl and R. Wittkower, *British Art and the Mediterranean* (1948), 14, emphasises the foreign parallels. Lawrence Stone, *Sculpture in Britain in the Middle Ages*, Pelican History of Art (1955), 10–12, discusses the difference in the way Northumbrian carvers handled these foreign themes.

5 M. D. Whinney, *The interrelation of the Fine Arts in England in the Middle Ages* (1930), *passim*.

6 E. W. Tristram and W. G. Constable, *English medieval Wall-paintings: 12th century* (1944), 64.

7 M. D. Anderson, 'The twelfth-century design sources of the Worcester Cathedral misericords', *Archaeologia*, XCVII (1959).

8 M. R. James, 'On two series of paintings formerly at Worcester Priory', *Cambridge Antiq. Soc. Proc.* No. 42, 99 ff.

9 M. R. James, *The Sculptured Bosses in the Cloisters of Norwich Cathedral* (1911).

10 *The Trinity Apocalypse*, ed. M. R. James, Roxburghe Club, 1909.

11 Bertram Colgrave, 'The St. Cuthbert paintings on the Carlisle Cathedral stalls', *Burl. Mag.*, LXXIII, 17 ff.

12 J. A. Knowles, 'Medieval methods of employing cartoons for stained glass', *Master Glass Painters' Journal*, I, No. 3, 35 ff.

Part III: The Recrod of Social History

I   PRINCES OF CHURCH AND STATE   *pp.* 177–93

1 G. H. Cook, *Medieval Chantries and chantry chapels* (1947), 53.

2 Katherine of Aragon and Mary, Queen of Scots, were both buried in Peterborough cathedral but their original monuments have been destroyed.

3 J. Harvey, *The Plantagenets* (1948).

4 *Livery Collars.*

F. H. Crossley, *English Church Monuments* (1921), and Arthur Gardner, *Alabaster Tombs* (1940), illustrate the following examples:

S.S. Collar. Three tombs at Elford (Staffs); others at Bottesford (Leics), Malpas (Ches), Higher Peover (Ches), Lowick (Northants) and Turvey (Beds). Other examples on memorial brasses occur at Digswell (Herts), Little Casterton (Rutland), Mugginton (Derbs) and Apsley Guise (Beds).

Suns and roses collars occur on effigies at: Norbury (Staffs), Stanton Harcourt (Oxon), Macclesfield (Ches), Holme Pierrepont (Notts), Kinlet (Salop), Berkeley (Glos), Melbury Sampford (Dorset).

On brasses at: Little Easton (Essex), Broxbourne (Herts), Rougham (Norfolk). For further examples see Mill Stephenson, *A list of Monumental Brasses in the British Isles*, 1926.

5 W. W. Rees-Jones, *The Order of St. George and St. George's, Stamford* (1937).

6 Arthur Gardner, *Alabaster Tombs* (1940), 27.

7 The arms on the Tickhill tower are identified in Hunter's *South Yorkshire*, 1828–31.

8 F. J. C. Hearnshaw, *An outline of the History of the British Isles* (1938), 148.

9 John A. Cory, 'Notes on fortified churches in Cumberland', *Arch. Journ.*, XVI (1859), 318.

10 W. G. Bannister, *Guide to Tewkesbury Abbey* (1923).

11 W. Brown, 'The Brus Cenotaph at Guisborough', *Yorks. Arch. Soc. Journ.*, XIII (1895), 226 ff.

12 Colonel G. F. T. Leathers, 'The Flodden window at Middleton, Lancs', *Berwickshire Naturalists Club*, XXX, 82.

13 A. W. B. Messenger, 'The Heraldry of Canterbury Cathedral; the Great Cloister vault'. Supplement to the *Friends of Canterbury Cathedral Reports*, I.

14 A. R. Wagner, *Historic Heraldry in Britain* (1939), 17.

15 The explanation of this curious device, which was used by other families besides the Stanleys, lies in the legend of Sir Thomas Lathom being carried off by an eagle while still an infant. Carved on the Dean's stall in Manchester cathedral, we see a huge nest in a tree, with the babe lying in it, while a group of people hurry to the castle to tell what they have seen. Misericords in Bolton parish church and Whalley (Lancs) show the eagle and the swaddled baby. It appears in its heraldic form as the crest on the helm of Sir John Stanley's effigy at Elford (Staffs).

16 A. C. Fox-Davies, *Heraldic Badges* (1907), 29–41, cites a grant or exemplification of the Stafford badges, to the number of eighteen, put into evidence in the Stafford Peerage Case. This book lists many of the best-known badges which are likely to be seen in medieval churches.

17 W. H. St. John Hope, 'The Last Testament and Inventory of John, de Vere, Thirteenth Earl of Oxford', *Archaeologia*, LXVI.

18 F. H. Cripps Day, 'Arms and Armour in Churches in England', *Arch. Journ.*, XCI (1934), 59.

19 The de la Pole leopards' heads also appear on the fonts at Hull, Holy Trinity, and Hedon (Yorks, E.R.). In the south chancel aisle at Hull we can see both the old de la Pole arms: two bars nebuly, and their later coat: azure, a fess between three leopards' heads or.

20 F. J. Allen, *The great Church Towers of England* (1932), 115.

21 G. T. Rivoira, *Lombardic Architecture* (1910), ii, 239.

22 Châlons-sur-Marne, Lyons and Geneva. See also J. N. Dalton, *The Collegiate Church of Ottery St. Mary* (1917).

23 Immediately after his consecration Richard of Gravesend crossed to France with the Earls of Gloucester and Leicester to negotiate peace terms and he accompanied Henry III on a similar mission the following year (D. N. B.).

24 J. S. Purvis, 'The use of Continental woodcuts and prints by the Ripon school of wood-carvers in the early 16th century', *Archaeologia*, LXXXV (1936), 107.

2 THE CRUSADERS *pp.* 195–9

1 G. Zarnecki, *Later English Romanesque Sculpture* (1953), 39–41, discusses the marks of French influence on Rochester cathedral and the churches at Barfreston and Patrixbourne in Kent.

2 R. M. Serjeantson, *Notes on the History of the Church of the Holy Sepulchre, Northampton.*

3 W. H. St. John Hope, 'Round-naved churches in England and their connection with the Orders of the Temple and the Hospital of St. John of Jerusalem', *Archaeologia Cantiana*, XXXIII (1918), 63 ff.

4 T. W. Shore, *History of Hampshire* (1892), 138 ff.

5 A. W. Clapham, *English Romanesque Architecture after the Conquest* (1934), 134, 137.

6 G. W. Minns, *North Baddesley Church and the Knights Hospitallers* (n.d.).

7 J. S. Coltart, *Scottish Church Architecture* (1936), 144–6.

8 F. H. Crossley, *English Church Monuments* (1921), 177.

9 E. S. Prior and A. Gardner, *Medieval English Figure Sculpture* (1912), 594. The wooden effigy of a Knight Templar of the Weston family in the church at Weston-under-Lizard (Staffs) is represented drawing his sword.

3 THE PILGRIMS *pp.* 200–7

1 G. Zarnecki, *Later English Romanesque Sculpture* (1953), 9–15.

2 *Ibid.*, 12.

3 The helmet is in the Historical Museum at Stockholm and this detail is reproduced in H. S. Schetelig and H. Falk, *Scandinavian Archaeology*, plate 62.

4 W. L. Hildburgh, 'Iconographical peculiarities in English Alabaster Carvings', *Folklore*, June 1933.

5 G. McN. Rushforth, *Medieval Christian Imagery* (1936), 95–6.

6 John Stabb, *Old Devon Churches*, iii, 35.

7 J. J. Jusserand, *English Wayfaring life in the Middle Ages* (1891), 379.

8 E. W. Ganderton and Jean Lafond, *Ludlow stained and painted glass* (1961), 46 ff. repr.

9 F. C. Elliston Erwood, *The Pilgrims' Road* (1923), 115.

10 Tancred Borenius, *St. Thomas à Becket in Art* (1932).

11 H. Munro Cautley, *Suffolk Churches and their Treasures* (1938), 202.

12 E. W. Kemp, *Canonisation and Authority in the Western Church* (1948), 123.

13 The existing monument to Simon de Montfort at Evesham is modern, but one of the windows from the Abbey, now in Fladbury church (Worcs), shows a shield bearing his lion rampant with a forked tail, together with the shields of other knights who fell in the Battle of Evesham in 1265. These include the arms of Lord Despenzer (see Fig. 7), de Boteler, Lord of Sudeley, Henry de Montfort and Ernaud de Blois, Hereditary Steward to the Earls of Leicester.

14 E. W. Tristram, 'The wall-paintings at South Newington', *Burl. Mag.*, March 1933.

15 T.C.F., 'On a fragment of glass in Nettlestead church', *Archaeologia Cantiana*, VI, 29.
16 M. D. Anderson, *A Saint at Stake* (1964), 169–91, gives examples of such comparisons and also examines the semi-magical aspect of some medieval procedures.

4 MERCHANTS AND MARINERS *pp. 208–21*

1 A. H. Thomson, *The historical growth of the English Parish Church* (1911), 24–48.
2 Sir John MacClean, 'Armoury and Merchants' Marks in the ancient church of Cirencester', *Bristol and Glos. Arch. Soc. Trans.* (1892–3), 268 ff.
3 F. A. Girling, *English Merchants' Marks* (1962). J. P. Rylands, *Merchants' Marks and other medieval personal marks* (1910).
4 Reproduced in *Country Life*, Nov. 12th, 1948.
5 Henry H. Trivick, *The craft and design of Monumental Brasses* (1969), 86 ff, includes many reproductions.
6 *Victoria County History of Gloucestershire*, II, 215–38.
7 *Regist. Test. Ebor.*, V, 108. Quoted from J. A. Knowles, 'Gild Windows', *Master Glass Painters' Journal*, VII.
8 H. W. Macklin, *The Brasses of England* (1914), *passim*.
9 F. H. Crossley, *English Church Craftsmanship* (1941), 101, estimates that about 150,000 brasses were laid down of which only about 3,000 survive.
10 H. H. Trivitt, *op. cit.*, 28 ff., compares the Continental and English examples of large quadrangular brasses with many illustrations. Macklin, *op. cit.*, lists examples of foreign brasses at: King's Lynn, St. Albans, North Mimms (Herts), Aveley (Essex), Newark (Notts), Topcliffe (Yorks), Newcastle-on-Tyne, Ipswich and London.
11 F. H. Crossley, *English Church Woodwork* (1933), 21–4.
12 W. G. Constable, 'Some East Anglian Roodscreen paintings', *The Connoisseur*, 1929.
13 H. R. Plumer, *Wynkyn de Worde and his contemporaries* (1925), 22–4.
14 G. R. Crone, *The Hereford World Map* (1948).
15 R. and R. C. Anderson, *The Sailing Ship* (1925), 86.
16 H. Clifford Smith, 'Some medieval ships', *Country Life*, May 9th, 1925.
17 A. B. Emden, 'Graffiti of medieval ships from St. Margaret-at-Cliffe, Kent', *The Mariner's Mirror*, VIII. Further scratch drawings of ships occur in the crypt at Doncaster, and at Combpyne (Devon). Reset in the tower of Whitchurch Canonicorum (Dorset) is a carving of a ship said to be Saxon, but its position makes date and construction hard to ascertain.
18 H. H. Brindley, 'The Ship in the St. Christopher window in Thaxted church with remarks on early methods of reefing sails', *Cambridge Antiq. Soc. Proc.* (1911), XV, 26.
19 G. Callendar, *The Naval side of British History* (1924), 25.
20 R. C. Anderson, *op. cit.*, 133
21 B. C. Clayton, 'The sculptured ships on Tiverton Church', *Apollo*, October 1934, gives clear illustrations of some of these sailing galleys. See also E. K. Prideaux, 'Late medieval sculpture from the church of St. Peter, Tiverton', *Arch. Journal*, LXXV.
22 G. W. Minns, 'The Slavonian Tombstone at North Stoneham', *Hampshire Field Club*, II (1893), 357 ff.
23 J. F. Wadmore, 'Sir Thomas Smythe Knt', *Archaeologia Cantiana* (1893).

5 THE COUNTRY GENTLEMAN TURNED ARCHITECT *pp.* 222–8

1 See *Country Life*, December 27th, 1946. The parson was Dr. Thomas Cattell, who lived in the reign of George III.
2 For medieval building administration, see D. Knoop and G. P. Jones, *The Medieval Mason* (1933), and John H. Harvey, 'The medieval Office of Works', *British Arch. Ass. Journal*, 3rd series, VI (1941).
3 Two churches in Charleston, U.S.A., St. Philip's and St. Michael's, have spires based on designs by Gibbs. Reproduced in *Country Life*, May 26th, 1950.
4 Marcus Whiffen, *Stuart and Georgian churches outside London 1603–1837* (1948), 59.
5 *The Wren Society*, XIX.
6 Nikolaus Pevsner, *Worcestershire*, Buildings of England series (1968), 172.

6 THE COMMON PEOPLE *pp.* 229–37

1 H. Munro Cautley, *Suffolk Churches and their Treasures* (1937), 279.
2 J. C. Cox, *The Parish Registers of England* (1910), 59–60.
3 Francis Bond, *Fonts and Font Covers* (1908), 263.
4 Katherine Esdaile, *English Church Monuments 1510–1840* (1946), 112.
5 J. C. Cox, *op. cit.*, 86.
6 The Scold's Bridle was introduced into England from Scotland *c.* 1620, but was rarely used after 1800, although one was used at Shrewsbury in 1846. They must have been plentiful at one time for, in 1886, there were still six examples in Shropshire alone. (See letter in *The Times*, Aug. 19th, 1949.)
7 J. C. Webster, *The Labours of the Months* (1938).
8 George Zarnecki, *English Romanesque Lead Sculpture* (1957), 17.
9 F. Bond, *Misericords* (1910), 96.
10 Octavius Morgan, *Some Account of the ancient monuments in the Priory Church of Abergavenny* (1872).
11 E. Morris, *Legends of the Bells* (n.d.), 15, 42.

COUNTY INDEX

All these appear in General Index

ENGLAND

BEDFORDSHIRE
Apsley Guise
Blunham
Cockayne Hatley
Dunstable
Turvey
Wymington

BERKSHIRE
Abingdon
Aldermaston
Buckland
Cumnor
Drayton
Harwell
Lambourn
Little Shefford
North Moreton
Radley
Reading
Stratfield Mortimer
Wickham
Windsor

BUCKINGHAMSHIRE
Broughton
Datchet
Dinton
Drayton
Drayton Beauchamp
Edlesborough
Eton
Gayhurst
Hillesden
Langley Marish
Little Horwood
Little Kimble
Parslow
Quainton
Taplow
Water Stratford
West Wycombe

CAMBRIDGESHIRE and ISLE OF ELY
Babraham
Burwell
Cambridge
Ely
Guilden Morden
Hauxton
Isleham
Kingston
Landwade
Madingley
Pampisford
Whittlesford
Wilburton

CHESHIRE
Barthomley
Bunbury
Chester
Disley
Gawsworth
Grappenhall
Higher Peover
Macclesfield
Mal pas
Nantwich
Sandbach
West Kirby

CORNWALL
Altarnun
Bodmin
Breage
Falmouth
Forrabury
Golant
Hayle
Kilkhampton
Lanivet
Lansallos
Lanteglos-by-Fowey
Launcells
Madron
Menacuddle
Mevagissey
Morwenstow
Padstow
Pelynt
Penmachno
Phillack
Poughill

T

LEICESTERSHIRE

Ashby-de-la-Zouch
Bottesford
Breedon-on-the-Hill

Hallaton
Scraptoft
Staunton Harold

Stockerston
Swithland
Twycross

LINCOLNSHIRE

Aslackby
Bardney
Barholm
Barton-upon-Humber
Boston
Corby
Crowland
Epworth

Grantham
Heckington
Kirkstead
Kirton
Lincoln
Linwood
North Cockerington
Saltfleetby All Saints

Springthorpe
Stamford
Syston
Tattershall
Temple Bruer
Welbourn

MIDDLESEX

Harrow-on-the-Hill
Hayes

Little Stanmore
Ruislip

West Drayton

NORFOLK

Antingham
Barnham Broom
Barton Turf
Binham
Blakeney
Burlingham St. Andrew
Burnham Deepdale
Burnham Norton
Castle Acre
Cawston
Cley
Colton
Crostwight
East Dereham
East Harling
Felbrigg
Feltwell
Fritton
Gooderstone
Great Plumstead
Gresham

Heacham
Hempstead
Hingham
Horsham St. Faith
Houghton-in-the Dale
King's Lynn
Little Melton
Ludham
Mattishall
North Elmham
North Tuddenham
Northwold
Norwich
Paston
Pulham St. Mary
Ranworth
Rougham
Salle
Salthouse
Seething
Sloley

Smallburgh
Tacolneston
Thornham
Trimingham
Tunstead
Upper Sheringham
Walpole St. Peter
Walsingham
West Lynn
West Walton
Weston Longueville
Wiggenhall St. German
Wiggenhall St. Mary
  Magdalen
Wiggenhall St. Mary the
  Virgin
Wighton
Wiveton
Wymondham

NORTHAMPTONSHIRE

Barnack
Brixworth
Croughton

Earls Barton
Fotheringhay
Gayton

Guilsborough
Hemington
Higham Ferrers

T 2

SCOTLAND

ABERDEENSHIRE
Aberdeen

ANGUS
Fowlis Easter

DUMFRIESSHIRE
Durisdeer   Middlebie   Ruthwell

FIFE
Inchcolm Abbey   St. Andrews

LINLITHGOWSHIRE
Torphichen

ROXBURGHSHIRE
Linton

WEST LOTHIAN
Abercorn   Dalmeny

WIGTOWNSHIRE
Kirkmadrine   Whithorn

ORKNEY
Orphir

Iona

IRELAND

Monasterboice   Seir Kieran   Waterford

GENERAL INDEX